Current issues in industrial economic strategy

Current issues in industrial economic strategy

edited by
Keith Cowling and Roger Sugden

Manchester University Press
Manchester and New York
Distributed exclusively in the USA and Canada by St Martin's Press

Published by Manchester University Press
Oxford Road, Manchester M13 9PL, UK
and Room 400, 175 Fifth Avenue,
New York, NY 10010, USA

Distributed exclusively in the USA and Canada
by St Martin's Press, Inc.,
175 Fifth Avenue, New York, NY 10010, USA

British Library Cataloguing-in-Publication Data
A catalogue record for this book is available from the British Library

Library of Congress Cataloguing-in-Publication Data

Current issues in industrial economic strategy / edited by Keith Cowling and
   Roger Sugden.
      p.   cm.
   Includes index.
   ISBN 0-7190-3811-1
   1. Industry and state–Congresses. 2. Industrial promotion–Congresses.
3. Industry and state–Case studies–Congresses. 4. Industrial promotion–Case
studies–Congresses. I. Cowling, Keith. II. Sugden, Roger.
   HD3611.C87   1992
   338.9–dc20   92-9050

ISBN 0 7190 3811 1 *hardback*

1000633374 T

Typeset in Great Britain
by Megaron, Cardiff, Wales
Printed in Great Britain
by Biddles Ltd, Guildford & King's Lynn

Contents

PART V: THE EUROPEAN COMMUNITY

PART VI: EASTERN EUROPE

Contributors

Professor Michael H. Best, Professor of Economics, Department of Economics, University of Massachusetts, Amherst, MA 01004, USA.

Professor Patrizio Bianchi, Professor of Economics and Finance of the European Communities, Nomisma-Laboratorio di Politica Industriale, Strade Maggiore, 44-40125 Bologna, Italy.

Dr Ivo Bicanic, Department for Macroeconomics and Economic Policy, Faculty of Economics, University of Zagreb, Trg J F Kennedy ja 6, 41000, Zagreb, Croatia.

Mr Dan Coffey, Lecturer in Economics, School of Business and Economic Studies, ESS Building, The University of Leeds, Leeds LS2 9JZ, UK.

Professor Keith Cowling, Professor of Economics, Department of Economics, University of Warwick, Coventry CV4 7AL, UK.

Dr Michael Dietrich, Lecturer in Economics, School of Management and Economic Studies, University of Sheffield, PO Box 598, Crookesmoore Building, Conduit Road, Sheffield S10 1FL, UK.

Dr Colin Haslam, Principal Lecturer, Business Studies Department, East London Polytechnic, Longbridge Road, Dagenham, Essex RN8 2AS, UK.

Professor Gentaro Matsumoto, Professor of Economics, 3-1, 3-Jo 7-chome, Nishioka, Toyohira-ku, Sapporo, 062 Japan.

Professor James Peoples, Assistant Professor, College of Letters and Science, Department of Economics, University of Wisconsin-Milwaukee, Bolton Hall 6415, PO Box 413, Milwaukee, WI 53201, USA.

Dr Christos N. Pitelis, Barclays Bank Lecturer in Industrial Organization and Corporate Strategy, The Judge Institute of

Management Studies, and Fellow in Economics, Queens' College, University of Cambridge, Mill Lane, Cambridge CB2 1RX, UK.

Dr Harvie Ramsay, Senior Lecturer, Department of Human Resource Management, University of Strathclyde, Marland House, 50 Richmond Street, Glasgow G1 1XT, UK.

Professor Malcolm Sawyer, Professor of Economics, School of Business and Economic Studies, ESS Building, The University of Leeds, Leeds LS2 9JZ, UK.

Professor Hans Schenk, Associate Professor of Corporate Strategy and Industrial Strategy, Graduate School of Management, Erasmus University, PO Box 1738, Burg Oudlaan 50, 3000 DR Rotterdam, Netherlands.

Dr Ajit Singh, Lecturer in the Department of Applied Economics and Fellow of Queens' College, University of Cambridge, Austin Robinson Building, Sidgwick Avenue, Cambridge CB3 9DD, UK.

Professor K R Stollery, Department of Economics, University of Waterloo, Waterloo, Ontario N2L 3G1, Canada.

Dr Roger Sugden, Senior Lecturer in Industrial Economics and Director of the Research Centre for Industrial Strategy, Department of Commerce, Birmingham Business School, University of Birmingham, Edgbaston, Birmingham B15 2TT, UK.

Professor Horst Tomann, Professor of Economics, Department of Economics, Fachbereich Wirtschaftswissenschaft, Institute for Wirtschaftspolitik, Fachrichtung Planung under Steuerung von Wirtschaftsprozessen, Freie Universitat Berlin, FB 10, WE 4. Reichsteiner Weg 1A, 100 Berlin 33, Germany.

Professor John Williams, Professor of Economic History, Department of Economics, University College of Wales, Penglais, Aberystwyth, Dyfed SY23 4DB, UK.

Mr Karel Williams, Senior Lecturer, Department of Economics, University College of Wales, Penglais, Aberystwyth, Dyfed SY23 4DB, UK.

Professor Johan Willner, Professor of Economics, Department of Economics, Nationalekonomiska Institutionen, vid Abo Akademi, Fanriksgaten 3B, 20500 Abo, Finland.

Introduction
Developing research in industrial economic strategy

Economists researching industrial policy have traditionally focused attention on relatively narrow, albeit important, issues, such as monopolies and mergers regulation. Indeed it is a sad indictment of the economics profession that in many ways policy has received comparatively little thought. In more recent years, however, wider concerns have begun to emerge, for instance in the light of German, Italian, Japanese and Pacific Rim experiences. This trend may well continue and moreover it is very important that it does so, not least because the experience of various countries suggests that an appropriate industrial strategy can have an enormous influence on people's welfare.

To reflect this trend and, more significantly, to promote its continuation, 1991 saw the first Warwick/Birmingham Workshop on Industrial Strategy. The papers in this volume are derived from the workshop proceedings. (A full list of workshop participants is provided at the end of this introduction.) The contributions focus on prominent issues facing industrial economists now and in the future. They are of interest individually and are thus readable in isolation but in many ways build upon each other. Furthermore, collectively the contributions illustrate the greater breadth and imagination that are needed in policy discussion and analysis, without ignoring the important more traditional areas.

Part I contains four papers concentrating on theoretical foundations, although many later contributions return to these issues as part of their more specific concerns. With Malcolm Sawyer's paper, we begin very much at the beginning. It characterizes, compares and contrasts three approaches to industrial policy, namely: the market failure, Austrian and industrial strategy approaches. To do so it focuses on the meaning, nature and effects of competition; the role of markets, firms and governments; the nature of the state; the relevance of ownership and control for performance; and policy objectives. Michael Dietrich then takes up what Sawyer calls an industrial strategy approach. Dietrich's starting point is that critics of neo-liberal thinking on economic policy often point to different interventionist practices in Germany and Japan, but without a framework to justify the intervention. His chapter contributes to rectifying this omission; it criticizes orthodox positions and thus develops an alternative, dynamic perspective. The significance of strategic management systems, networking, path-dependent development and power structures are all emphasized. Industrial strategy approaches are also the concern of Hans Schenk in Chapter 3. He uses literature on firms' strategic management to delineate the characteristics which make an activity strategic. Receiving particular attention are the problems in accomplishing mission-derived objectives, and the idea that an industrial policy authority is engaged in strategy only if it is competing with rivals from other areas in a small numbers game. In exploring the latter, Schenk contemplates the possibility of authorities taking an entrepreneurial approach and therefore following different paths from their alleged rivals.

Johan Willner's paper contributes to the theoretical foundations of industrial strategy in a different way from the other papers in Part I. This contrast is revealing; it supports the view that different types of analysis are relevant and necessary. Moreover the paper has implications for governments' privatisation/nationalisation strategies. Willner formally models a Cournot–Nash mixed oligopoly (i.e. one with both private and public actors) with endogenous costs. It is suggested that a publicly owned firm can promote welfare gains even though it will be observed to have higher costs and lower profitability than privately owned rivals.

Concern with the details of production is the distinguishing feature of the papers in Part II, which begins with Michael Best's contribution. This discusses theoretical foundations but concentrates very firmly on production processes; it thus provides an obvious link between Parts I and II. The chapter also begins to turn our attention to particular countries, organisations and regions. Starting with a necessarily brief appreciation of Jamaica's economic problems, Best criticises IMF and 'non-IMF' (i.e. state planning plus nationalisation) paths of development and hence advocates a production-led strategy. He considers mass production techniques (using Ford as an example), just-in-time production and flexible specialisation. Identifying interchangeability, flow and flexibility as the fundamental issues, Best presents a general approach which is then explored by returning to the Jamaican example. The interest in Ford is maintained and pursued in Chapter 6, which presents a relatively detailed account and characterisation of Model T production at Highland Park. Contrary to widespread belief, it is argued that recent Japanese success is a rediscovery and resumption of Ford's earlier success under different circumstances. Karel Williams, Colin Haslam and John Williams conclude that industrial policy intervention should not be confined to what they see as the strategic level. It is felt that the re-conceptualisation of manufacturing activity needs further development before more appropriate policies can be formulated. Production experience in the car industry is also a subject of Dan Coffey's paper, which builds a challenging argument from casework at Rover's Longbridge plant. He takes up the issues of production flexibility and just-in-time manufacture. It is suggested that the need to forecast demand for a complex product is a severe obstacle to achieving reliable delivery in response to customers' orders; that just-in-time production is in itself not a means of overcoming this obstacle; and furthermore that just-in-time production imposes a discipline which constrains the production process (for example, it has a low tolerance for complex products). Coffey concludes that an acceptable just-in-time strategy requires reduced complexity and in this sense reduced flexibility.

Alternative policies for the Jamaican economy, criticism of the IMF and discussion of inappropriate neo-liberal policies are all seen in Parts I and II. They are also brought together in Part III, which comprises Ajit Singh's chapter on future industrial policies in the Third World in general. Singh is pessimistic about the chances for success of current initiatives, indeed suggesting that in some cases they might harm development. His alternative is based upon various parameters, such as a continuing social imperative for fast growth and a slow expansion in world manufactures demand. The advocated interventionist strategy points to a greater reliance on internal factors as the main dynamic for change. One of the more general points illustrated by this volume is that whilst it is appropriate to give the Third World special attention – hence our positioning of Singh's contribution as a distinct part–problems of successful development cross all borders and all cultures. This is not to deny that every country needs a unique approach, specifically designed for its own circumstances. Nevertheless, countries in the Third World, for instance, require strategies with considerable similarity to those needed elsewhere.

One of the constant themes seen throughout the volume, indeed in this introduction, is that the formulation of industrial economic strategies can and should build upon past experiences in different countries. This theme is given particular attention in Part IV, which concentrates on experience in Japan, North America and Western Europe. Most attention is given to Japan, a country where dramatic development has raised numerous questions and in some ways has given industrial economic strategy greater prominence in 'the more advanced industrialised countries'. In Chapter 9, Gentaro Matsumoto explains and evaluates the role of the Ministry of International Trade and Industry in Japanese postwar economic success, and is generally less enthusiastic than many (non-Japanese) commentators. He suggests that MITI's approach has been based not on neoclassical price theory but on, for example, improvements in comparative technical advantage. MITI is seen as an arbitrator and co-ordinator. It is also seen as a body which has not always had its own way and a body whose influence is likely to decline. Moreover, the most important characteristics of postwar Japan are seen as flexibility in industrial organisation and a competitiveness between companies, features which he feels cannot be attributed to MITI. Matsumoto argues that there have been industries where MITI's restrictions unwittingly stimulated new entry. Thus he identifies and explores entrepreneurship as a more important determinant of Japanese success. In contrast to this relatively detailed look at an aspect of Japanese strategy, Chapter 10 provides thumbnail sketches of experiences with industrial policy in various countries. Each sketch is written by a native of the particular country in question. The pieces on Canada (by Ken Stollery), Britain (Malcolm Sawyer), Finland (Johan Willner) and Italy (Patrizio Bianchi) provide potted histories, whereas those for the USA (James Peoples) and Germany (Horst Tomann) focus on recent events. Even such brief examinations reveal that there is a lot to be learnt from different countries, and that there are thought-provoking comparisons and contrasts to be built upon.

Our spotlight then turns on Europe more generally. Part V looks at the European Community. It begins with a contribution by Patrizio Bianchi. This focuses on perspectives towards European integration. It explores the idea that policy and policy-making have moved from a centralised 'French' approach to a decentralised 'German' approach. Bianchi examines the role of supranational, national and regional governments, and explores the argument by looking at Italian policy towards small and medium-sized firms. This provides an obvious follow-on from Part IV, which ended with the sketch of Italian experience. Harvie Ramsay also presents a perspective on European integration, but from a different angle. Rather than explicitly focusing on centralised versus decentralised approaches, he argues that the Single European Act is a Euro-champions policy, for instance breathing new life into the preoccupation with creating a European big business counter-challenge to the USA. This analysis has significant, largely implicit, implications for any alleged decentralisation in other aspects of policy. Ramsay criticises the approach on various grounds and reaches a gloomy conclusion about the effects of the 1992 initiatives. His particular concern with the role of transnational corporations is also taken up by Christos Pitelis, who proposes a competitive strategy for the European Community but in a more international context. Pitelis' paper begins with a discussion of the competition concept in theory and practice, and then develops various theoretical propositions as the general basis for a competition policy. These emphasise Pareto criteria. Pitelis uses the propositions to formulate a Community strategy. In an analysis sensitive to inter-country differences, he is especially concerned with 'European and non-European' transnationals, conscious promotion of competition, and the avoidance of 'fortress Europe'.

From the European Community, our attention shifts in the last part to another aspect of European development receiving considerable and growing attention: the problems of transition in Eastern Europe. Ivo Bicanic examines privatisation in Poland, the Czech and Slovak Federation, Hungary, Yugoslavia, Romania, Bulgaria and Albania. He argues that privatisation has been seen in an idealised sense, arousing expectations that are not and will not be fulfilled. Bicanic identifies various pressures decelerating the transition process and giving the state significant policy possibilities, including the chance to implement a proactive industrial strategy focusing on such things as investment, technological change and training. Horst Tomann's chapter considers the theoretical basis for transition mechanisms, drawing on the Austrian tradition and on monetary theory. Unlike Bicanic, he argues against gradual change, seeing a 'socialist planning system' and a capitalist market economy as mutually exclusive. The case of Germany is used to explore the consequences and requirements of rapid transition. The German Monetary Union, wage policy and again privatisation are given relatively detailed consideration.

Participants at the 1991 Warwick/Birmingham Workshop on Industrial Strategy

David Bailey	University of Birmingham
Marco Bellandi	Università degli studi di Firenze
Michael Best	University of Massachusetts
Patrizio Bianchi	Università di Bologna
Ivo Bicanic	University of Zagreb
Martin Chick	University of Edinburgh
Dan Coffey	University of Leeds
Keith Cowling	University of Warwick
Michael Dietrich	University of Sheffield
John Edmonds	GMB
Monica Giuletti	University of Warwick
Pat Hanlon	University of Birmingham
Stephen Littlechild	Office of Electricity Regulation
Gentaro Matsumoto	University of Sapporo
Marco Mazzoli	University of Warwick
Mansoob Murshed	University of Surrey
James Peoples	University of Wisconsin, Milwaukee
Christos Pitelis	University of Cambridge
John Prescott, MP	
Harvie Ramsay	University of Strathclyde
Alan Roe	University of Warwick
Malcolm Sawyer	University of Leeds
Hans Schenk	Erasmus University
Paul Schreyer	OECD
Sudi Sharifi	University of Birmingham
Ajit Singh	University of Cambridge
Ken Stollery	University of Waterloo

Paul Stoneman	University of Warwick
Roger Sugden	University of Birmingham
Jim Tomlinson	Brunel University
Horst Tomann	Freie Universität Berlin
Michael Waterson	University of Warwick
Karel Williams	University of Aberystwyth
Johan Willner	Åbo Akademi University

PART I

THEORETICAL FOUNDATIONS

1 *Malcolm Sawyer*

On the theory of industrial policy

Introduction

Much discussion of industrial policy, at least in the Anglo-Saxon world and especially amongst industrial economists, is heavily influenced by the 'market failure' approach, which involves an essentially static approach to the workings of the economy as well as a particular view of the way in which markets work and the relevant objectives for industrial policy. One purpose of this paper is to sketch the nature of that approach and of two other approaches (the Austrian and an approach which we label industrial strategy). But each approach can only be understood on its own terms, and much misunderstanding arises in discussion on industrial policy through consideration of one approach using the intellectual frameworks of other approaches. These misunderstandings are exacerbated by the use of the same words with different meanings, of which the term 'competition' is a particular example. Specifically, the industrial strategy approach has its own ideas and theories concerning the operation of unfettered market forces which then inform its policy conclusions, and those conclusions cannot be understood apart from an appreciation of the underlying view of the operation of a market economy. The major point behind this paper is the relatively simple one: different views of how market economies operate lead to quite different policy conclusions. An approach to policy, such as the industrial strategy one, can be seriously examined only in the context of the relevant theoretical framework. Further, although an elaboration is beyond the scope of this paper, the methodological stances of the three approaches are quite different over, for example, the usefulness of equilibrium analysis.

Our discussion of different approaches to industrial policy is organised in terms of the following range of issues:

(a) the meaning and nature of competition and its effects on the economy and society;
(b) the appropriate roles for markets, firms and government intervention;
(c) the nature of the state (e.g. creature of capital, neutral agent acting in the interests of society);
(d) the relevance of ownership and control for economic performance;
(e) the objectives of industrial policy.

These considerations are rather broader than those generally explicitly discussed in the context of industrial policy. It is argued that, in general, each approach to industrial policy deals with these issues, as indeed it has to. However, the treatment is often implicit and in part the aim of this paper is to make the treatment explicit. We seek (albeit briefly) to indicate the manner in which three approaches to industrial policy deal with the five issues outlined above. These are not, of course, independent of one another.

In the next section we discuss the market failure view (which could be seen as the traditional approach of industrial economists in the UK and USA). This is followed by discussion of the Austrian approach (which could be seen as having had some influence on the British government during the 1980s). The third approach is difficult to label as it tends to mix ideas from a number of different traditions which range over the Marxian and monopoly capital ones as well as notions of cumulative causation drawn from the work of Myrdal and Kaldor and recent writings from a radical political economy perspective which stress the role of worker participation.[1] I would argue that, with some augmentation, ideas drawn from these traditions have strongly influenced those advocating a pro-active industrial policy (e.g. Cowling, 1990). Based on that argument, I will label the third approach the industrial strategy approach.

The definition of industrial policy presents some difficulties. It is not only that each approach has some problem in delineating industrial policy and that the boundaries of industrial policy differ between approaches. It is also that each approach has to some degree built within it a definition of industrial policy: in other words the definition of what constitutes industrial policy is paradigm-specific. From the 'market failure' approach, industrial policy can be identified as microeconomic measures designed to influence the structure, behaviour or performance at the level of the industry. Policy instruments such as interest rates and rates of taxation, which are seen as influencing the whole economy and are regarded as part of macroeconomic policy, are thereby excluded, even though they may have significant impact on industrial performance. In the Austrian approach, entrepreneurship and competition are seen as the driving forces for beneficial economic evolution. Governments are able to raise or lower barriers to competition through regulation. Beneficial industrial policy is then linked with the reduction or complete removal of barriers to entry into industry and the exercise of competition.

In the industrial strategy approach, the objectives of industrial policy would include industrial development and efficiency (though this is discussed further below). But this approach would define industrial policy more in terms of policy *intention* than policy *instruments*. For example, in Britain, variations in interest rates are usually seen to have the intention of influencing variables such as the stock of money or the exchange rates, and as such are seen as part of macroeconomic policy. But if such variations were used with the primary intention of influencing the pace of investment and industrial development, they could reasonably be seen as part of industrial policy. The stated intention of the industrial strategy of the 1974–79 Labour government can be seen in this light for ideas of subordinating short-term macroeconomic policy to the needs of medium-term industrial development (see discussion in Sawyer, 1991a). The approach, which we have labelled industrial strategy, could have been labelled productionist (see also Part II of this volume) for it is particularly concerned with production (including the development of new products and the nature of the labour process), whereas the other two approaches focus on the conditions of exchange, with the implicit assumption of productive efficiency. Neoclassical and Austrian economics have both been essentially concerned with exchange, and production seen as exchange with nature whereby inputs are exchanged for outputs. In contrast, the industrial strategy approach involves consideration of the conditions of production.

The market failure approach

The 'market failure' approach views situations of oligopoly and monopoly as involving welfare losses in comparison with a situation of perfect competition (the other forms of 'market failure' such as externalities are not of immediate concern here). The role of government can then be seen as the correction of 'market failure', either through the implementation of perfect competition or through the regulation of prices, profit rates, etc. (particularly if perfect competition is unattainable, as in the case of economies of scale).

We can now look at the issues raised above. Competition is considered in a structural and static sense (with perfect competition defined in terms of number of firms and ease of entry). More competition is generally viewed as preferable to less (which means more firms and/or lower barriers to entry), though caveats based on the theory of second-best are often entered. The notion of contestability and the benefits of a perfectly contestable market fit into this general approach, although there is a stress on the absence of entry barriers rather than on number of firms in the market. Competition is viewed as generally beneficial for static economic efficiency, and no consideration is given to any wider impacts on society. In particular, no attention is given to any distributional issues (which are seen here as including distribution of decision-making as well as of income).

The role of government intervention is clearly seen to be the correction of 'market failure'. This has been criticised as assuming 'government perfection', whereas there may also be 'government failure', and the government is modelled as having perfect infor-mation, etc. Substantial government intervention may be implied by the 'market failure' approach if the view is taken that oligopoly and monopoly (and/or externalities) are extensive, though there is a general suggestion that markets are pervasive. But it is still the case that there is regulation of markets by government.

The state is seen as operating in the interests of society, where those interests are judged on the basis of standard welfare econ-omics. There is some ambiguity within the 'market failure' approach about whether it provides a positive or a normative approach to state operations: the welfare elements clearly signal a normative aspect, with the positive aspect derived from a prediction that governments do operate to correct market failure. In either case the state is viewed as a neutral agent, paying proper regard to the welfare of all, whatever their economic or political influence.

The form of ownership is rarely discussed in connection with the 'market failure' approach, though there would appear to be a general presumption that private ownership is the norm. Regulation (particularly of natural monopolies) may take the form of public ownership, although in the last decade or so much more attention has been given to the use of regulatory agencies for private monopolies. At the limit, under perfect competition the form of ownership becomes irrelevant as each firm is forced to conform to the dictates of the market and survival requires profit maximisation. Within this there is the general view that private owners will seek profit maximisation, and that such maximisation leads to technical efficiency.

The objectives of industrial policy are generally seen to be the improvement of economic welfare (and hence of economic efficiency). The 'market failure' is a static approach, with perfect information and technical efficiency assumed. Thus a range of concerns (such as the dynamism of the industrial sector, the creation of new products, improvement of productive efficiency) just do not arise. There is clearly no reason to have as the objective of policy the improvement of productive efficiency when such efficiency has been assumed to exist. Thus industrial policy is left to focus on changes in the industrial structure leading to improvements in industrial performance, and thereby generating a close affinity between industrial policy and competition policy. Further, there is no scope with the structure–conduct–performance approach (on which the 'market failure' approach relies) for consideration of the relationships between the financial and productive sectors of the economy or of those between employers and employees.

The Austrian approach

We now consider the Austrian approach in terms of the issues identified above. Competition is seen as a dynamic process for which there is no final position of rest towards which the economy or market moves. Competition is viewed not in a structural sense or in terms of rivalry, but rather in terms of the ability of entrepreneurs to take advantage of opportunities; as Reekie (1979, pp.10–11) argues, competition is to be viewed as 'mobility, not equilibrium.

We ought to mean the unbarred movement of factors of production'. The effects of competition are seen as beneficial, virtually by assumption in the sense that new opportunities have been taken and would only have been taken if they were perceived to be beneficial.

The appropriate role of government is seen to be that of a minimalist state, enforcing laws which safeguard the exchange processes and property rights. The co-ordination of economic activity should take place through the market. Firms as organisations and co-ordinators of economic activity have typically not been the focus of attention. An associated feature is the emphasis on the importance of exchange to the neglect of production. The central role in economic activity is given to the entrepreneur, who profits from perceiving and taking beneficial initiatives. However, it would appear that the enterprise considered is limited to that which involves market activities and undertaken for reasons of individual profit derived from a position as residual claimant (to use the phrase of Alchian and Demsetz, 1972). A related aspect of the Austrian approach is the notion that there is limited information, and that the exploitation by entrepreneurs of the differentially available information (and perceptions) is one of the engines of the economic system. Exploitation of differential information by entrepreneurs is the source of profits and '[i]f all entrepreneurs were to anticipate correctly the future state of the market, there would be neither profits nor losses' (Mises, 1949, p. 291). From our perspective, it is important to note that entrepreneurship is linked with the exploitation of superior information, but it appears that the exploitation of superior information occurs through the market and leads to profits. Thus the concept of entrepreneurial activity is a rather circumscribed one.

The state is generally seen as counterposed to the market in that state activity limits and constrains market activity. State workers do not face the market constraints faced by other workers nor are there people with a profit interest in ensuring technical efficiency, which leads to a tendency towards over-expansion of the state and inefficiency. There are the presumptions that '*no government interference with exchange can ever increase social utility*' and that '*the free market benefits all its participants*' (Rothbard, 1956, pp.252, 250; emphasis in original). The general thrust is for the role of the state to be restricted to that of 'nightwatchman' enacting and enforcing laws to protect property rights and market exchange.

Private ownership is viewed as essential for good economic performance. Alchian and Demsetz (1972) argue for the importance of a residual claimant who monitors the performance of the labour force in search of profits and efficiency. The residual claimant argument postulates inefficiency arising not only from state activities but also from organisations such as workers' co-operatives and management-controlled firms.

In one sense, industrial policy (or indeed any economic policy) is not provided with any objectives in terms of the achievement of specific economic (or other) goals. Instead the objective is urged to be minimal state intervention since any interventionist industrial policy can only harm economic performance. Further, it is left to the market and the entrepreneurs to determine what happens.

The industrial strategy approach

The view which underlies this section is that there are a number of ideas, generally advanced by economists working outside the mainstream, which serve to underpin the general notion of an industrial strategy approach.[2] This approach is not widely known and is less well defined than those discussed above, and we seek to elaborate the approach by considering the five issues listed above.

Capitalist firms are profit seeking, and the pursuit of profits brings firms into conflict with one another. However, when the rivalry intensifies and threatens profits and survival, firms often seek agreements and mergers. Competition involves winners and losers, and thereby a process of concentration and centralization, with market power emerging from the competitive struggle. At the industry (and economy) level, this throws up problems of monopoly power. But, unlike the 'market failure' approach where there is no mechanism transforming atomistic competition into oligopoly, there is a basic tendency here pushing in that direction. Capitalist firms are owned by private individuals and are run to a greater or lesser extent in the interests of the owners. However, this approach also points to the possibilities of a transformation of capitalist firms into more democratic, participative organisations, as discussed below.

There are also winners and losers in the spatial dimension, with some regions and nations succeeding whilst others are relative failures. Thereby, the operation of unfettered market forces generates uneven development. Governments find difficulty in offsetting these forces, for not only are the forces strong but the spending and other powers of government are reduced in the less successful regions or nations.

The forces of cumulative causation (Myrdal, 1957) and centripetalism (Cowling, 1987) which are involved in the operation of market (and other) forces sustain and exacerbate disparities between regions (nations). The relatively poor regions not only find difficulty catching up with the relatively rich regions but also exhibit unemployment and underemployment. There is then a strong tendency for the market process to display cumulative causation, and for higher-level activities to gravitate towards the centre.

The industrial strategy approach does not see there being a sharp dichotomy to be drawn between allocation through markets and allocation through planning. This dichotomy has been strongly influenced by the equivalence in static general equilibrium theory of the two forms of allocation. But that theory ignores important elements such as competition through new products, strategic planning and uncertainty. In the industrial strategy approach, there is a degree of complementarity between the market mechanism and industrial policy. For, as Best (1990, p. 20) argues, '[t]he first element in a successful industrial policy is a creative use and shaping of the market. Industrial policy fails when it overrides or ignores the market and is based upon the presumption that plans and markets are alternative means of economic coordination. The purpose is not to substitute the plan for the market but to shape and use markets.'

Whilst the roles for market, firms and the government have yet to be discussed with any precision within this approach, the starting point is the potential complementarity between the three. There can clearly be cases where government (market) action limits the effectiveness of markets (government). The Austrian view is that government action almost always limits the effectiveness of markets, and the 'market failure' view is that governments should and do restrain and correct the operations of the market. Whilst there is a need for anti-monopoly and regulatory policies within the industrial strategy approach, there is also the need for a developmental role for the state, which involves the active promotion of industrial development under which the state adopts an entrepreneurial role, either in its own industrial operations and/or in its promotion of private business. The state is thereby able to create opportunities which would not otherwise exist. If successful, the operation of the state enhances the operation of markets.

A variety of relationships between firms themselves and between firms and government can be involved, with substantial differences emerging as between different economies. In particular, beneficial relationships between firms are not restricted to arms-length exchange relationships.

> [A]llowance must be made for consultative coordination or cooperation amongst mutually interdependent firms each of which specializes in distinct phases of the same production chain. The pressure for inter-firm cooperation comes, in part, from the competitive lead that accompanies problem solving at a time of rapid technological change. For suppliers and buyers can be a source of ideas as well as sellers of inputs and purchasers of outputs. (Best, 1990, p. 16)

The state is not seen as a neutral agent acting in the social interest, and the debates here concern the extent to which the state can operate against the interests of capital, particularly when those interests conflict with the interests of consumers and/or workers. Capital often has the advantage of direct access to government and relative fewness of numbers (as compared with workers and consumers).[3] Even when there is common interest between workers and capitalists for industrial development, there are still likely to be distributional (of income and power) consequences, and hence who controls state policy will be important. This difficulty is perhaps the major one facing the industrial strategy approach, for the implementation of such a policy requires the acceptance of the underlying philosophy by those charged with its implementation (i.e. civil servants) and a state able and willing to challenge interest groups in the cause of industrial development. For example, a more democratic style of management clearly requires a decline in the power of existing management.

The industrial strategy approach pays particular regard to the enhancement of democracy in at least two dimensions. First, it argues that participation by workers at the work-place can improve productivity (as briefly discussed below). Second, a more open style of government can help restrain the power of small groups who have access to government decision-making.

In an approach which emphasises the role of democratic participation, the objectives of industrial policy should emerge from the

wishes of the relevant electorate. It was argued above that the
objectives of industrial policy are intimately linked with the analysis
of the approach concerned. Instead of discussing the objectives of
policy, we discuss briefly what could be achieved by a proactive
industrial policy. It must though be stressed that what would
actually be obtained would depend on the political forces at work.
However, the industrial strategy approach would include a less
inequitable distribution of income amongst its goals, and that may
be combined (as in the work of Bowles *et al.*, 1990) with the notion
that there is *not* a trade-off between equality and efficiency.
Similarly, participation in decision-making is often viewed as
desirable *per se* and also enhancing economic efficiency.

The improvement of economic efficiency was seen as the sole
objective of the 'market failure' approach, and then limited to
allocative efficiency. The usual focus is on static efficiency. In so far as
efficiency over time is discussed, it is related to the allocation of
consumption and production over time in line with people's time
preference. The industrial strategy approach would seek to move
the focus to dynamic efficiency. This concept is difficult to define
with any precision, but would include a concern (in an industrialised country) than an economy is developing new products and able
to maintain its position in international competition.

The industrial strategy approach is obviously not averse to the
improvement of economic efficiency but would see the sources of
such improvement in a much broader context.[4] Here we highlight
four. The first arises from the organisation of production and the
gains from worker participation. Bowles *et al.* (1990), for example,
argue that 'the keys to high-productivity work performance are
commitment and cooperation. The keys to commitment and
cooperation, in turn, are participation in the design and execution of
work and a share in the gains of a job well done' (p. 174). The
Austrian approach emphasises the use of information by entrepreneurs but identifies the entrepreneur with property ownership
(the requirement for a residual claimant). However, much information and knowledge reside with individual workers and groups of
workers, who in the right institutional setting could use that
information and knowledge fruitfully. The ability of workers to
exploit their specialised knowledge would enhance efficiency. Restricting the role of entrepreneur to profit-making through
exchange in the market is far too narrow, and it is argued here that a

much wider view of the possibilities for enterprise should be acknowledged.

The second area where efficiency could be improved is the diminution of the waste generated by the capitalist market system of rivalry as discussed by, for example, Baran and Sweezy (1966) and more recently by Bowles *et al.* (1990). These costs of rivalry include excessive advertising, product differentiation and change generated by the competitive process.

The third draws on the notion that unfettered market forces lead to disparities between regions, sectors and groups. Relatively backward regions display unemployment and workers in the secondary labour markets suffer from underutilisation of their talents. A broadly conceived industrial policy would be concerned to offset regional disparities and the lack of training and education.

We mention briefly the fourth, namely the losses from unemployment and underutilisation of capacity which arise from a combination of an insufficiency of aggregate demand and the use of unemployment as a means of maintaining factory discipline and dampening down inflationary pressures.

The industrial strategy approach does not lead to the advocacy of central planning – in part because the informational and incentive requirements for successful planning are impossible to achieve. Instead, the government accepts a strategic role under which a broad view on future developments is evolved, and in which public support is forthcoming for productive activities (rather than exchange or financial ones). Much of the co-ordination of economic activity is undertaken through the market, though it is recognised that substantial parts of such co-ordination take place within firms and within households.

Concluding comments

In this brief paper, we have been able to present only a rather cursory outline of different approaches to industrial policy. Our aim has been not a full description or evaluation of those approaches but rather to provide evidence for the view that there are major differences between the approaches, in terms of the underlying view of the workings of a capitalist economy and the nature of the state, leading to differences in policy recommendations. Further, the policy recommendations of any particular approach can be understood only by reference to the underlying view of the economy which is adopted.

Notes

This paper was written after the Warwick/Birmingham Industrial Strategy Workshop held at the Birmingham Business School, 22 July to 1 August 1991. It draws on some ideas in Sawyer (1992) presented at the workshop and brings in ideas stimulated by the presentations of others (notably Michael Dietrich). I owe the development of some of the ideas in this paper to John Hillard.

1   I have discussed ideas in this general approach elsewhere, e.g. Sawyer (1989), Chapter 13, Sawyer (1991b), with an emphasis on the importance of the forces of cumulative causation.

2   In Chapter 2, Dietrich provides further discussion of an industry strategy approach, with more emphasis than I give on the strategic aspects. See also Schenk in Chapter 3.

3   For example, anti-monopoly policy would impact in any particular case on the interests of one firm but on millions of consumers. It is clearly easier for the single firm to lobby government than it is for millions of consumers to present a united front.

4   Indeed, within the industrial strategy approach, the definition of economic efficiency becomes problematic. Higher labour productivity in terms of output per unit of labour time cannot be identified with increased efficiency since the increase may be a result of more labour effort.

References

Alchian, A. and Demsetz, H. (1972), 'Production, information costs and economic organisation', *American Economic Review*, 62.

Baran, P. and Sweezy, P. (1966), *Monopoly Capital*, New York: Monthly Review Press.

Best, M. (1990), *The New Competition*, Oxford: Polity Press.

Bowles, S., Gordon, D. and Weisskopf, T. (1990), *After the Wasteland: A Democratic Economics for the Year 2000*, New York: M. E. Sharpe.

Cowling, K. (1987), 'An industrial strategy for Britain', *International Review of Applied Economics*, 1.

Cowling, K. (1990), 'The strategic approach to economic and industrial policy', in K. Cowling and R. Sugden (eds), *A New Economic Policy for Britain*, Manchester: Manchester University Press.

Mises, L. von (1949), *Human Action: A Treatise on Economics*, London: Hodge.

Myrdal, G. (1957), *Economic Theory and Underdeveloped Regions*, London: Duckworth.

Reekie, W. (1979), *Industry, Prices and Markets*, Deddington: Philip Allan.

Rothbard, M. (1956), 'Towards a reconstruction of utility and welfare economics', in M. Sennholz (ed.), *On Freedom and Free Enterprise*, Princeton: van Nostrand.

Sawyer, M. (1989), *The Challenge of Radical Political Economy*, Hemel Hempstead: Harvester-Wheatsheaf.

Sawyer, M. (1991a), 'Industrial policy', in M. Artis and D. Cobham (eds), *Labour's Economic Policies 1974–79*, Manchester: Manchester University Press.

Sawyer, M. (1991b), 'Analysing the operation of market economies in the spirit of

Kaldor and Kalecki', in J. Michie (ed.), *The Economics of Restructuring and Intervention*, Aldershot: Edward Elgar.

Sawyer, M. (1992), 'Reflections on the nature and role of industrial policy', *Metoeconomica*.

The foundations of industrial policy

Introduction

For more than a decade in the UK, economic debate has been dominated by neo-liberal thinking, particularly in the political arena and to a lesser extent within academic economics. In terms of the subject matter to be discussed in this paper the policy conclusions have emphasised a passive role for the state in microeconomic/industrial affairs; the metaphor 'levelling the playing field' is apt in this context. Any alternative perspective is dismissed with claims that the state cannot pick winners, and that civil servants, with no real material responsibility, are in no position to improve the decision-making of private sector managers. Critics of this dominant framework frequently make reference to best practice in other countries, for example pointing out the interventionist tradition in Germany and Japan. But such a response is essentially arbitrary because it is not grounded in a framework to justify the intervention. This is symptomatic of the lack of understanding of the subject matter concerned, which in turn has reinforced the neo-liberal hegemony.

In this context, this paper discusses the foundations of industrial policy. The next section critically examines the orthodox position with regard to microeconomic/industrial intervention. This leads on to an alternative framework within which the rationale for industrial policy can be understood. Following this, the nature and forms of industrial policy intervention are discussed. Finally some conclusions are drawn. It should be stated at the outset that this discussion, given its nature and objectives, is essentially theoretical. Hence examples are used for illustrative purposes rather than fully developed applications.[1]

Industrial policy and economic orthodoxy

Industrial policy can be characterised as long-run supply-side initiatives aimed at restructuring or promoting the activities of particular firms or sectors. Following Saunders (1987) we can, for the moment, highlight the following industrial policy tools: selective promotion of particular sectors or branches of an economy; financial aid to investment and R&D; and/or regulation of foreign trade in the interests of a national (or international) economy. In practice, therefore, it is clear that such tools overlap with other arms of government activity, perhaps most notably regional, training, competition and even defence objectives. Consequently, industrial strategy must acknowledge such interdependencies if mutually self-supporting policies are to be developed. In addition, any concrete analysis of industrial policy must recognise that it can be 'disguised' under other policy headings.

A further point on the definition of industrial policy concerns a distinction between positive and negative aspects of such initiatives. The former refers to moving resources into areas to develop new industries or new products/processes for existing firms. Negative restructuring refers to the movement of resources away from particular activities. Market processes are particularly powerful at achieving the latter. On the other hand, positive restructuring is a more problematic process, and is feasible only to the extent that private appropriation of the benefits of innovative activity is possible. Private appropriation is facilitated by the following 'appropriability devices' (Dosi, 1988, p. 1139): patents; secrecy; lead times; costs and time required for duplication; learning-curve effects; superior sales and service efforts; and technical efficiency advantages due to scale economies. However, the effectiveness of these appropriability devices implies the inhibition of diffusion, which may present a policy problem because it is only with use that the economic benefits of innovation are generated.

Against this background, orthodox economics presents the following justifications for industrial policy:[2]

(1) a general lack of information about the potential of new technologies and/or managerial/organisational methods;
(2) the public goods characteristic of information;
(3) a divergence between private and social rates of return because of (a) producer and consumer externalities which can exist in

new areas; and/or (b) excessive private sector discount rates
because of risk aversion;

(4) the infant industry argument, where first-mover advantages
    need to be broken down and initial capital requirements are
    substantial and/or significant potential cost reductions arise
    from learning effects or scale economies.

These justifications are clearly based on an optimising framework
within which allocative and technical efficiencies act as normative
benchmarks. At the same time, however, the rhetoric surrounding
industrial policy frequently emphasises dynamic and proactive
aspects of shifting developmental paths and reorienting strategic
objectives. For example, a recent Labour Party document (1991, p.
5) outlines three principles upon which their industrial policy for
the 1990s would be based: the modernisation of manufacturing
industry; a long-term emphasis; and partnership between industry
and government, not in the form of subsidies but as co-operation to
meet specific objectives. In addition, specific reference is made to
the encouragement of near-market research (p. 15), rather than just
a pre-competitive emphasis where the earlier mentioned market
failures are likely to dominate.

Thus a gap appears to exist between our conceptualisation
of industrial policy within a static optimising framework and
rhetoric in terms of a stress on dynamic, strategic benefits.
This gap weakens the case for an active policy stance and is
an important reason why any reference to non-UK best practice
is arbitrary and frequently unconvincing. This tension between
static and dynamic perspectives mirrors a tension in economic
theory about the conceptualisation of competition. On the one
hand, neoclassical theorists, and in particular the structure–
conduct–performance tradition in industrial economics, stress
the nature of competition as a market structure, with the resultant allocative and technical efficiency benchmarks and the
earlier mentioned justifications for industrial policy. On the
other hand, there is a heterodox tradition within economics that
stresses competition as a process, frequently with cumulative
(dis)advantage. The intellectual roots of this paper are based
in the latter tradition, which facilitates the development of an
alternative framework which is required to understand the dynamic
context of much industrial policy practice. In particular, emphasis

will be placed here on a further source of market failure, that of 'missing markets'.[3]

Successful industrial policy, and the resulting economic restructuring, implies that an economy will experience non-steady-state growth. In such conditions relative prices and profitabilities will change over time. Consequently, when economic decisions are temporally non-separable, as is the case when investment in human and non-human assets is undertaken, static decision-making is no longer appropriate. The resource allocation complexities involved in such conditions are conventionally analysed in one of two ways. Neoclassical economists posit comprehensive futures and insurance markets which generate future prices and profitabilities. This framework, while perhaps being an interesting intellectual curiosity, is clearly a nonsense in terms of understanding actual resource allocation processes.

An alternative means of solving the 'missing markets' problem is suggested by Austrian-inspired economists by invoking the entrepreneur (see, for example, Kirzner, 1973). The economic dynamism of an economy supposedly revolves around this economic actor who perceives and exploits market opportunities by organising the production of goods and services for unmet consumer needs, the reward being the profit thereby obtained. Invoking the entrepreneur appears to solve the analytical problem of how resources are allocated to future activities in non-steady-state conditions. But, without wishing to remove entrepreneurial activity from the economic stage, a problem exists with this Austrian 'solution'. The existence and nature of individual preferences, technologies and entrepreneurs themselves are assumed exogenous. This inevitably leads to the 'conclusion' that economic restructuring must, fundamentally, be left to individual entrepreneurs. Apart from government activity to 'level the playing field', outside influences and control will blunt competitive forces. Consequently industrial policy is marginalised to a passive role.

Industrial policy: an alternative framework

The above discussion indicates that an alternative to orthodox analyses is required if the potential role of industrial policy in an economy is to be appreciated. A dynamic emphasis is required which goes beyond, but accommodates, their insights. The alternative framework suggested here starts from the proposition that in non-steady-state conditions, when the 'missing markets' problem just discussed is evident, any organisation can effectively adapt to, exploit and mould the evolving changes only if (formal and/or informal) strategic management activity is undertaken.[4] The recognition of this centrality of strategic management shifts the analytical centre of gravity significantly. In particular, such activity allows us to analyse entrepreneurship rather than simply assert its importance, and facilitates a movement away from the overt methodological individualism of Austrian economics, but in a way that incorporates active human agency.

An underlying theme in much strategic management literature is that any analysis should not be constrained within a narrow mechanistic framework whereby input:output relationships are understood in a deterministic manner. The bounded rationality of economic actors implies that ambiguity and co-ordination breakdown would inevitably result. Therefore modern management theorists[5] stress social, cultural and political aspects of intra-firm strategic resource allocation. These aspects create the assumptions and beliefs that are shared within an organisation, and reproduce and legitimise organisational practices. Therefore, all formal and informal (strategic) management activities are guided and structured by their social, cultural and political context. In addition, the consistent relative success, or failure, of firms can be understood in terms of the idiosyncracies of such practices (Peters and Waterman, 1982, Clutterbuck and Goldsmith, 1984). In more narrowly economic terms, decision-making and management control process economies are evident by moving beyond a mechanistic framework.

The shift away from equilibrium theorising implied by strategic management activity means that orthodox allocative and technical optimality norms can no longer be taken as unproblematic indicators of efficiency. Rather than abstract rules, human motivation is centrally important. For example, Peters and Waterman (1982) stress the centrality of decentralised, informal organisational processes and self-esteem for corporate success, an argument that Knight and Sugden (1990) take up to argue for economic democracy on efficiency grounds. In short, entrepreneurial activity, as embodied in detailed organisational practices, responds to a series of non-monetary, as well as monetary, incentives.

This argument for strategic accountability and intra-organisational power sharing is central to an efficient industrial policy. If universal neoclassical efficiency norms are inappropriate in dynamic circumstances, an alternative theorisation of what constitutes efficient practice is needed. It is clear that, outside a self-equilibrating framework, strategic decisions endogenise market processes (as analysed below) and hence function in the interests of those in senior hierarchical positions who have effective control over organisational practices (Cowling and Sugden, 1991). Consequently, organisational processes should recognise the needs of intra-organisational efficiency (in its widest meaning). It is not pertinent to discuss the details of such processes here; suffice it to say that power sharing and accountable senior management, in terms of major strategic issues, are basic requirements so that decisions can recognise the aspirations and objectives of currently subordinate organisational actors. To avoid any ambiguity it should perhaps be stated that accountable strategic management does not imply elimination of hierarchy, or line authority, for operational decisions. While power sharing and accountability are likely to reduce shirking and opportunism, it is utopian to assume their non-existence. At the same time, however, senior management shirking and opportunism must be equally controlled. In short, intra-organisational processes define in whose interests organisations function and are important determinants of the nature of social, political and cultural aspects of (strategic) resource allocation.

To act as a basis for understanding the role and functioning of industrial policy, the above comments must be developed by recognising the importance of networks within and between the public/private and commercial/non-commercial sectors. Networking is characterised by enduring rather than transient relationships and may involve research, marketing, distribution and production and involve franchising, contracting-out and joint ventures, or more generally strategic alliances (Wright, 1988, Badaracco, 1991). Recent work (for example, Dietrich, 1991b, Semlinger, 1991) stresses the way in which networking combines the development of trust, characteristic of intra-firm management, with the incentives of markets.[6]

Such ideas have been dormant in economics for some time. Richardson (1972) suggests that the uniqueness of a firm is characterised by a body of know-how. Resource allocation for activities that are necessary for a firm but are outside the character-istic body of skills and expertise will be controlled by market-based relationships. However, the inherent uncertainty of arms-length trading, both operationally and strategically, when innovation is evident means that networks are of central importance, as Lundvall (1988) stresses.

Methods of governing resource allocation between markets and intra-firm management are becoming increasingly important for reasons identified by Badaracco (1991). He draws a distinction between product and knowledge links. Product links are strategic alliances based on knowledge that is readily communicable, com-mon objectives being cost reduction and rapid market penetration. Hence they can be best described as defensive responses to competitive pressures, which have accompanied the current period of restructuring. Knowledge links, on the other hand, involve the joint use of more than one (traditionally separate) knowledge input that is not readily communicable except by direct use. As such these links, representing attempts to manage innovative developments, have become increasingly important given the opportunities offered by current technological change.

It is perhaps worth making the obvious point that the detailed structuring and functioning of networked activity will reflect dominant practices of the organisations involved. In turn, such practices will affect not only the general efficiency of the networks (as measured, for example, by how information rich they are) but also the interests that are represented in the relationships. Relatedly, while networking fosters trust between economic agents, this does not eliminate rivalry and competition. Hence individual returns depend on relative power and motivation.

The elements of the discussion can now be pulled together. When economic restructuring, and hence non-steady-state growth, are evident, resource allocation will be based on strategic management systems and (increasingly) networking as well as markets. But the particular characteristics of these three aspects of resource alloca-tion, and the way that they interact and the resulting economic performance, are not predetermined. To this extent, neo-liberal references to 'free markets' are a conceptual nonsense because markets always embody supply-side idiosyncracies as well as the relative power of the organisational actors involved. It is in these respects that industrial policy is central.

The existence of this institutional complexity implies that market processes are endogenous to strategic decisions. In particular, path-dependent economic processes are evident rather than a self-equilibrating market mechanism. Langlois (1986) argues that if firms that would be profit maximising in equilibrium are badly adapted to disequilibrium they may be selected out before the equilibrium is reached by firms that can more effectively exploit disequilibrium, hence endogenising long-run outcomes. A situation of this sort is implied by the analysis of this section. In equilibrium, static efficiency will dominate competition, but in disequilibrium the ability to exploit an evolving situation is important. Thus firms that have effective strategic management systems and forge effective networked relationships will possess a dynamic comparative advantage. But effective non-market institutions imply investment in systems and activities that are irrational from a static perspective.

More recent work by Arthur (1988, 1989) similarly links path dependency to the dynamics of resource allocation. If choice between technologies follows a random walk, one technology will inevitably become locked-in if falling unit costs with use are evident. In addition, the chosen technology will not necessarily be the most efficient. Hence multiple equilibria, with indeterminate outcomes, can exist. Evolutionary paths become dependent on 'chance' events. The relevance of this is obvious. The use of information is characterised by increasing returns (Arrow, 1974), hence organisations and networks, whose very existence is based on information externalities, will generate path dependencies (North, 1990) which reflect organisational practices and the power relations that they embody. In short, in non-steady-state conditions, path dependency will be the rule rather than the exception (Dosi *et al.*, 1988).

A dynamic industrial policy

Path-dependent dynamics set the parameters within which industrial policies, aimed at facilitating economic change and efficiency, must operate. To this extent the public sector is involved in picking developmental paths, or visions of the future, even if this is in the negative sense of reinforcing current paths by default. The standard market failure arguments fit into particular strategic policy orientations. It follows that proactive industrial policy is selective and restricted to restructuring those parts of an economy deemed strategically important (Cowling, 1990). The majority of a mature economy is consequently autonomous in terms of direct strategic policy objectives. In addition, however, if industrial policy is defined as a set of long-run supply-side initiatives, in this dynamic context it should also be concerned with fuelling institutional change to facilitate the emergence of developmental paths in a more decentralised way. In particular it is worth reiterating the importance of intra-organisational power sharing as discussed in the previous section.

A more dynamic industrial policy can be analysed in terms of two levels: the firm, and system-wide characteristics. With respect to the firm, a fairly obvious point is that, if radical corporate restructuring is required, managerial systems will have to be correspondingly transformed. It follows that progressive strategies are useless if they are not supported by consistent intra-firm practices. More pertinently, competitive pressures will not automatically promote positive strategies because of the problems involved in the transformation of corporate beliefs and assumptions. The power of conservatism and inertia can itself inhibit the development of the dynamism necessary for fundamental microeconomic change.

Reorienting the strategic directions of a firm is a significant management problem usually referred to as 'turnaround'. In the business literature this is usually discussed as an organisation-specific problem,[7] emphasis being placed on new senior management, tighter financial control and so on. In practice, however, successful turnaround appears to depend on outside agencies as well as intra-firm restructuring. In Japan and Germany the banking systems play major supporting roles; and in Japan groups of companies, either based on sub-contracting relationships around a main company or as a redevelopment of the old Zaibatsu system (Aoki, 1988) carry out firm-based turnaround activities. In the UK, such networks appear not to exist. An accurate generalisation might depict actors (particularly financial institutions) protecting interests after corporate failure rather than preventing collapse by turnaround. The arms-length nature of the relationships involved, with the corresponding underdeveloped information flows, will inevitably result in reactive rather than proactive behaviour. It follows that a major industrial policy problem is to facilitate institutional restructuring to allow effective strategic reorientation, a matter discussed shortly.

The general principle involved with system-wide factors is clear. Feasible corporate beliefs and assumptions will be constrained by dominant economic and societal practices and cultural norms. This does not imply a unique one-to-one mapping from extra- to intra-corporate systems, or that no feedback effects are evident. In short, system-wide characteristics define general, but evolving (path-dependent) bounds to firm-level decision-making. Rather than attempt the impossible task, given the limited objectives of this paper, of a general discussion of system-wide characteristics, two particular factors will be isolated: public–private sector relationships, and general organisational–technological imperatives.

The Anglo-Saxon tradition with respect to public–private sector contacts can perhaps best be described as a scepticism with regard to an active role for the state. In terms of analytical categories this can be described in terms of a markets–hierarchies framework: the characteristic arms-length relationships revolve around formal contracting. This has been expanded into a markets–hierarchies–state framework (Pitelis, 1991). The equivalent arms-length contacts imply public sector responsibilities in terms of, for example, a general legal framework and taxation. Given these parameters, private sector decisions are usually considered autonomous. The industrial policy implications are clear; emphasis is placed on, for example, (de)regulation and tax incentives.

It is clear from earlier discussion, however, that the simple markets–hierarchies paradigm is breaking down with the development of networking. Therefore, it would appear to be worth considering the possibility that the efficiency of industrial policy could be equivalently improved by being based on long-run, enduring contacts rather than arms-length relationships.

The previous section indicated that the economic advantages of networking are based on the joint use of different knowledge inputs, and the combination of trust with market incentives. It is clear that public and private sector research activities are complementary (Teece, 1988), with the former accommodating market failures, hence corresponding knowledge links would appear to be necessary to ensure technological restructuring. In addition, however, if the arguments developed above are accepted, networked relationships can, in principle, be used as an alternative to nationalisation for the strategic reorientation of an economy. This might involve public sector share-holding agencies at national and regional–local levels (see below), with all this implies in terms of representation and responsibility. Such structures would facilitate not only (static) economic efficiency, which is one of the main justifications for privatisation, but also the development of trust, rather than scepticism or antagonism, which is essential for the management of dynamic gains.[8]

Before developing the implications of networked policy in more detail, it will be useful to consider the second system-wide factor to be discussed here. It is generally recognised that firm-level restructuring is being channelled by fundamental organisational – technological change. A shift away from previously dominant mass production of homogeneous products, with characteristic technologies and organisational processes based on rigid hierarchy, is occurring, towards more flexible production processes, based on microelectronic and other technologies, with flatter, more decentralised hierarchies (Piore and Sabel, 1984, Freeman and Perez, 1988). While the recognition of these trends is important, the emphasis sometimes placed on a resulting increasing comparative advantage of smaller firms (for example, Dosi, 1988) would appear to be misplaced. The rise of an oligopoly-based or monopoly capitalism is based on financial, marketing and R&D advantages of large firm size (Prais, 1976, Hannah, 1983), technological changes are correspondingly relatively unimportant. To be more precise, Penrose's (1959) distinction between economies of size and expansion can be used. The advantages of large size are dynamic as much as static. It follows that technological change, and its effect on economies of size, need not lead to the reversal of increasing market concentration and the internationalisation of economic activity. Rather, current organisational–technological imperatives, if they unfold in a deregulated environment, will overlay existing historical trends (Amin and Dietrich, 1991a,b). It follows that, if technological potential is to be realised, in terms of creating dynamic small–medium-sized firm activity, industrial policy must recognise the constraining dynamic non-technological factors.

Given these firm- and system-level parameters, the appropriate forms of industrial policy necessary to achieve supply-side restructuring and generate strategic reorientation can be discussed.[9] Policy initiatives would appear to be necessary on three nested layers: international, national, and regional – local. The first of these is necessary because of the international focus of strategically important activities, which requires a regulatory structure of corresponding scope. In terms of the UK, the European Community is obviously a natural focus (see also Part V of this volume). But current EC industrial policy practices have obvious short-comings (Dietrich, 1991a). They are overly passive and their 'top–down' nature is reliant on the leading firms involved. These problems reinforce current organisational practices. Hence a more general proactive EC industrial policy would require movement 'downstream' into innovation and diffusion activities (Grahl and Teague, 1990).

National-level industrial policy initiatives are important because the detailed characteristics of socio-economic norms are over-whelmingly nationally based. It is clear from earlier discussion that strategic management systems nest into these wider characteristics. Hence resource allocation practices cannot be simply implanted into one society from another. Industrial policy frameworks must be 'home-grown' in terms of their detailed functioning.

Socio-economic and organisational norms have constrained the UK's economic development along a dominant trajectory defined by Cowling (1987, 1990) in terms of three characteristics: trans-nationalism, centripetalism and short-termism. Thus, to counter these characteristics and shift the UK's development path, signif-icant institutional change is necessary. Basic requirements would appear to be a Strategic Development Agency and a National Development Bank (Cowling, 1990). But, to counter problems of bureaucratisation, these nationally based agencies should be as small as is feasible and work with regional–local equivalents. In addition, these many loci of autonomous public–private strategic initiatives, and inter-agency networking and institutional compet-ition based on differing skills, will help overcome the problem of public sector activity itself being path dependent. (This problem is discussed by Hans Schenk in Chapter 3.)

The idea behind regional–local initiatives is to improve the capacity to supply goods/services by exploiting particular compar-ative advantages and needs. To this extent they complement intra-organisational power sharing as important elements of an efficient and responsive industrial policy. Current technological changes provide an opportunity in this respect. However, the ability to exploit this potential is contingent upon effective marketing, R&D (innovation and diffusion) and financial support systems. The dynamic advantages of large size in these areas, as discussed earlier, inhibit small–medium-firm development. Thus an effective decentralised industrial policy can be based around public–private networking involving one or more of these factors. This networking may be based on either direct public sector provision or the public sector facilitating the formation of private sector collective institutions. The transaction costs and learning effects involved with the latter possibility imply that public sector subsidy may be appropriate. Thus, what may be called 'strategic havens' can be developed to exploit economies in support services. In addition, such 'strategic havens' can facilitate firm-based strategic reorientation and turnaround activity. It is perhaps no accident that areas with thriving innovative small firm activity are based around either the strategic protection of mutually supporting public–private institutions, as in Emilia Romagna in Italy, or that of core firms, as in Japan (Best, 1990).[10]

Conclusion

This paper has attempted to provide a dynamic framework that can be used to close the gap between industrial policy rhetoric and academic analysis. The framework suggested here is based on the breaking of path-dependent behaviour by selective targeting and proactive intervention in strategically important activities. One important loose end involves justification of the assumption that the state should take on responsibility for strategic reorientation. The reasoning here is clear: the very logic of locked-in activity implies that it is in no one firm's interest to attempt to develop alternative growth paths. This is not just a matter of the opportunity costs of organisational and technical asset development, with the attendant problems of private appropriability. It is also concerned with the development of a strategic consensus within which decentralised (strategic) decision-making is located and focused.[11]

This leads on to a further issue. Neo-liberal, and perhaps Marxist, economists may see a neo-corporatism in the framework suggested in this paper, and hence point to failed experiments in the UK. There are perhaps two ways of confronting this issue.[12] First is a casual empiricism that seems to suggest a correlation between public sector proactive intervention and long-run economic success. On a more analytical level, however, there are clear differences between an obsolete corporatism and the framework suggested here. The arguments presented recognise that economic processes embody power relations that industrial policy must explicitly acknowledge. Furthermore, the framework is based on the evident restructuring that is providing a new sectoral and organisational economic dynamic, and hence emphasises selective state activity that is decentralised to its relevant level. Perhaps most importantly, however, an emphasis on public sector failure obscures the reality that static and dynamic market failures are pervasive. Hence the choice is between an industrial policy based on public sector involvement to facilitate long-run proactive development that responds to popular need, or short-run defensive restructuring with its attendant supply-side weakness.

Notes

This paper has benefited from discussion at the 1991 Warwick/Birmingham Workshop on Industrial Strategy. Needless to say I am solely responsible for the form in which any comments have been included (or excluded), and correspondingly for any remaining mistakes, confusions, etc.

1 See Dietrich (1991a) for a more complete application, in the context of European integration, of aspects of the framework developed in this paper.

2 See Stoneman and Vickers (1988), Shepherd (1987), Odagiri (1986) and Shonfield (1981).

3 Economic theory suggests two reasons why markets might be 'missing'. One involves a dynamic analysis, as suggested in the text. The other involves recognising the costs of contracting, or operating markets which may be larger than any benefits derivable. This second reason is frequently located in a transaction cost framework (see Dietrich, 1991b). A discussion of the conceptual problems involved if these two reasons are combined into a single analytical framework is beyond the scope of this paper, hence missing markets due to excessive contracting costs will be ignored.

4 The analysis of strategic management in the text is based on Dietrich (1990).

5 In this context, modern management theorists are taken to be writers such as Johnson and Scholes (1988) and Mintzberg (1991).

6 While the efficiency of networking is apparent in some contexts, it should also be recognised that it may be a second-best option to full integration (Kay, 1991).

7 A useful summary of the turnaround literature is provided in Bowman and Asch (1987). A more detailed discussion is Slatter (1984).

8 In a different context we can cite the system of monetary control that existed in the UK in the 1970s, important aspects of which involved persuasion. Arguably this system was more successful than that introduced in the 1980s based on arms-length relationships between the public and private sectors.

9 The forms of industrial policy discussed in the text are similar to those suggested by Coriat and Petit (1991) as being necessary to exploit, in a positive way, the opportunities offered by the emerging economic dynamic.

10 There is some evidence of a shift towards the development of decentralised strategic havens in the area of R&D support in Canada, Denmark, the Netherlands, Norway, Switzerland and Germany (OECD, 1990). For Germany this is a continuation of its traditional industrial policy stance. Also note that this list does not include the UK.

11 The consensus building to facilitate strategic reorientation should not be confused with traditional indicative planning (see Estrin and Holmes, 1983). The latter is based on the exogeneity of corporate assumptions and policies.

12 A complete discussion of this issue would involve an extended socio-economic analysis, concentrating in particular on the non-neutrality of the state. Such a discussion is obviously beyond the scope of this paper.

References

Amin, A. and Dietrich, M. (1991a), 'From hierarchy to "hierarchy": the dynamics of contemporary corporate restructuring in Europe', in Amin and Dietrich (1991c).

Amin, A. and Dietrich, M. (1991b), 'Deciphering the Terrain of European restructuring', in Amin and Dietrich (1991c).

Amin, A. and Dietrich, M. (eds) (1991c), *Towards a New Europe? Structural change in European economy*, Aldershot: Edward Elgar.

Aoki, M. (1988), *Information, Incentives and Bargaining in the Japanese Economy*, Cambridge: Cambridge University Press.

Arrow, K. J. (1974), *The Limits of Organization*, New York: W. W. Norton.

Arthur, W. B. (1988), 'Self-reinforcing mechanisms in economics', in P. W. Anderson, K. J. Arrow and D. Pines (eds), *The Economy as an Evolving Complex System*, Redwood, CA: Addison Wesley.

Arthur, W. B. (1989), 'Competing technologies, increasing returns and lock-in by historical events', *Economic Journal*, 99, 116–31.

Badaracco, J. L. Jr (1991), *The Knowledge Link*, Boston, MA: Harvard Business School Press.

Best, M. H. (1990), *The New Competition: institutions of industrial restructuring*, Cambridge: Polity Press.

Bowman, C. and Asch, D. (1987), *Strategic Management*, Basingstoke: Macmillan.

Clutterbuck, D. and Goldsmith, W. (1984), *The Winning Streak*, London: Weidenfeld & Nicolson.

Coriat, B. and Petit, P. (1991), 'De-industrialisation and tertiarisation: towards a new economic regime?', in Amin and Dietrich (1991c).

Cowling, K. (1987), 'An industrial strategy for Britain: the nature and role of planning', *International Review of Applied Economics*, 1, 1–22.

Cowling, K. (1990), 'The strategic approach to economic and industrial policy', in K. Cowling and R. Sugden (eds), *A New Economic Policy for Britain: essays on the development of industry*, Manchester: Manchester University Press.

Cowling, K. and Sugden, R. (1991), 'A strategy for industrial development as a basis for regulation', mimeo, University of Warwick/Birmingham.

Dietrich, M. (1990), 'Corporate management and the economics of the firm', *British Review of Economic Issues*, 12(28), October, 21–35.

Dietrich, M. (1991a), 'European economic integration and industrial policy', *Review of Political Economy*, 3(4), October, 418–40.

Dietrich, M. (1991b), 'Firms, markets and transaction cost economics', *Scottish Journal of Political Economy*, 38(1), February, 41–57.

Dosi, G. (1988), 'Sources, procedures, and microeconomic effects of innovation', *Journal of Economic Literature*, 26, 1120–71.

Dosi, G., Freeman, C., Nelson, R., Silverberg, G. and Soete, L. (eds) (1988), *Technical Change and Economic Theory*, London: Pinter Publishers.

Estrin, S. and Holmes, P. (1983), *French Planning in Theory and Practice*, London: Allen & Unwin.

Freeman, C. and Perez, C. (1988), 'Structural crises of adjustment: business cycles and investment behaviour', in Dosi *et al.* (1988).

Grahl, J. and Teague, P. (1990), *1992 – the Big Market*, London: Lawrence & Wishart.

Hannah, L. (1983), *The Rise of the Corporate Economy*, 2nd edn, London: Methuen.

Johnson, G. and Scholes, K. (1988), *Exploring Corporate Strategy*, 2nd edn, Hemel Hempstead: Prentice Hall.

Kay, N. M. (1991), 'Multinational enterprise as strategic choice: some transaction cost perspectives', in C. N. Pitelis and R. Sugden (eds), *The Nature of the Transnational Firm*, London: Routledge.

Kirzner, L. M. (1973), *Competition and Entrepreneurship*, Chicago: University of Chicago Press.

Knight, K. G. and Sugden, R. (1990), 'Efficiency, economic democracy and company law', in K. Cowling and R. Sugden (eds), *A New Economic Policy for Britain: essays on the development of industry*, Manchester: Manchester University Press.

Labour Party (1991), *Building a World Class Economy, Modern Manufacturing Strength*, London: The Labour Party.

Langlois, R. N. (1986), 'Rationality, institutions, and explanation', in R. N. Langlois (ed), *Economics as a Process: essays in the new institutional economics*, Cambridge: Cambridge University Press.

Lundvall, B. A. (1988), 'Innovation as an interactive process: from user–producer interaction to the national system of innovation', in Dosi *et al.* (1988).

Mintzberg, H. (1991), 'The Effective Organization: forces and forms', *Sloan Management Review*, Winter, 54–67.

North, D. C. (1990), *Institutions, Institutional Change and Economic Performance*, Cambridge: Cambridge University Press.

Odagiri, H. (1986), 'Industrial policy in theory and reality', in H. W. de Jong and W. G. Shepherd (eds), *Mainstreams in Industrial Organization*, Lancaster: Klewer Academic Publishers.

OECD (1990), *Industrial Policy in OECD Countries, Annual Review 1990*, Paris: OECD.

Penrose, E. T. (1959), *The Theory of the Growth of the Firm*, Oxford: Basil Blackwell.

Peters, T. S. and Waterman, R. H. (1982), *In Search of Excellence*, New York: Harper & Row.

Piore, M. and Sabel, C. F. (1984), *The Second Industrial Divide: possibilities for prosperity*, New York: Basic Books.

Pitelis, C. (1991), 'The Nature of the capitalist state', mimeo, University of St Andrews.

Prais, S. J. (1976), *The Evolution of Giant Firms in Britain*, Cambridge: Cambridge University Press.

Richardson, G. B. (1972), 'The organisation of industry', *Economic Journal*, 82, 883–96.

Saunders, C. T. (ed.) (1987), *Industrial Policies and Structural Change*, Basingstoke: Macmillan.

Semlinger, K. (1991), 'New developments in subcontracting: mixing market and hierarchy', in Amin and Dietrich (1991c).

Shepherd, J. (1987), 'Industrial support policies', *National Institute Economic Review*, November, 59–71.

Shonfield, A. (1981), 'Innovation: does government have a role?', in C. Carter (ed.), *Industrial Policy and Innovation*, London: Heinemann.

Slatter, S. (1984), *Corporate Recovery*, Harmondsworth: Penguin.

Stoneman, P. and Vickers, J. (1988), 'The economics of technology policy', *Oxford Review of Economic Policy*, 4(4).

Teece, D. (1988), 'Technological change and the nature of the firm', in Dosi *et al.* (1988).

Wright, M. (1988), 'Redrawing the boundaries of the firm', in S. Thompson and M. Wright (eds), *Internal Organisation Efficiency and Profit*, Oxford: Philip Allan.

3   *Hans Schenk*

Some comments on the competitive strategy aspects of industrial policy

'Strategy is about winning.' (R. M. Grant, 1991)

Introduction

The focus as well as content of industrial policies is strategic. Although this attribute is often mentioned in government white papers as well as academic discourse, one sometimes gets the impression that the adjective 'strategic' is simply added to signal that the activities under discussion are 'very important'. The business literature is no exception in this respect: one frequently encounters such terms as strategic inventory management, strategic human resources management, strategic accounting and strategic budgeting. Even strategic management textbooks are frequently so vague about the exact *meaning* of the term 'strategic' that it is generally uncertain what makes strategic management strategic. Likewise, it is uncertain *why* industrial policy is – or should be qualified as – strategic and what precisely are the *implications* of that. This paper is therefore meant to clarify the strategic characteristics of industrial policy so that it can be treated as strategic activities should be treated.

By investigating precisely what makes an activity (or a decision-making process) strategic, the first section will deal with issues of domain. The next section checks whether industrial policy is in fact a strategic activity and tries to find out what this implies. I then briefly discuss some models of strategic or rather strategy management in an effort to find the appropriate model for the derivation of some principles of industrial policy. The ultimate aim of the paper is to make a contribution to clarifying what distinguishes a good industrial strategy from a bad industrial strategy.

What is strategy?

A strategy is the final manifestation of a process that has involved problem recognition, analysis of alternative courses of action and the selection of the most desirable alternative. This process may have been either an implicit process which can be distilled *ex post* or a consciously managed process designed to lead from one stage to the other. Managing 'the strategy (formation) process' in a conscious or deliberate way is usually called 'strategic management', but I prefer the term 'strategy management', as will be explained shortly. A dissection of this process (see Figure 3.1) reveals the following ingredients. Something is a strategic problem whenever it creates either grand opportunities for, or existential threats to, the organisation in question. This is the case when it is related to what is commonly called the 'domain' of the organisation. The domain of an organisation is understood here to be very similar to its 'mission', the sole difference being that the latter is the more or less articulated version of the former – sometimes having even been written down in a 'mission statement'. Both are concerned with the scope of an organisation's activities. A mission concerns the basic philosophy of an organisation, i.e. its purpose, image and character. It is the explicit projection of the central and overriding concepts on which the operations of e.g. a firm are based. Strategic problems often – though not necessarily – have major resource implications and they are likely to affect the long-term direction of an organisation. Thus, in the first place, the strategic management process involves making a firm's scope explicit in order to establish its overall purpose and direction, thus distinguishing it from, or positioning it vis-à-vis, other firms. Other reasons for being explicit on an organisation's scope include the establishment of unanimity of purpose among its members, providing an initial overview of the directions in which resources are to be utilised, providing a starting point for thinking beyond current business involvement, allowing for the development of a scenario that will provide future aspirations (Greenley, 1989; also see, e.g., Jauch and Glueck, 1988, Johnson and Scholes, 1988). Deciding the mission can be a complicated matter, depending on the complexity of the firm's environment, in particular the

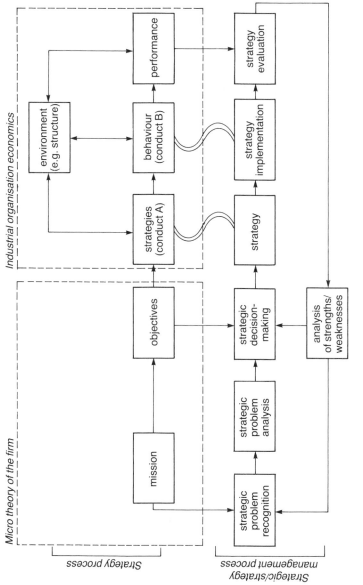

Figure 3.1   Strategy and strategic management: an ideal-type model

complexity of its collection of stakeholders. This complexity is bound to be great when the firm is not of the one-product, one-plant type but a conglomerate. At present, most large firms resemble the conglomerate in the sense that they are multi-product, multi-plant and multi-divisional companies, and a considerable number of them are outright conglomerates, i.e. firms with activities in unrelated industries or technologies. The more complex the circumstances, the greater the need for mission (and domain) analyses.

Once a strategic problem is recognised, it has to be analysed. This simply means that it has to be broken down into causes and effects: it has to be understood. Strategic decision-making involves evaluating the options available for meeting the problem in relation to both the objectives of the organisation and its strengths and weaknesses.[1] Objectives state what is to be achieved and when the results are to be accomplished. Whereas missions are hard to formulate in closed terms, objectives are the crystallised expressions of missions implying that mission and objectives should square. The *strategies* of an organisation state how those results are to be achieved. A strategy is quite commonly defined as a pattern or plan that integrates an organisation's mission, objectives and action sequences into a cohesive whole (see, e.g., Quinn, Mintzberg and James, 1988). Putting these strategies to work means implementing them, and the result of all this is what outsiders can observe: strategic conduct or behaviour.

It is instructive to discuss here briefly the differences between operational management and strategic management as the latter has been defined above. Operational management is normally understood to be concerned with the effective use of *current* levels of expenditure and revenue plus the efficient use of *existing* capacities (see Greenley, 1989). One could, however, easily make a further distinction between short-term and long-term operational management, as we will see below. In that case, it would be more appropriate to define operational management as being closely related to issues of strategy implementation. Although most texts are rather vague on this issue, it could be argued that these relations themselves are the manifestations of *tactics*. Tactics then are schemes for action. In the traditional understanding of these terms, however, what is defined as strategic or tactic or operational largely depends on where one sits – which evidently is bound to create confusion. Glancing over the strategic management literature, one is indeed soon convinced that such confusion is the order of the day.

Moreover, focusing on the procedural aspects of strategy as has been done above cannot capture the substantive essence of strategy. It does not illuminate why strategic behaviour is possible at all, or why it is a fact of life.[2] For example, why can firms not just confine themselves to long-term operational management? To grasp the significance of strategy, it is necessary to note that strategic behaviour is non-existent in what (neoclassical) economists call a perfectly competitive environment. Recall that this is defined as a situation in which the multitude of competitors guarantees that the actions of no one individual firm can have a perceptible influence on market outcomes (most significantly: price), or alternatively a situation in which each player is so insignificant that their decisions can have no effect on any other players. In such a situation the only option available to firms, at the cost of being wound up, is to maximise profits, i.e. to select the point on the production function at which profits are maximised (or exit the industry). Recall also that this means – for entirely mathematical reasons – that it is necessary to assume subsequently that firms cannot be allowed any scope to determine the nature of the production functions: 'the production function is a datum which the firm accepts, and nothing the firm does can alter the production function' (Moss, 1981, p. 10).[3] Of course, the situation of perfect competition is entirely hypothetical. Nevertheless, it reminds us of the fact that strategic behaviour can only be present where competition is *im*perfect, more particularly where the market environment is characterised by some variant of oligopoly (which the business literature takes for granted, even when it is not fully aware of its implications). Fortunately, oligopoly is the normal state of affairs in real markets so that it is not surprising at all to find that it is a normal – even essential – part of business activity to violate that most basic assumption of perfect competition. It is precisely the indeterminacy of the oligopoly problem that allows firms degrees of freedom, i.e. the possibilities to exercise a substantial measure of choice between strategic alternatives and to practise what I will call strategy management.

All is not as nice as it sounds, however. This freedom of choice is at the same time quite limited too – most importantly by the fact that firms under oligopoly realise that their actions are interdependent.[4] Whereas mutual dependency certainly exists under perfect competition as well, agents will not and need not perceive it: all the information that is relevant is incorporated in the market prices, which are assumed known. We may therefore say that firms are 'trapped in a *large* numbers game' to such an extent that competition is, in fact, ruled out. When it is assumed, on the other hand, that players know that other players are conscious actors and are aware of the mutual interdependencies, we may rather qualify their position as 'being trapped in a *small* numbers game'. In practice, this may mean that their strategic options are quite limited as well, especially in the case that the players have to deal with imperfect and incomplete information and the game's payoffs are far away. Speculations as to what may be the outcome of such games are not just interesting but quite important for industrial policy as well. We will therefore return to this issue later on in this paper.

For the moment, let us focus on the fact that firms cannot just be content with operational management *because there is rivalry*: an aggressive struggle between interdependent competitors for the patronage of buyers (see Brenner, 1987). Without such rivalry, the concept of strategy is empty and strategic management reduces to something which – as was already implicitly suggested above – could be labelled as long-term operational management. It would 'only' be concerned with establishing objectives, forecasting future developments and planning resource deployments in the light of these. This means that the substantive definition of strategy should make explicit reference to the phenomenon of rivalry. Most textbooks on strategic management tend to forget this crucial issue (mostly because they are so preoccupied with procedural matters) but there are a few exceptions, albeit that these arrive at their conclusions while heavily leaning on military analogies instead of oligopoly theory. Grant (1991, p. 11) for example refers to strategy as the 'overall plan for deploying resources to establish a favourable position . . . strategy is concerned with winning the war'. Quinn (in Quinn, Mintzberg and James, 1988, p. 3) speaks of strategies as plans which are based on among others 'anticipated *changes in the environment*, and contingent moves by *intelligent opponents*' (emphasis in the original). Note that both Grant and Quinn refer to a 'plan', which implies that strategies are developed consciously and purposefully in advance of the actions to which they apply.[5] This need not be the case, however, since strategies can also have 'emerged' for one reason or another. They may even have taken the actor by surprise. Following Mintzberg (1985), the former type of strategy is usually designated as 'deliberate', the latter as 'emergent'. Keeping that in mind, a combination of these two definitions would lead to strategy being defined as 'the deployment of resources to achieve a favourable position against competition from intelligent opponents' (see also James, 1985). Thus, a strategic move need not be designed to influence the behaviour of others (as classic and frequently cited treatments such as in Schelling, 1960, would maintain), although it will certainly be designed or meant to influence other firms' expected payoffs or at least the ratio of their respective payoffs. This can essentially be done in two ways (Morris *et al.*, 1986). First, a strategy can have lasting effects on cost and/or demand conditions: investments in capacity, R&D, advertising, brand introduction, etc. Secondly, it can influence the beliefs of competitors – even while not affecting cost and demand conditions – by signalling. Strategies of the first type will obviously have both major resource implications and long-term consequences, whereas signalling strategies may or may not have these consequences.

Note, also, that the Quinn definition refers to changes in the environment. As far as these changes have been created in the process of rivalry, they are captured in our understanding of strategy. But environmental changes may also be the result of more general causes (like initiatives to reduce trade barriers on a significant scale; a speeding up of technological change). Since we would be sailing under false colours if we tried to deal with this kind of problem here as well (and my impression is that precisely that is one of the causes for paradigmatic confusion among strategists), it seems appropriate to let this be clear from the start. I therefore prefer the term 'competitive strategy' (see Porter, 1980). Likewise, I prefer to use the term 'strategy management' rather than 'strategic management'.

Summing up, activities (or decision-making processes) will be rightfully called strategic:

- if they relate directly to strategic problems, i.e. problems which are of existential importance to the mission or the domain (and thus goals) of the organisation in question, and
- if they are responses to acts of rivalry or rivalrous acts themselves.

Thus, I would suggest for example that the act of vertical integration (frequently considered a strategic move in its own right) can be defined as strategic only if it is undertaken in order to influence the expected payoffs of rivals (through such activities as pre-empting, market closure, price squeezing). In all other cases it would 'merely' be operational.[6]

One last point should be mentioned here. Strategic decisions are normally – and especially so in the case of business firms – taken by the 'leaders' of the organisation. While it is unlikely in practice that these decisions are the pure preserve of top managers (it will normally take contributions from different hierarchical parts of the organisation in the sense of ideas, but there will also be a lot of bargaining, negotiation, compromises, etc.), they do have the authority to force or persuade business units to comply with the decisions once these have been taken. Of course, there normally will be ample opportunities for undermining or evading the hierarchical flow of things in a firm, but at the same time the arsenal of rewards and punishments that can be applied by the leaders of the firm will be large too. Only when an organisation has the disposal of this authority of implementation can we rightly describe it as a strategic actor *pur sang*.

What is so (un)strategic about industrial policy?

From the preceding section it can be concluded that industrial policy can be correctly described as strategic if it fits into Figure 3.1. That involves two things: there have to be problems that can be interpreted as threats to or opportunities for accomplishing mission-derived objectives, and the industrial policy body must be operating in a small numbers game, i.e. in competition with rivals. In addition, when management of the process of strategy formation is on the agenda, the industrial policy authority (say, the government) must be *able* to control or supervise all the different strategic management stages: the government must be able to act as a strategic principal. Industrial policy is normally understood as a policy that seeks to influence the process of industrial change (the objective) through microeconomic intervention, i.e. intervention in the general mechanisms of production and resource allocation or in the actual allocation of resources among sectors of production (e.g. Lindbeck, 1981). Others are more applied in a sense but not different in principle; they speak of business firms instead of mechanisms and resources, so that industrial policy is seen as intervention in the decision-making procedures used by firms or in the actual outcome of those for the purpose of influencing the process of industrial change. The accepted definition of industrial policy – while being useful as a working definition – does not make any reference to the rivalry aspect, thus suggesting that its domain is rather a fight 'against nature'. As we will see shortly, that is not in accordance with the evidence. But the received definition does make a few things clear: industrial policy is not competition policy,[7] and industrial policy is selective policy.[8]

Let us now try to imagine a situation that is in accordance with the conditions just mentioned. Assume that domestic firms are losing ground to foreign firms, within their domestic markets or abroad. Since this type of international competition can be described as a struggle for market share among a small number of oligopolists, we here have a situation of rivalry in which strategic behaviour is not only likely but essential to survival. Assume further that governments see it as one of their tasks to assist their domestic firms in this battle. In that case, governments are in effect considering the country (nation) as a relevant unit of competition. When the Dutch government supports Philips in its development of megabit chips and in developing an international market for these (which it did with hundreds of millions of ECU during the late 1980s) it is viewing the Netherlands as in competition with, for example, France and Japan in a core industry, not just considering Philips as competing against Thomson and Fujitsu. When the French government helps Air France to acquire its biggest domestic competitor UTA – in fact it was orchestrating the merger in early 1990 – in order to reap a stronger international market position, it is not just considering Air France as an ordinary airline firm in competition with British Airways or KLM but it is viewing France as in rivalry with other European countries.

These examples are clearly cases of strategic behaviour on the part of governments in rivalry with other governments. First, it is clear that they are not concerned with trivial problems: these are issues that are of major relevance to a nation's competitive stance. Secondly, they have major resource implications and long-term consequences. Thirdly, they illustrate selective policies instead of generic policies, implying that choices had to be made. The last argument, however, may be doing more justice to industrial policy than is justified by the evidence since at this point in our discussion it is not clear at all whether, for example, the Philips case involved a deliberate strategy or not. Could it be that the decision to support Philips had been forced upon the Dutch government in some way or another? We will return to this issue shortly.

The examples mentioned can be supplemented by many others illustrating that governments are at present heavily involved in strategic processes of international rivalry. This, however, has not always been so. The intensification of international competition during the 1980s inevitably led to a generally stronger focus of governments on the competitive position of domestic industry in a worldwide perspective (Dankbaar, Groenewegen and Schenk, 1990). But when government white papers of the 1980s are compared with those produced in the 1970s one is struck by the sudden appearance of international competition as the major legitimisation of the policies discussed or proposed. This is only paralleled by the role that has been awarded to technology, to technology policy and consequently to those industries which are considered to be promising high-tech or sunrise industries.[9] The 1970s, on the other hand, were characterised by manifold references to the selectively appreciable consequences of (what was seen at the time as) a general deterioration in economic conditions. Consequently, industrial policy was justifiably focused on the support of ailing industries and firms.

Despite this change in focus, it is noteworthy that the measures chosen to realise both of these strategies are remarkably similar, thus causing doubt about the supposedly strategic content of the policies in question. An overview of Western industrial policies shows that two measures are of special importance: while only the French distinguished themselves with a quite intensive national-isation programme at the beginning of the 1980s, it is subsidies and the promotion of firm size which have generally and lavishly been applied across Western Europe (Schenk, 1992). At present, the financial support of industry in a selective sense is, indeed, impressive. It is typically between 4% and 7% of industrial GDP in the major European countries (i.e. excluding supranational sup-port) and sometimes on an average yearly basis as high as 42% of value added in a specific industry like steel (calculated across the EC10 over 1981 – 86; see also Chapter 11 on European Community countries). In many cases the financial support of firms as well as industries was and still is coupled with measures aiming at the establishment of higher concentration ratios. In the earlier period, special semi-government institutions were even set up to promote this process in, for example, Great Britain (the IRC, Industrial Reorganisation Corporation) and the Netherlands (the NEHEM, an acronym for the Dutch Restructuring Corporation, modelled on the IRC).

Another aspect of industrial policies in both the 1970s and 1980s strikes the eye: the similarity of policies *across countries*. As far as the policies to support ailing firms/industries are concerned, this should not be a surprise: for their justification was found in *generally* deteriorating circumstances, or was it not? But what really causes concern is the fact that the focus as well as the extent of the 'picking winners' policies of the 1980s are so similar (Roobeek, 1988, Schenk, 1992). For *these* policies are supposed to be really strategic. What type of strategy is this that we are dealing with here?

Let us first deal with the strategies of the earlier period. Since selection of the candidates for support was mainly on a first-come/worst-case basis and the existing managerial hierarchies were almost never affected in the sense that incumbent managers were removed or their decision-making authority curtailed (Schenk, 1987), it would appear that government subsidies could hardly be seen as intervention that was meant to change the general mechanisms of production and allocation or the (strategic) behaviour of firms – one of the two major elements in the received definition of industrial policy. It has to be concluded, indeed, that subsidies were merely meant to help the firms concerned in their struggle with general economic problems along established strategic routes. Thus, these industrial policy actions would have to be described as actions in a game 'against nature' rather than a game against rivals. That is, they were not explicitly meant to improve the competitive position of domestic firms in international rivalry in a structural way. They nevertheless had this effect. Describing these measures as elements of an industrial *strategy* would seem to be a tall order, however. Only in so far as they were explicitly meant to *match* subsidies that foreign governments were allocating to their ailing firms, which was occasionally the case, may it be concluded *ex post* that governments were conscious of the fact that they were operating in a competitive situation and that the support given was to change the balance of payoffs that were expected in case of inaction. Since in general a clear mission was lacking and government action was primarily (and consequently) *ad hoc*, the best we can say is that the industrial policies of the 1970s can be described as emergent instead of deliberate strategies to change the *de facto* allocation of resources through a redistribution programme – the second element in the received definition of industrial policy. My impression is, however, that we should really describe this type of industrial policy as an imposed strategy, i.e. a strategy that has been dictated in its patterns of action by the environment either through direct imposition (say by a strong business lobby) or through implicitly pre-empting or bounding the government's choice (see Mintzberg in Quinn, Mintzberg and James, 1988).

What about the focus on industrial market concentration as well as aggregate concentration during the 1970s? Apart from the familiar size mystique surrounding many of these efforts, the main reasons for pro-merger attitudes were quite traditional. Against a background of stagnating consumer demand and labour-saving technological advance, scale economies and the reduction of competition were thought to result in more viable firms. France, however, may have been one of the first European countries in which it was explicitly recognised that the already increasing internationalisation of competition was part of the problem. Its well-developed machinery for encouraging national leaders to become in effect 'national champions' – probably originally created in order to facilitate the transmission of more general political and macroeconomic demands from government to industry (Groenewegen, 1987) – was maintained and partly revived in response to worries that – following an influential monograph by Servan-Schreiber (1967) – French enterprises were too small to be able to compete with their American rivals. These worries were also for the first time aired at the level of the European Community by the so-called Colonna Report of 1970 (see also Harvie Ramsay's discussion in Chapter 12). It took more than a decade, however, before the European Commission translated these worries into programmes deliberately designed to stimulate co-operation and alliances in the area of technology. But it should be admitted that the EC's lenient attitude towards mergers and acquisitions in the meantime was so apparent that one can speak of an industrial strategy anyway. The worries about the comparative size of European enterprises have recently been boosted again against the background of the 1992 programme. While many national

European markets are considered too small to allow the capturing of the benefits of scale economies, the 1992 initiative not only aspires to reducing the remaining internal trade barriers in Western Europe, but also 'looks forward to what it sees as an inevitable restructuring of European industry, one that will facilitate the growth of large pan-European firms able to compete on a par with their US or Japanese rivals' (Geroski, 1989, p. 29).[10] Developments in the area of mergers and acquisitions during the second half of the 1980s corroborate this: their frequency and size were unprecedented. Added to this was a generally favourable attitude towards alliances and collaborative ventures, especially in the field of technology. The picture that has emerged is comparable to a vast collection of intertwined spiders' webs: it is difficult to find a firm that is going it alone, or with fewer than five others. Government programmes in high technology look like offprints of a single menu: telecommunications, microelectronics, biotechnology, etc., these are the areas that are collectively found to be worthy of increasing attention. R&D support is typically a mere reflection of R&D priorities that are in vogue in the international ball park. The new industrial policy has received wide acclaim, especially in the economics and business profession – which is in stark contrast with the 'backing losers' policies of the 1970s, which were generally criticised (at least *ex post*).

Only a few connected questions remain. Is there really a fundamental difference between the industrial policies of the 1970s on the one hand and those of the 1980s on the other, as official public reports and academic analyses would have us believe? And why do governments align so easily with the *modus vivendi* of the corporate economy? Why do they not break away from established and collectively shared trajectories? In other words: can we regard the average West European government as a purposive strategist, choosing deliberately a particular strategy under circumstances {Y} and choosing again but accidentally a similar strategy under circumstances {X}? Unless this me-too and matching behaviour is the result of original, rational assessments during the strategic decision-making stage (Figure 3.1), which would seem too easy an answer, the answer I would suggest is perhaps hidden in the properties of the small numbers game.

Above, I have made the suggestion that the interdependencies which are the essence of such games may lure the players into a trap.

While the budget requirements are sizeable, strategic games in the areas of innovation, mergers, foreign direct investment, etc., are fraught with great uncertainties concerning modalities as well as payoffs. What is known is that the normalised failure rates are potentially very high, but that the rewards may occasionally be very high as well. Especially since many of the players in game *a* (the R&D game) may or will meet again in game *b* (the takeover game) and again in game *c* (the Foreign Direct Investment game) – which resembles the situation of multi-market contacts – so that the leadership may rotate, it is not far-fetched to assume that players in those circumstances will adopt strategies that aim at the minimisation of the largest possible *ex post* regret over chosen alternatives. Such a minimax regret strategy is akin to minimising the risk of overlooking opportunities which have been (rightly or wrongly) grasped by competitors. Quite often, it would seem, the only way of realising this strategy would be to follow a first mover. If this first mover is backing the wrong horse, the followers will also be at a loss. *Comparatively* speaking, however, the competitive situation *ex post* would not be much difference from that *ex ante*. Following the leader then becomes a rational way of countering, and countering becomes a form of insurance (cf. Knickerbocker, 1973). The final result would be that firms will forge R&D alliances to know what rivals are going to undertake (thereby making come true that innovations are connected instead of particular), will match competitors in the merger arena (thereby creating the customary waves), and will display bandwagon behaviour in FDI (creating a sudden apparent attractiveness of region *x* today and region *y* tomorrow). Thus, swimming with the tide assures the players of a further turn in the ball park, and that this may be of vital importance has among others been shown by Teece (1990): a firm that did not participate in the development and production of one generation of dynamic random access memories (DRAMs) had only a slim chance of being able to participate in the next.

When we add to all this that managers have a limited capacity to design strategies, are even sometimes accused of being unable to think strategically (as is illustrated in most introductory chapters of strategic management textbooks; e.g. Johnson and Scholes, 1988), it is clear that at the least it will be impossible for all possible strategic options to be evaluated. Rather, one will find that managers use 'successive limited comparisons', implying that the strategy process is characterised by 'logical incrementalism' (Quinn, 1980). This means that those options most approximating to past decisions are likely to be looked upon most favourably because they build on the experience of the organisation and its managers.

As yet, there is no reason to expect that a government, particularly in its policies towards those firms and their managers, i.e. in its industrial policy, will be able to persuade them into breaking away from their established strategic routines. First, the small numbers game offers not only a trap, but also a quite rational way of strategy making which consequently has a strong appeal to business decision-makers. Secondly, firms cannot be considered as the business units of governments, so that agents who could execute dissenting industrial policies are lacking. Thirdly, while it is to be applauded that governments have increasingly become aware of the fact that the phenomenon of rivalry has transcended the laws of economies of scale and comparative advantage, participating in international processes of rivalry means participating in a small numbers game too. Since both categories of game are heavily and increasingly intertwined we must conclude not only that industrial policy hasn't exactly become a classic example of deliberate strategic problem solving, but also that it will be rather difficult to change all this. Yet, the ultimate in strategy is being able to operate as a strategic actor *pur sang*, to design your own trajectory, to break away from this 'kind of dynamic "lock-in" phenomenon' (Teece, 1990, p. 62). Are there any leads that can direct a strategic decision-maker, in either business or industrial policy, in doing exactly that?

Towards strategic industrial policy

Asking the question implicitly supposes that it is *possible* for firms or industrial policy authorities to break away from the *mores* of the small numbers game. Right from the start we should point to the fact that not everybody in strategic management shares this belief. In particular, proponents of what Mintzberg (1990) has called 'the environmental school' would maintain that strategy formation is a passive process and that power over it rests not in the organisation but in its environment. In commenting upon the views of this school, Mintzberg rightfully stresses, however, that debating whether organisations are able to make strategic choices is 'about as useful as debating whether people are happy' (1990, p. 178). On the other hand, assuming that strategy results, just like that, as the end-product of decomposing the strategy process into specified components and then assembling these according to a blueprint (a premise of what has become known as the 'planning school') is, again according to Mintzberg, committing the fallacy of formalisation. Such decomposition typically leads to endless series of black boxes on paper that 'instead of showing how to create strategies merely implore managers to do so' (1990, p. 123). What we typically see in organisations that believe in strategic planning is truckloads of forecasting, scheduling, programming and budgeting techniques, all of which take you into routine games instead of out. Nor is the 'design school' a way out of procedure-focused strategic management. It advises strategic managers to disconnect thinking from action in order to be able to design a full-blown and explicit strategy, but does not focus on the actual content of strategies; again, they are the almost automatic result provided that the strategic actor follows the prescribed steps in the process, and the designers need not worry about issues of implementation. The motto is: it does not matter much which strategy you follow, as long as you do it procedurally correctly. Making strategy 'grand' and explicit, however, is bound to promote inflexibility since the more clearly it is formulated, the more difficult it is to change. And frequent change in particular is of extreme importance since, no sooner than your trajectory seems attractive, rivals will join in so that a new small numbers game is born and you will have to break away again. Thus, two of the most established schools of strategic management cannot tell us how to break away: their procedures encourage incremental change instead of quantum change, doing things correctly instead of breaking the rules, generic thinking instead of creative thinking, attention to established categories instead of creating new ones, tedium instead of surprise and, rather unexpectedly for allegedly long-term activities, short-termism at the expense of long-term perspectives because they encourage stepwise thinking. In the end, they do not tell us how to eliminate path dependency – whereas that is precisely what counts. Moreover, they are hardly concerned with competitive processes, however strange that may sound. Their focus is on long-range planning and on forecasting environmental change: setting long-term goals and developing budgeting and control systems that anticipate future flows of funds and ensure more or less consistent decisions along the path to the future. In our terminology, they should be classified under long-term operational management.

In summary, the supposedly scientific (for 'compartmentalised') approach to strategy must be sacrificed to an approach that stimulates creative thinking, is flexible, does not separate design from implementation, and, through its awareness of small number dependencies, focuses on how to outsmart rivals by avoiding them. What we are looking for then, in fact, is an entrepreneurial approach to industrial policy, i.e. an industrial policy in which the state plays a major role as public entrepreneur (see Minns and Rogers, 1990). This is different from being a public *enterprise* since it focuses – in accordance with the established Schumpeterian understanding of the term – on innovation and new ventures. This paper is not the place to present a full outline of such an entrepreneurial role for the state. But, apart from the suggestions that arose automatically from the discussion above, it is possible to develop a few principles.

Perhaps the most important guiding principle is Porter's finding that nations gain advantage because of differences, not similarities (Porter, 1990). This difference, moreover, is not inherited but can be created. It just needs the courage to abandon the ball park – like the classic Schumpeterian entrepreneur – and think of something new. That requires intuition, wisdom, experience, judgement, etc., but above all vision as to which product/market combinations would be accessible for the state as entrepreneur. While finding profitable market niches is ultimately difficult for private firms, governments have two advantages in that respect. First, all missions of government include taking care of public welfare, which means that of all possible product/market combinations a small number have already been preselected as falling in the domain of government. It is not very difficult to make a targeted selection of as yet unmet public needs and to annex priority product/market combinations from that list. Secondly, governments only need to 'fulfil the aim of launching and managing new initiatives . . . as effectively as the private sector pursues profit' (Minns and Rogers, 1990, p. 61). Thus, instead of pushing and pulling private firms into doing particular activities or abstaining from others, the state itself takes up the gauntlet. In this manner, the government achieves what it could not and cannot achieve via the established routes of industrial policy: control. Since it selects new areas for action, and these selections will initially be purely aimed at domestic suppliers, markets and needs, there is no competitive arena yet. While taking the initiative can provide a crucial advantage, the suggested concentration of resources may be decisive for a breakthrough, as has been shown to be the case in private markets (James, 1985). Since we are dealing here with new initiatives, it is likely that small and medium-sized firms will be the obvious candidates for taking over the initiatives once these have reached a privatisation stage.

Conclusions

'Industrial policy', says Johnson (1984, p. 74), 'is first of all an attitude, and only then a matter of technique.' This, indeed, is what needs to be communicated to industrial policy-makers (and strategists in general). We have seen that the elaboration of strategic management techniques can lead to little more than the provision of the means for programming the strategies that have been created according to some other mechanism. Thus, no matter how well the small numbers game is played, it remains a game that cannot cope well with creative strategic jumps. Governments that address their industrial policies predominantly to supporting their national favourites can therefore not expect to contribute to structural improvements in the strategic behaviour of these firms. Thus, we conclude that the pure type of industrial strategy requires that a government breaks away from these games, which in turn requires it to start acting as an entrepreneur. It must then fully participate in competitive market processes but not – at least not primarily: matching will be unavoidable to some extent – in the role of supporter cum participant in international small numbers games (with the high risk of either becoming hostage to the international business community or ending up in minimax regret behaviour or both). On the contrary, it should aspire to the role of a real strategic actor seeking insulation from the uncertainties of this game by developing its own trajectory of publicly needed innovations. Whereas participating in international rivalry implies (if done 'well') such strategies as bluffing and counterbluffing, threat and deterrence, but ultimately will not result in much more than variations on familiar themes, the suggested focus implies a continuous search for innovation in those fields that are part of its public mission.

Notes

Thanks are due to the participants at the 1991 Warwick/Birmingham Workshop on Industrial Strategy for stimulating comments. They, of course, are not to be blamed for any flaws in the argument.

1 Going through the first two stages in the process is therefore commonly called conducting a SWOT analysis (Strengths/Weaknesses/Opportunities/Threats).

2 Compare recent debates on the theory of the firm (upper left corner of Figure 3.1). While the firm is an accepted and fully recognised economic institution and everybody knows what firms do, economists try to elucidate the firm's existence as such (and have come up with different theories as well: Coasian, Schumpeterian, Penrosian, to name just a few of the most important ones). The general neglect of this issue in the business literature may well be the cause of the paradigmatic vacuum that is still being observed in the field of strategic management (see, e.g., several contributions in Frederickson, 1990). Our approach implicitly leans on a couple of others (predominantly industrial organisation and evolutionary economics) in order to establish what may be called 'the core business of strategy'.

3 As Moss (1981) has argued, the maximising problem cannot be solved without this second assumption since (constrained) maximising problems can be solved only if the constraint functions and the objective functions are exogenous to the problem.

4 There are, of course, many more limitations to strategic choice in terms of learning, path dependencies, selection and transaction costs. Some of these will return later in the paper.

5 This is not to imply that these authors would not share what follows next. On the contrary. Quinn in particular has stressed that actual strategy formation processes are usually fragmented, evolutionary and largely intuitive (see Quinn, 1980).

6 Of course, this is a highly stylised impression of things: it will be hard to find important cases of vertical integration that have not been motivated by the desire to reap a competitive advantage – which if realised should ultimately or at least theoretically show itself by a transfer of revenues from rivals to the focal organisation.

7 Rightfully so. By doing this, however, an interpretation of industrial policy as structural policy is repudiated. While such an interpretation is not unusual in the Netherlands and Germany (see Schenk, 1989), it surely implies a rather laborious combination of industrial policy with competition policy where it would be better to distinguish the two explicitly – not only because there are basic differences between the two but also because in practice they are quite often in conflict. As a recent illustration, recall the conflict which arose within the European Commission as well as between the Commission and both France and Italy in late 1991 over the proposed takeover of the Canadian-based Boeing subsidiary De Havilland by Aerospatiale (France) and Alenia (Italy). According to the Commissioner for Competition Policy, the takeover would result in a worldwide monopoly in the market for regional aeroplanes, whereas the French Secretary for Industry dismissed this argument as being in conflict with the goals of European industrial policy which would require far-reaching market concentration.

8 Thus, Tyson and Zysman (1983) have emphasised that the distinction between selective policies and policies that apply across all industries would perhaps be the most decisive standard for what constitutes an industrial policy. And according to Bellon and De Bandt: 'la politique industrielle a une action sélective et spécifique' (1988, p. 841).

9 Although the subsidy data do not exactly show that the focus has indeed changed, we may accept the argument that these processes take much time to become

manifest (see calculations in Schenk, 1992, based on data supplied in EC, 1989).

10 The American situation is not much different. The Reagan administration, for example, advocated the promotion of horizontal mergers arguing that "if our industries are going to survive there have to be additional consolidations to achieve needed economies of scale" (cited by Acs and Audretsch, 1990).

References

Acs, Zoltan J. and Audretsch, David B. (1990), 'Small firms in the 1990s', in Z. J. Acs and D. B. Audretsch (eds), *The Economics of Small Firms. A European Challenge*, Dordrecht/Boston/London: Kluwer Academic Publishers, pp. 1–22.

Bellon, B., and De Bandt, Jacques, (1988), 'La Politique industrielle', in R. Arena, L. Benzoni, Jacques De Bandt and Paul-Marie Romani (eds), *Traité d'Économie Industrielle*, Paris: Economica, pp. 840–57.

Brenner, Reuven (1987), *Rivalry. In business, science, among nations*, New York/Cambridge: Cambridge University Press.

Dankbaar, Ben, Groenewegen, John and Schenk, Hans (1990), 'Recent developments and the prospects of industrial organization', in Ben Dankbaar, John Groenewegen and Hans Schenk (eds), *Perspectives in Industrial Organization*, Dordrecht/Boston/London: Kluwer Academic Publishers, pp. 1–26.

EC (1989), *First Survey on State Aids in the European Community*, Brussels/Luxembourg: Commission of the European Communities.

Frederickson, J. W. (ed.) (1990), *Perspectives on Strategic Management*, New York: Harper & Row.

Geroski, Paul A. (1989), 'European industrial policy and industrial policy in Europe', *Oxford Review of Economic Policy*, 5(2), 20–36.

Grant, R. M. (1991), *Contemporary Strategy Analysis. Concepts, Techniques, Applications*, Oxford/Cambridge, MA: Basil Blackwell.

Greenley, G. E. (1989), *Strategic Management*, London: Prentice Hall.

Groenewegen, John (1987), 'L'État Développeur: The French Way' (in Dutch), in Schenk (1987), pp. 97–119.

James, B. G. (1985), *Business Wargames*, Harmondsworth: Penguin.

Jauch, L. R. and Glueck, W. F. (1988), *Business Policy and Strategic Management*, 5th edn, New York: McGraw-Hill.

Johnson, Ch. (1984), 'The industrial policy debate re-examined', *California Management Review*, 27(1), 71–89.

Johnson, G. and Scholes, K. (1988), *Exploring Corporate Strategy*, 2nd edn, London: Prentice Hall.

Knickerbocker, F. T (1973), *Oligopolistic Reaction and Multinational Enterprise*, Boston: GSBA, Harvard University.

Lindbeck, A. (1981), 'Industrial policy as an issue of the economic environment', *World Economy*, 4(4), 391–405.

Minns, R. and Rogers, M. (1990), 'The state as public entrepreneur', in Keith Cowling and Roger Sugden (eds), *A New Economic Policy for Britain. Essays on the development of industry*, Manchester/New York: Manchester University Press, pp. 53–71.

Mintzberg, H. (1985), 'Of strategies: deliberate and emergent', *Strategic Management Journal*, 6, 257–72.

Mintzberg, H. (1990), 'Strategy formation. Schools of thought', in Frederickson (1990), pp. 105–235.

Morris, D. J., Sinclair, P. J. N., Slater, M. D. E. and Vickers, J. S. (eds) (1986),

Strategic Behaviour and Industrial Competition, Oxford: Oxford University Press.

Moss, Scott J. (1981), *An Economic Theory of Business Strategy. An Essay in Dynamics without Equilibrium*, Oxford: Martin Robertson.

Porter, M. E. (1980), *Competitive Strategy*, New York: Free Press.

Porter, M. E. (1990), *The Competitive Advantage of Nations*, London: Macmillan.

Quinn, J. B. (1980), *Strategies for Change: Logical Incrementalism*, Homewood, IL: Irwin.

Quinn, J. B., Mintzberg, H. and James, R. M. (1988), *The Strategy Process*, Englewood Cliffs, NJ: Prentice-Hall.

Roobeek, Annemieke (1988), *A Race without Finish. The Role of Government in the Technology Race* (in Dutch), Amsterdam: VU Publishers.

Schelling, T. C. (1960), *The Strategy of Conflict*, Cambridge, MA: Harvard University Press.

Schenk, Hans (ed.) (1987), *Industrial and Technology Policy. Analysis and Perspectives* (in Dutch), Groningen: Wolters-Noordhoff.

Schenk, Hans (1989), 'Structural policy for the 1990s' (in Dutch), *Economisch Statistische Berichten*, 74(3720), 804–8.

Schenk, Hans (1992), *Industrial Policy and Competitive Strategy*, Rotterdam: GRASP (forthcoming).

Servan-Schreiber, J.-J. (1967), *Le Défi Américain*, Paris: Denoël.

Teece, D. J. (1990), 'Contributions and impediments of economic analysis to the study of strategic management', in Frederickson (1990), pp. 39–80.

Tyson, L. and Zysman, John (1983), 'American industry in international competition: government policies and corporate strategies', *California Management Review*, 25(3), 27–52.

To create competition without regulation
A mixed oligopoly with endogenous cost differences

Introduction

Why public ownership?

How can we encourage growth and innovativeness without allowing excess profits, and how can we restrict excessive profits without distorting incentives to innovate? That question arises if, for example, the authorities identify and support potential success industries. Large and successful firms tend to cause allocative inefficiency because success usually means that competition is not perfect. Therefore there exists a tension between emphasising growth and development on the one hand and justice and fair pricing on the other. This dilemma is sometimes described as the conflict between dynamic and static efficiency: to focus on the former makes the policy too permissive of monopolistic abuse but in the opposite case we impose excessive restrictions on innovative firms.[1] In what follows we shall suggest a strategy of state intervention in the form of ownership which, we believe, causes dynamic private firms less harm than a traditional anti-trust policy.

Although unfashionable at present, public ownership still plays an important role. Successful growth and development strategies include not only intervention but also state ownership. In most countries the state owns at least the railways, telecommunications and power stations; private companies need their services even if the policy otherwise favours private enterprise. There are other reasons for state ownership as well. The economic history of, for example, Finland shows that the state can provide more than just the infrastructure in the absence of private risk capital.

Why, then, are public firms mistrusted? Most readers would, in addition to the poor performance of socialist economies, mention the popular view that public firms are 'inefficient'. It is not difficult to find examples of inefficiency.[2] However, it is not true that public production in general performs badly. Public firms in Finland are usually no less efficient than similar private companies (*Valtionyhtiöt markkinataloudessa*, 1989). Borcherding, Pommerehne and Schneider (1982) and Stiglitz (1986) find several cases of inefficient public production but examples of the opposite as well. First, public production seems to be efficient if it meets competition. Secondly, a number of public firms are inefficient but they would have been unprofitable under private ownership as well.

The point that public firms can be profitable if they are required just to make profits is of course important. However, it would be foolish to compare only costs and profits if other objectives (like employment, growth of firms in other industries, regional development and the trade balance) dominate. Given the abundance of often conflicting targets that public firms should fulfil, they are likely to fail at least some criteria of what is good performance. Therefore, the only sensible criterion is 'the extent to which a public enterprise achieves the objectives which have been set for it' (Rees, 1984, p. 11). To set and grade the objectives should be part of a rational industrial strategy.

In this contribution we focus on one particular objective, namely forcing private firms to cut their profit margins without imposing detailed and restrictive regulations. In other words, instead of policing undesirable behaviour, the state creates competition where private firms are too strong. With such an objective, a public firm will have higher costs and lower profitability as part of the strategy.

What is a mixed oligopoly?
We shall in what follows examine a *mixed oligopoly*. This is characterised by the presence of a firm which is not only publicly owned but also acts as an aggressive, 'disloyal' competitor. By disloyalty we mean that the public firm maximises welfare, not profits.

The idea is known in the literature, but unknown among policy-makers. To mention an example, a working party suggesting major privatisations in Finland has recommended that there should not be both private and public firms in the same industry because it is then more difficult to accomplish the necessary mergers (*Visio yksityistämisestä Suomessa*, 1991). Not surprisingly, it is in practice often hard to distinguish the objectives of public and private firms. In the present climate it can even be expected that public firms will be required to be more concerned about profits than before.

Since objectives are crucial, public ownership is not a sufficient condition for welfare maximisation. Nor, strictly speaking, is it necessary. The disloyal firm could, for example, be co-operative as well.[3] On the other hand, the state has no direct control over the objectives of independent firms. Although the government may encourage co-operatives, they belong to the private sector and a normative analysis of private objective functions is beyond our scope. Moreover, if the mixed oligopoly works it could provoke price war threats. A co-operative firm which can go bankrupt may be unable to maintain its aggressive policy.

Earlier results and unsolved problems
In the earlier literature, the public firm is mostly assumed to maximise welfare, but in Merrill and Schneider (1966) it chooses the largest output that allows the private firms to break even. The public firms are constrained to set prices that give zero profits in Cremer, Marchand and Thisse (1989). Usually, it follows that the presence of a disloyal competitor is welfare improving (see Merrill and Schneider, 1966, Harris and Wiens, 1980, Beato and Mas-Colell, 1984, De Fraja and Delbono, 1989 and Cremer, Marchand and Thisse, 1989).

A couple of exceptions to this general rule have to be mentioned. According to De Fraja and Delbono (1989), it may sometimes be better for the public firm to maximise profits instead of welfare if all firms have Cournot conjectures. That happens, however, if the industry is 'almost' competitive. On the other hand, the mixed oligopoly is always superior if the welfare-maximising firm is a Stackelberg leader. There may also be counter-intuitive effects if products are not homogeneous. Cremer, Marchand and Thisse (1991) assume product differentiation. Private firms change the characteristics of their products in response to the public firm's choice. It turns out that the performance of the mixed oligopoly crucially depends on the number of firms: if they are between two and six in number, a private oligopoly is better than a mixed.

However, a number of issues need further elaboration. Given that attention is currently focused on cost efficiency, it is unsatisfactory to ignore cost differences between public and private production. It may be true that a nationalised industry has the largest welfare (De Fraja and Delbono, 1989), but few would be convinced unless the costs are analysed. On the other hand, just to assume that costs are higher under public production, as in Cremer, Marchand and Thisse (1989), is unsatisfactory. If costs in the public firms are too high, the mixed oligopoly becomes unduly expensive, but in the opposite case private production cannot survive. It follows that it is important to know *why* costs differ.

The cost structure of public and private firms is important not only for whether or not the mixed oligopoly improves welfare. For example, in Cremer, Marchand and Thisse (1989), exogenous sunk costs and constant marginal costs explain why the break-even constraint is binding and why it is better to nationalise than to establish a new firm. It follows that it is important to know more not only about the marginal costs of different types of firms but about their fixed costs as well.

In reality, firms choose their capacity and that is an important determinant of both fixed and marginal costs. Capacity constraints are not always ignored in the literature, but they usually take the form of a given and definite limit to output after an interval of constant marginal costs. An alternative way to understand limits to the firms' capacity to expand is to assume that marginal costs are globally increasing. If, on the other hand, capacity is endogenous and if it is not absolutely limiting, we can partly understand how costs can differ according to firms' objectives. Will the public firm then have higher or lower unit costs in a mixed oligopoly?

An outline of a mixed oligopoly approach with endogenous cost differences

There are several reasons why costs are not necessarily equal in private and public production. For example, public firms which cannot go bankrupt may have to pay more than their private competitors either to monitor their employees or to provide incentives. However, as several authors point out, arguments of that type are highly oversimplified (see, for example, Pint, 1991, Estrin and Pérotin, 1991, and De Fraja, 1991).

Our purpose is to ask how the mixed oligopoly performs if there are cost differences which can be derived from the firms' objective functions. We concentrate on the capacity choice and ignore other reasons for cost differences. Total costs depend on capacity and output in the same way, but, given the choices made, different firms have different relationships between output and unit costs. In the earlier literature on capacity choice, the investments set an absolute limit to what can be produced. We generalise in the sense that marginal costs are constant until a capacity limit is reached. Firms can exceed this limit but only at higher (and increasing) marginal costs. The cost functions become kinked, although the firms can choose the point at which marginal costs start to increase.[4] If firms choose to extend their capacity, the variable unit costs fall but fixed costs increase. There may be other fixed costs as well, but to rule out natural monopolies they are small enough to allow at least two firms to make a profit. The private firms choose the profit-maximising output and capacity while the public firm maximises welfare.

We apply a two-step procedure: first we examine how firms choose output given their capacity, and then we turn to their capacity choice. The obvious question to ask is whether the mixed oligopoly has favourable effects under the circumstances we focus on. In addition, is the public firm likely to be more or less efficient than private firms in the optimal solution? Will the private sector be marginalised by the policy? Is it better to establish a new firm or to nationalise an existing oligopolist? When will it be sensible to privatise?

At least in the model, the mixed oligopoly offers a fairly attractive industrial strategy. Unless imperfect competition produces negligible welfare losses, industry performance is better than if all firms are profit maximisers. Moreover, since the optimal solution implies that both public and private firms operate beyond the linear part of their total cost schedule, they are profitable (unless there are exogenous and large fixed costs). It then turns out to be better to create a new firm than to nationalise. On the other hand, it may appear worrying that under some circumstances welfare maximisation forces the private firms to operate on the fringe of the industry.

We find it equally important that the public firm always has higher unit costs and lower profitability as part of the welfare-maximising strategy. Judgements based on comparing the size of the unit costs in different types of firms are therefore misleading even when we ignore macroeconomic priorities and distributional issues.

How would purely private and public oligopolies work?

A description of the model
Throughout the paper we shall think in terms of a fixed number of producers (n) that operate in a market for a homogeneous good. In our thought experiment we shall see what happens if all of them are private and compare that situation with the case in which one firm is public. For comparison we also need the case in which all firms maximise welfare, although the model is not designed for analysing nationalised industries.

Following a large part of the literature, we assume that the demand function is linear. Let a and b be two positive parameters and let x stand for quantity and p for price; the inverse demand function is then:

$$p = a - bx. \tag{4.1}$$

The firms in the industry are assumed to know demand. They are Cournot–Nash competitors in the sense that they choose their optimal output assuming their competitors' output to be unchanged. When introducing the public firm we make the more controversial assumption that it, too, takes the other firms' output as given. Some authors would prefer to make the public firm a Stackelberg leader taking reaction functions rather than output as given. On the other hand, why should the public firm be able to be the leader in a market with large and smart oligopolists? If we do not know why, symmetric conjectures are no less reasonable.[5]

In earlier studies we find both increasing and constant marginal costs with and without an absolute capacity limit.[6] There is a large literature showing that marginal costs are indeed constant over some interval. We shall combine features that different assumptions in the previous literature have emphasised. Let x stand for industry output and x_i for the i'th firm's output. For each firm i we define a limit $\hat{x}_i$ which we call capacity. It is possible to produce more, but it is then more expensive: $\hat{x}_i$ restricts the amount that can be produced at the constant marginal costs c_i, implying that cost functions are kinked. If production exceeds capacity, costs will increase more than proportionately. They will depend on $(x_i - \hat{x}_i)^2$ with the coefficient c_2 if $x_i > \hat{x}_i$. We may have in mind a situation in which the firm uses obsolete machinery or hires additional equipment if its own capacity is insufficient. The definite limit is a special case because c_2 may be infinite. Each firm has fixed costs as well and that causes a trade-off. A firm can cut marginal costs by investing in larger capacity, but then the fixed costs increase in the proportion c_3.[7]

The firms have identical cost functions in the sense that they depend on x_i and $\hat{x}_i$ in the same manner. However, at given and different levels of capacity the relationship between costs and output is different. The kinked cost function can be written as follows:

$$TC_i = \left\{ \begin{array}{l} c_1 x_i + c_2 (x_i - \hat{x}_i)^2 + c_3 \hat{x}_i, \quad for \ x_i \geq \hat{x}_i \\ c_1 x_i + c_3 \hat{x}_i, \quad for \ x_i < \hat{x}_i \end{array} \right\} \qquad (4.2)$$

The marginal cost function is illustrated by Figure 4.1.

In this figure, the marginal costs MC_i are constant up to the point $\hat{x}_i$ and thereafter increasing with the slope $2c_2$. If, on the other hand, capacity is extended to $\hat{x}'_i$, marginal costs become constant up to that larger limit. Beyond that they increase with the same slope $2c_2$.

A description of a private and public oligopoly

To evaluate the mixed oligopoly we need points of comparison. A hypothetical mixed oligopoly must be compared with an oligopoly in which all firms maximise profits. Another point of comparison is an 'ideal' allocation. Keeping the number of firms fixed at n means that competition cannot be perfect and therefore we assume that in the ideal allocation they all co-operate to make welfare as large as possible.

Suppose first that all firms maximise profits. Consider the i'th firm in a private Cournot–Nash oligopoly. We start by profit maximisation with given capacity to obtain output as a function of $\hat{x}_i$. Thereafter we turn to the capacity choice and maximise the profits which depend on $\hat{x}_i$ via the optimal output and the cost function.[8]

Suppose first that the firm plans an output level which is larger than its present capacity. Its profit function is then:

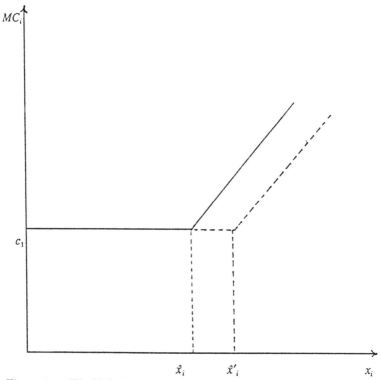

Figure 4.1 *The kinked marginal cost curve*

$$\pi_i = (a - bx)x_i - c_1x_i - c_2(x_i - \hat{x}_i)^2 - c_3\hat{x}_i. \tag{4.3}$$

It can be shown (more details are presented in Willner, 1991) that the price, industry output and capacity per firm will be:

$$p^\star = \frac{a + n(c_1 + c_3)}{n + 1} \tag{4.4}$$

$$x^\star = \frac{n(a - c_1 - c_3)}{(n + 1)b} \tag{4.5}$$

$$\hat{x}^\star_i = \frac{a - c_1 - c_3}{(n + 1)b} - \frac{c_3}{2c_2}. \tag{4.6}$$

Because of symmetry, $\hat{x} = n\hat{x}_i$. For the same reason, $x^\star = nx^\star_i$.

What would be the case if the firm chose to produce less than $\hat{x}_i$? Marginal costs would then be constant, so that the terms containing c_2 would disappear. The maximum profits, $[(a - c_1)^2/(n + 1)^2b] - c_3\hat{x}_i$, would be a decreasing function of capacity. Therefore, we need to consider only the case $x_i > \hat{x}_i$. However, it is possible that the firms choose not to invest in capacity at all, and the model then breaks down to a well-understood standard case. To avoid that, we shall assume that demand is large enough for firms in a conventional oligopoly to choose a non-zero capacity. In formal terms, this is equivalent to the condition that $a > c_1 + [2c_2 + (n + 1)b] c_3/2c_2$.

What is the aggregate surplus under private oligopoly (where surplus is the area under the demand curve minus the sum of total costs in each firm)? It can be shown that the expression is:

$$W\star = \frac{(a - c_1 - c_3)^2 (n + 2)n}{2b(n + 1)^2} + \frac{nc_3^2}{4c_2}. \tag{4.7}$$

Next, consider the case in which the industry consists of only n benevolent public firms. The authorities are able to choose x and $\hat{x}$ so as to maximise welfare. This means that the industry is modelled as consisting of a multi-plant state company. Let welfare be defined by the following function:

$$W = \int_0^x a - bydy - c_1x - [c_2(x - \hat{x})^2/n] - c_3\hat{x}. \tag{4.8}$$

The expressions for the industry output, the price and the capacity per firm are:

$$x_0 = \frac{a - c_1 - c_3}{b} \tag{4.9}$$

$$p_0 = c_1 + c_3 \tag{4.10}$$

$$\hat{x} = \frac{a - c_1 + c_3}{nb} - \frac{c_3}{2c_2}. \tag{4.11}$$

As might be expected, output is higher but cheaper than in the private oligopoly. Would the firms break even and what unit costs would they have? Let x_j stand for the output of a firm in a market in which all firms are either private or public. Note that $x_j - \hat{x}_j = c_3/2c_2$ in both types of markets. The unit costs are therefore:

$$AC_j = c_1 + c_3 - \frac{c_3^2}{4c_2} \frac{1}{x_j} \tag{4.12}$$

Compare (4.10) and (4.12) and note that average costs increase with output. If there are no large exogenous fixed costs, firms break even but they have higher unit costs than in the private oligopoly.

The mixed oligopoly

How would the mixed oligopoly perform?
Consider now what happens if one of the n firms maximises welfare. The private sector maximisation problem is the same as in section 2.1 as long as the public firm's output, x_g, and capacity, $\hat{x}_g$, are given. The public firm's objective function is:

$$W = \int_0^{x_g} a - b(x_p + y)dy - \sum_{i=1}^{n} c_1 x_i - \sum_{i=1}^{n} c_2 (x_i - \hat{x}_i)^2 - \sum_{i=1}^{n} c_3 \hat{x}_i. \tag{4.13}$$

Technically, we derive the reaction functions for the private and public firms for a given capacity to get output as a function of capacity. In the next step we insert the output levels in the objective functions and maximise once again to get the optimal capacity. After inserting this in the first reaction functions, we get the solutions for the output levels; summing up and inserting the inverse demand function yields the price. It turns out that the private firms would choose a zero capacity (this is a corner solution). However, if a is sufficiently large for firms in a private oligopoly to have a positive capacity, as we have assumed, the public firm in a mixed oligopoly would also have a positive capacity. The public firm's output, x_g, the sum of the private firms' output, x_p, and the capacity in the public firm, x_g, are:

$$x_g = \frac{a - c_1 - c_3}{b} - \frac{c_3(n-1)}{b + 2c_2} \tag{4.14}$$

$$x_p = \frac{(n-1)c_3}{b + 2c_2} \tag{4.15}$$

$$\hat{x}_g = \frac{a - c_1 - c_3}{b} - \frac{c_3(b + 2c_2 n)}{2c_2(b + 2c_2)}. \tag{4.16}$$

Since all private firms are equal, the output of the i'th firm is obtained by dividing (4.15) by $n - 1$.

However, does the optimal output give the private firms positive profits or would they prefer not to produce? It turns out that they will indeed be active. Each private firm will get positive profits (unless there are large non-capacity-related fixed costs):

$$\pi_i = \frac{c_3^2(b + c_2)}{(b + 2c_2)^2}. \tag{4.17}$$

Thus, a mixed oligopoly is feasible in the sense that the private and public firms would co-exist. Would it perform better than the private oligopoly? Would private firms be forced to operate on the fringe of the industry? That issue is only indirectly related to the efficiency of the industry but it may nevertheless be important from a policy standpoint. Lastly, how does the mixed oligopoly compare in terms of unit costs and profitability?

Add x_g and x_p and insert the inverse demand function. It follows that price and output in the industry are the same as if all firms were maximising welfare. On the other hand, is it possible that costs will be so large that the private oligopoly is preferable? The public firm has the option of behaving like a private oligopolist, but it chooses to produce more. This is not sufficient to prove the superiority of the mixed oligopoly. We have shown only that (4.14) is optimal given that the private firms choose not to invest in capacity, not that welfare in the mixed oligopoly (W_0) is superior to welfare when all firms maximise profits ($W^\star$). The surplus in the mixed oligopoly case is:

$$W_0 = \frac{(a - c_1 - c_3)^2}{2b} + \frac{c_3^2}{4c_2} + \frac{c_3^2(b + c_2)(n - 1)}{(b + 2c_2)^2}. \tag{4.18}$$

Looking at $W_0 - W^\star$ shows that welfare is always higher under the mixed oligopoly if c_2 is large enough compared with b. In particular, welfare is improved if marginal costs are almost vertical for $x_i > \hat{x}_i$. If that is not the case, it may happen that the private oligopoly performs better. More precisely, it happens either if the demand intercept *a* is very small compared with c_1 and c_3 or if *n* is very large. The intuition is that, unless c_2 is large enough, the cost disadvantage in the mixed oligopoly will dominate the gain in output.[9] With a small demand intercept, the profit margin is small and, if the number of firms is large, the industry is fairly competitive. Thus, the mixed oligopoly improves welfare provided that there is some scope for improvement.

Given earlier results that welfare maximising under certain conditions allows only for public production, we may ask whether the public firm may become too large in relation to the private firms.[10] It is obvious that the public firm is the largest in the industry. With sufficiently large values of *a* and c_2 compared with c_1 and c_3, the public firm would even have a larger market share than all private firms taken together. If a dominance of that kind is undesirable, a public firm may improve welfare by pursuing a more modest target.[11]

Next, consider profitability and relative costs. Will the public firm be able to make profits or does it have to be supported by public funds? As it turns out, the public firm will earn positive profits (unless there are exogenous fixed costs which are large):

$$\pi_g = \frac{c_3^2}{4c_2} \tag{4.19}$$

As follows from (4.19) and (4.17), the public firm will even earn higher profits than the private firms. On the other hand, that is not particularly interesting given that it will be bigger than each private firm. Indeed, it can be shown that profits per turnover are smaller in the public firm than among the private firms. Moreover profits per costs are also smaller in the public sector.

We know that costs may sometimes be higher in a mixed than in a private oligopoly, because otherwise $W_0 > W^\star$ would hold true for all values of *a* and *n*. In a mixed oligopoly, will production in the public firm be more expensive than in the private firms? The answer is that the unit costs in the public firm are always higher than in the private firms (formal proofs can be found in Willner, 1991). It follows that the public firm will give an impression of being less successful although it promotes welfare.

Changes in ownership – some comments about policy conclusions
The model suggests that the current trend to privatise is misplaced.

However, apart from natural monopolies, there exist industries in which the public sector owns more than is necessary to allow a mixed oligopoly to work. Entry in a completely private industry is likely to be expensive and it may be financed by reducing public ownership where it is excessive.

However, the mixed oligopoly strategy may provide another reason for privatisation. The strategy, as we have presented it, requires that only one firm per industry belongs to the state. If the managers are inefficient, the firm can be privatised because the state can buy another firm or establish a new firm to maintain its influence.

As follows from the previous section, the mixed oligopoly might perform less well than a private oligopoly if demand is elastic and/or the number of firms is large. If the state owns a firm in such an industry, should it then privatise? That does not necessarily follow. Strictly speaking, the result concerns objective functions, not ownership. Therefore it might be preferable not to privatise but to require profit maximisation until, for example, mergers have changed the situation.

The mixed oligopoly policy appears radical because it forces private oligopolists to set prices equal to long-run marginal costs. However, the policy does not necessarily favour nationalisations. It follows from (4.18) that welfare is increasing in n. Therefore, nationalisation dominates entry only if there are fixed costs that are large enough to eliminate the private firms. This result contradicts Cremer, Marchand and Thisse (1989) because they put great emphasis on the exogenous fixed costs. If in our model nationalisation is better than entry, no private firm would be profitable.

Some final comments

The public firm in the model would have higher unit costs and lower profitability even under the best management as part of the optimal solution. However, it is often argued that private production offers better incentives. Does the mixed oligopoly require extremely altruistic managers?[12] That is not necessarily the case. The public firm in a mixed oligopoly operates in an environment of competition and is thus more likely to be efficient than under monopoly. The public and the private firms may in other words force each other to perform better. Moreover, bad performance can be punished because the state does not have to own the same firm forever.

There are a couple of other problems that need further elaboration. In this version, the mixed oligopoly is not designed to correct negative externalities, but can state ownership still have a constructive role? What incentives are needed for public firms to work properly under a natural monopoly? What happens if strong pressure groups associated with private oligopolists sacrifice profits in order to try to prevent the mixed oligopoly from succeeding?

Nevertheless, our analysis confirms the general impression that the performance of an industry is improved if there is a public firm that acts as a disloyal competitor. If applied in a large number of industries, the policy is likely to improve not only efficiency but real wages as well and may therefore offer greater social justice. The fact that, in most cases, no restrictive regulation is needed is an additional advantage. Despite its radical consequences, the mixed oligopoly does not eliminate the scope for private sector innovativeness but may even promote the use of new methods.[13] It seems reasonable that the possibility of *increasing* profits by being innovative offers a stronger incentive than if profits are persistently large, as under imperfect competition.

Notes

I wish to thank Jan Otto Andersson, Markus Jäntti, Anders Kjellman, Rune Stenbacka and the participants at the Warwick/Birmingham Workshop on Industrial Strategy for helpful comments. The shortcomings are my own.

    1   Some authors would argue that there should be a distinction between industrial policy and competition policy and that the former is concerned only with dynamic efficiency. However, I prefer to see competition policy as an integral part of an industrial strategy.

    2   Many examples of unsuccessful public production come from the UK; however, as Vickers and Yarrow (1988) point out, it is likely that the performance of the firms could have been improved substantially without privatisation.

    3   Interestingly enough, one of the motives for the co-operative movement is that co-operatives can enforce discipline among the private firms by keeping prices low. This argument is described for example in Aizsilnieks (1948).

    4   Naturally, if the marginal costs approach infinity above a certain point, we approach the special case where capacity sets a definite limit.

    5   The earlier contributions show a wide variety on this point. Harris and Wiens (1980) assume the public firm to be dominant. Beato and Mas-Colell on the other hand (1984) find it more reasonable to assume that the private firms maximise given the rule adopted by the public firm. Cremer, Marchand and Thisse (1989) assume Cournot behaviour. De Fraja and Delbono (1989) consider several cases, including nationalisation of the industry and mixed oligopolies with a profit- or welfare-maximising public firm, in the latter case with either Cournot or Stackelberg conjectures.

6 Merrill and Schneider (1966) and Cremer, Marchand and Thisse (1989) assume constant marginal costs; Merrill and Schneider additionally assume that there is a capacity limit. In general, prices cannot equal marginal costs in their models. Beato and Mas-Colell (1984), Harris and Wiens (1980) and De Fraja and Delbono (1989) assume convex cost functions; De Fraja and Delbono even increasing marginal costs. Since there are no fixed costs in the Beato and Mas-Colell version, the best prices in fact equal marginal costs.

7 As it will turn out, we can allow for exogenous fixed costs, F, as well without violating the break-even constraint, as long as they are small enough for at least two firms to break even. They might explain why perfect competition is not feasible and why nationalisations may sometimes be preferable to entry. However, that would add very little to our main point.

8 Applying the envelope theorem shows that each firm maximises its profits if $2c_2(x_i - \hat{x}_i) - c_3 = 0$. The intuitive interpretation is that the marginal reduction in variable costs caused by the capacity change should equal the marginal increase in the capacity-related fixed costs.

9 Note that the case in which all firms collude to maximise welfare is always superior, but it may be conjectured that the features which the model ignores may be quite important. However, if the mixed oligopoly is inferior to the private oligopoly, performance can be improved by having more than one public firm.

10 Welfare maximising in a simple model like that may imply yet another difficulty if there are fixed costs. With constant marginal costs, firms would get negative profits. That in turn means that we would have to weight the distortions from excessive prices and taxation to cover losses against each other.

11 Suppose that the public firm maximises revenues; let all firms have the same constant marginal costs c. Total output is then $[na + c(n-3)]/b(n+1)$. Welfare is improved without eliminating private production. The public firm produces $[a + c(n-1)]/b(n+1)$ and each private firm $(a-2c)/(n+1)b$. The public firm is the largest in the industry and it produces more than x_p unless $a > (n+1)c/(n-2)$.

12 There is another aspect of the principal–agent problem as well. Will managers of private and public firms collude to make the objective functions indistinguishable? The co-operative firms may provide a case in point because in most countries they are typically not seen as disloyal to their private competitors.

13 Increased profits under a mixed oligopoly could be seen as resulting from finding 'hitherto unnoticed opportunities', to use the language of the so-called Austrian school. According to, for example, Kirzner (1989), so-called *discovered* gains should be recognised as ethically justified.

References

Aizsilnieks, A. (1948), *Cooperationens mål och medel*, Falun: Kooperativa Förbundets Bokförlag.

Beato, P. and Mas-Colell, A. (1984), 'The marginal cost pricing rule as a regulation mechanism', in M. Marchand, P. Pestieau and H. Tulkens (eds), *The Performance of Public Enterprises*, Amsterdam: North-Holland, pp. 81–100.

Borcherding, T. E., Pommerehne, W. W. and Schneider, F. 'Comparing the efficiency of private and public production: the evidence from five countries', *Zeitschrift für Nationalökonomie*, Suppl. 2, 127 – 56.

Cremer, H., Marchand, M. and Thisse, J. F. (1989), 'The public firm as an instrument for regulating an oligopolistic market', *Oxford Economic Papers*, 41, April, 283–301.

Cremer, H., Marchand, M. and Thisse, J. F. (1991), 'Mixed oligopoly with differentiated products', *International Journal of Industrial Organization*, 9(1), 43–54.

De Fraja, G. (1991), 'Incentive contracts for public firms', Working Paper, University of Bristol.

De Fraja, G. and Delbono, F. (1989), 'Alternative strategies of a public enterprise in oligopoly', *Oxford Economic Papers*, 41, 302–11.

Estrin, S. and Pérotin, V. (1991), 'Does ownership always matter?', *International Journal of Industrial Organization*, 9, March, 55–72.

Harris, R. and Wiens, E. (1980), 'Government enterprise: an instrument for the internal regulation of industry', *Canadian Journal of Economics*, XIII(1), 124–32.

Kirzner, I. (1989), *Discovery, Capitalism, and Distributive Justice*, Oxford: Basil Blackwell.

Merrill, W. C. and Schneider, N. (1966), 'Government firms in oligopoly industries: a short run analysis', *Quarterly Journal of Economics*, 80, 400–12.

Pint, E. M. (1991), 'Nationalization vs. regulation of monopolies: the effects of ownership on efficiency', *Journal of Public Economics*, 44, March, 131–64.

Rees, R. (1984), *Public Enterprise Economics*, London: Weidenfeld & Nicolson.

Slade, M. 'Conjectures, firm characteristics, and market structure: an empirical assessment', *International Journal of Industrial Organization*, 4, December, 347–69.

Slade, M. (1987), 'Intrafirm rivalry in a repeated game: an empirical test of tacit collusion', *Journal of Industrial Economics*, XXXV, June, 499–516.

Stiglitz, Joseph E. (1986), *Economics of the Public Sector*, New York and London: Norton.

Valtionyhtiöt markkinataloudessa (1989), Helsinki: Liiketaloustieteellinen tutkimuslaitos (LTT).

Vickers, J. and Yarrow, G. (1988), *Privatization: An Economic Analysis*, Cambridge, MA, The MIT Press.

Visio yksityistämisestä Suomessa (1991), Helsinki: Kauppa- ja teollisuusministeriö (Ministry of Trade and Industry), 12.2.

Willner, J. (1991), 'The performance of a mixed oligopoly when average cost differences are exogeneous', Working Paper, Department of Economics, Åbo Akademi University.

PART II
PRODUCTION

A production-oriented industrial policy
The case of Jamaica

Two decades of economic decline

The golden years of the Jamaican economy were two short decades from the mid 1950s until 1973 during which annual growth rates of 5%, 6% and 7% prevailed.[1] For nearly 300 years Jamaica had been a plantation economy in which sugar was king, but the 1950s and 1960s' boom was led by bauxite earnings, which came to dwarf those of sugar.

The growth period was shortlived, however. Jamaican gross domestic product and per capita income peaked in 1973; since then a steady annual decline was arrested only briefly in the mid-1980s. Per capita income declined by 35% over the period from a peak of nearly $1,200 in 1972; however, owing to a shifting income distribution in favour of rent, interest and profits, the standard of living of Jamaican wage-earners was 45% lower in 1990 than it had been in the early 1970s (Levitt, 1990, p. 6 and Table 7).

The decline in output and income cannot be attributed to stingy international aid agencies. In fact, since the mid-1970s Jamaica has been the recipient of a massive inward flow of medium- and long-term official capital. External debt increased from the modest level of 31% of GDP in 1975 to 206% of GDP in 1985, transforming Jamaica from one of the least to one of the most indebted nations in the world. In that ten-year period total medium- and long-term public debt increased nearly sevenfold to $1,800 per person, the debt service ratio increased from 3% to 35% of gross domestic product and from 7% to 40% of export earnings (Levitt, 1990, Table 1 and pp. 8–9).

The results of the massive capital inflow overseen by the IMF and the World Bank have not been good. All of the indicators of ability to pay are worse than before the capital infusion: GDP and GDP per capita are both lower; the negative trade balance increased several-fold over the 15-year period as exports declined and imports soared; labour productivity in the industrial sector declined steadily over the entire period; and unemployment grew from 21% in 1973–76 to 25% in 1983–86, then dipped to 18.5% in 1988 before rising sharply again in 1989 and 1990.

Despite nearly $4 billion in foreign aid and eight IMF adjustment programmes, the economy has not been restructured and Jamaica remains desperately lacking in foreign exchange earning capacity. Today, bauxite and tourism generate over 60% of foreign exchange earnings; the rest comes mainly from sugar, bananas, farm worker remittances, and Free Zone production of garments.

Two failed visions of industrial policy

Jamaican economic policy-making in the declining decades has been guided by two radically different visions. The Michael Manley government of 1972–80 began office with a 'non-IMF path' based upon dependency theory. State planning, nationalisation, bureaucratic regulation of external and internal trade, and government production were pursued as means of achieving economic independence. However, by the mid-1970s, foreign exchange and fiscal deficits, inflation and devaluation were manifestations of a deteriorating economic base which led the Manley government to negotiate the first Standby Agreement with the IMF in 1977.

Ironically, the rhetoric of a 'non-IMF' path led to dependency on the IMF by the end of the first Manley government. Foreign official debt increased by two and half times between 1975 and 1980. Economic policy-making had to be consistent with the conditions required to access the extended fund facility of the IMF. The IMF, not the elected officials, was directing economic policy-making before the Edward Seaga government was elected in 1980.

However, after 15 years of IMF intervention, the results have not been any better. Neither the 'non-IMF' nor the IMF paths have stopped the Jamaican economy from the continuing decline. Today, the situation is much worse than in 1973 because of the huge debt servicing, which diverts funds away from the social services that Jamaicans enjoyed in the late 1960s. Education and health as a percentage of public expenditure have declined from

27% in 1973–75 to 17% in 1985–87 (Levitt, 1990, Table 7). Interest rates of 35–40% make productive investment prohibitive, and the massive exodus of skilled labour has deeply eroded the human resource base of the economy.

Both economic development visions, I would suggest, are informed by the same plan or market dichotomy of textbook economics. The free market version, which guides the IMF, defines the barriers to economic growth in terms of market restraints introduced by the government (see also Chapter 8 by Ajit Singh); the state planning version perceives the barriers to growth in terms of the anarchy of the market and the power of monopoly capital. The first seeks growth via freeing of markets; the second by replacing markets with planning and capitalists with central planners.

Each vision is the mirror-image of the other; both deny conceptual space to the organisation of production. Lacking a theory of production, both have pursued policies that have been antithetical to the development of a national industrial base capable of supplying the domestic needs of the populace. The first Manley government pursued an industrial policy like that of Eastern Europe: state planning and public ownership were perceived as the means of industrial growth. Here the task was one of replacing the market with the plan. The IMF years have sought to replace the plan with the market.

Both inadvertent industrial policies have worsened economic conditions for most Jamaicans because neither addressed the fundamental issue of production. Both free market and state ownership visions offer the illusion of a fast track to industrial development by government decrees, such as nationalising or denationalising property, announcing or denouncing free markets, regulating or deregulating prices. Lacking a concept of production, both visions obscure the related concepts of industrial restructuring and industrial policy.

The problem is not simply that the two competing visions lack conceptual space for production-related concepts. Worse still, the void is filled by an implicit industrial policy. The IMF vision is one in which industrial enterprises will spontaneously emerge by the invisible forces described by comparative advantage theory once prices and markets are freed from government interference. Here, industrial policy is about promoting the ideal of perfect markets, for only then can prices do the job of eliciting internationally competitive business enterprises.

The dependency school suggests that public ownership of the means of production is a prerequisite for economic development in the periphery. Here, industrial policy is about administering price controls and dictating to firms what to produce. The ideal is the perfectly administered plan created by an omniscient, centralised industrial accounting department.

What is clear is that neither vision has been successful in Jamaica. This paper is a brief outline of a third, production-led vision.

Towards a production-led vision of industrial development[2]

A production-led vision begins with the premise that the competitive strength of industrial enterprises demands careful attention to the principles of production and organisation of world-class firms. Furthermore, the 1980s and 1990s are a time of revolution in production methods, a revolution that is forcing restructuring in all manufacturing sectors everywhere in the world. The failure of enterprises to address these new developments will lead to business losses and economic decline. The failure of economic policy-makers to account for these new developments can lead to industrial strategies and economic policies that lock a nation's capabilities into low-productivity, price-competitive production systems. We start with an analysis of the old principles associated with mass production before turning to the new principles associated with both just-in-time production and flexible specialisation.

Mass production: economies of time versus size

Surprisingly, the industrial engineering principles of mass production are not widely understood even in advanced industrialised countries. The first principle, interchangeability of parts, was established decades before mass production became a vision of modern industrialisation. The application of interchangeability involved a revolution in production methods in that specialist machines run by machine operators replaced hand tools used by craftsmen. Before interchangeability of parts every product had to be constructed and assembled by custom fitting. In this production method, every product was slightly different and none could be made without fitting, which, in turn, required craft labour.

Application of the principle of interchangeability led to the redefinition of the product in terms of machining operations, each of which met certain tolerance limits which enabled the product to be assembled without altering any of the constituent parts. Interchangeability was first applied in military armouries in the United States in the second decade of the 1800s.

Interchangeability, however, does not define mass production; instead, it is a precondition to mass production. Efforts to undertake mass production which do not take into account the requirements of interchangeability are bound to fail. For, without interchangeability, economies of time (the defining feature of mass production) cannot be achieved. This can be illustrated using Ford's assembly line (which is also discussed in greater detail in Chapter 6).

Henry Ford described mass production as production without fitters. He was only partly right, for production without fitters had a long history before mass production appeared. Henry Ford's plants were organised according to a second constituent principle of mass production and this is what made Ford famous.

Mass production is the application of the principle of flow to the production of *a single product*. The idea was to maximise the rate of throughput in the production process, beginning with raw materials and ending with delivery to the customer. The primary focus, however, was on the production stage. The goal was to increase throughput or reduce the time required per unit output. The means was to rearrange machining and manual activities into the order of the operations required for the production of the product. Thus, instead of organising a plant according to machining operations in which the lathes would be in one department, the drills in a second, the planers in a third, etc., the machines were ordered according to the operations required to produce the product. Whereas under the pre-mass production system batches of intermediate or semi-finished products were shipped from department to department, under mass production batches were eliminated; in principle, no two products were ever at the same stage of assembly.

The vision of a flowline concentrated the attention of engineers on barriers to throughput. A barrier, or bottleneck, occurred wherever a machining operation could not process material at the same pace as the previous operation. Inventories indicated the existence of a production bottleneck. The pace of the machining operation that had the largest inventory before it determined the rate of throughput of the entire production process. The bottleneck machine was the activity that constrained the throughput not only at that machine but of the production system as a whole. Increasing the pace of work on any other machining activity could not increase output, only inventory. Thus the idea behind the principle of flow was to *synchronise* production activities so that each operation could process material without producing to inventory. Production for any non-bottleneck activity should be limited to the pace of the bottleneck activity. Production beyond this pace would only be producing to inventory; it could not increase the rate of throughput.

Henry Ford's Model T assembly line can be seen in this light. It was not the speed of the line that was revolutionary in *concept*, it was the idea of synchronising production activities so that bottlenecks did not constrain the whole production system. Unfortunately, all too often the basis of mass production was mistakenly defined in terms of economies of size, when it was really economies of speed based on synchronised production that drove the rate of throughput up and the per unit costs down.[3]

Henry Ford created a large plant to achieve synchronised production for two reasons. The first was because he produced in enormous volume. The second was because a supplier base did not exist at the time that could deliver parts and components in the volume and with the dependability of delivery times that was required to produce without machining bottlenecks.

Realising the principles of mass production did not always lead to huge managerial organisations. In the Baden-Württemberg region of Germany and the 'Third Italy' (the north central part of Italy, as distinct from the northern industrial heartland of Milan–Turin–Genoa and the agricultural south), production often was synchronised, not by building huge vertically integrated plants, but by networked groups of small specialised firms (Piore and Sabel, 1984). In fact, decentralisation of production into groups of small and medium-sized firms has made the transition to the new production principles considerably easier than in vertically integrated enterprises. Before turning to this 'flexible specialisation' vision we must first examine the weaknesses of mass production that emerged in practice and which were exposed by the development of a new set of production principles.

JIT: The principle of flow applied to multiple products[4]

The decades of the 1970s and 1980s witnessed a revolution in production organisation which began in the Japanese automobile and consumer electronics industries. The age of mass production is yielding to a new age of flexible production commonly referred to as just-in-time (JIT) production. The new production methods enable firms to gain a competitive edge on the basis of product-led as opposed to price-led competition. The winners are firms that can offer superior quality, shorter production lead times, more dependable delivery schedules and reduced new product development times; the losers are still seeking to compete on the basis of lower prices alone. What went wrong with mass production?

Mass production worked well as long as the plant made one product. Problems emerged with the need to produce multiple products *in the same facilities*. The fundamental weakness of mass production was the inflexibility of the production activities. The drive to increase throughput led process engineers to design ever more specialised and dedicated equipment. Too often the machines were linked in ways that made it impossible to use them for the production of any product except those for which the machine had been specially designed. In other cases it was possible to produce more than one product on a machine but only after a time-consuming take-down and set-up procedure.

The result was that inventories crept back into the system as engineers sought to reduce set-up costs per unit output by producing long runs. Mass production and multiple products meant a reversion to batch production. The insight of the link between synchronised production, no inventories and high throughput was lost. The principle of flow holds that throughput can be increased only by relieving the system-constraining bottleneck; this bottleneck was all too often hidden from view by the build-up of inventories at every stage in production. The result was that management focused its attention on increasing the productivity of each machine and each worker. Management accounting came to focus attention on individual factor productivity levels not on barriers to throughput. Not surprisingly, no matter how many machines were purchased or new control systems developed, throughput was unaffected unless they tackled the single bottleneck that regulated output.

The idea of JIT is to apply the principle of flow not to a single product but to a mixed range of products using the same production facilities. Mass production is about driving down the throughput time required to produce a single product; JIT is about driving down the production and new product development time required to produce a range of products. In this sense, moving from mass production to JIT production does not involve a revolution in the underlying principle of production; both are based on the principle of flow. The transition involves the application of the principle of flow to the production not of a single product but of multiple products on the same production line. But this small step involves a revolution in the organisation of production, including management structure, work organisation and supplier relations. Successful JIT production means reduced lead times, shorter runs, higher working capital turns, lower inventories, lower changeover times, and increased space productivities.

In the JIT plant, workers must be capable of operating, setting up and maintaining a range of machines, not simply operating a single machine as in the mass production plant. Thus, while the difference between the two production systems can be measured in terms of inventories, the real bottlenecks to JIT production are organisational: throughput cannot be increased without a revolution in the social practices of production.

For JIT, the production to inventory is a waste. It is better for resources to remain idle than to build up inventory. It is not simply that inventories add to working capital needs and increase financial costs. Inventories are costly in other ways: they have to be handled, transported, stored, counted, inspected; they take up space, they can be damaged and they hide defects. The goal of the JIT producer is one of inventoryless production. To produce a range of products with a minimum of inventory has lead to a drastic reduction in the length of product runs; this reduction has also created new opportunities for small-scale, flexibly specialised producers to compete in the marketplace.

The failure to define the manufacturing task of vertically integrated industrial enterprises as one of synchronising production activities has led to the establishment of factories everywhere in the world in which the principle of flow is not systematically applied. In fact, the proliferation of indirect labour, the scheduling congestion, and the long lead times of industrial enterprises can be attributed to a lack of understanding of the manufacturing challenge addressed by Ford.

Flexible specialisation: flow within industrial districts

Industrial enterprises of the Third Italy escape the material flow congestion of vertically integrated factories by remaining specialised in one link of the production chain and linking via long-term consultative relations with specialised enterprises in the chain. Competitive pressures amongst specialist firms force small batch, short set-up time, flexible work practices with similar effects to the directives of engineers implementing JIT at Toyota.

The industrial districts of the Third Italy combine co-operation and competition in ways that break down the plan–market dichotomy that has informed conventional economic theory and industrial policy-making. They suggest a concept of industrial policy as management of inter-firm co-operation with the goal of production rationalisation. Clearly, the production principles that guide rationalisation should not be followed slavishly. Third world countries may well find niches that do not depend upon implementation, at least in the form pursued in the advanced industrialised countries. But a strategic orientation is necessary if industrial investments are to have a chance of developing an independent industrial base. A strategic orientation means that enterprise investment strategies must be designed with an awareness of the strengths and weaknesses of industrial enterprises located elsewhere that are organised around world-class principles of production and organisation. Any version of flexible specialisation that ignores the role of the principles of interchangeability, flow and equalised cycle times (flexibility) can be no more successful as a vision for industrial policy than were the versions of mass production which confused economies of size with those of time.

Towards a production-led industrial policy

A productionist industrial policy starts with the existing industrial enterprises and builds a sector strategy. The aim is not to provide finance or to act as a lender of last resort. Rather it is to identify the sectors that have the best chance of success and the types of collective services that a local or regional government can develop to foster the development of multiple business enterprises within those sectors. Several stages can be identified:

(1) Conduct a strategic sector analysis. The first step is to visit a large number of firms in a sector and along the production chain with the purpose of analysing the strengths and weaknesses and challenges and opportunities facing the enterprises. The strategic dimension involves a comparison of the regional group of firms with leading regions in other parts of the world. A sector analysis must be conducted by an individual with knowledge of sources of competitive advantage of the world's leading firms and regions.

(2) Conduct wide-ranging discussions amongst industry insiders on the results of the sector analysis. The purpose is to shape a common vision, develop a shared language, establish a plan of action and identify common services.

(3) Develop benchmark analyses for individual companies. The purpose here is to contrast the performance indicators of target companies with world-class companies and to use the resulting gaps as targets for developing action plans.

(4) Establish implementation plans. This involves the development of pilot projects in individual companies, establishing workshops for attacking common problems and skill upgrading, sharing the results of implementing the pilot projects with all involved companies.

(5) Redefine the mission and upgrade the skills of individuals in the industrial policy bodies. A global, proactive, team approach to offering services to firms which share the common vision is superior to a firefighting, reactive approach.

(6) Diffuse the practical restructuring ideas widely in the sector. Videos, workshops, reports, contests and exhibits which illustrate principles with local examples can facilitate the diffusion of effective production practices.

(7) Develop performance indicators to track the progress of individual firms. The performance indicators should be production based, such as work-in-process turns, measures of waste, set-up times, defect rates and skill-upgrading programmes. These are all indicators of the transition to the fundamental principles of production, namely interchangeability, flow and flexibility.

Progression through each of these steps simultaneously creates a common language and reinforces the social fabric of community that distinguishes an innovative industrial district from atomistic, disconnected competitors. The existence of community provides the social context within which regionally specific inter-firm institutions develop and evolve. Examples of such institutions include marketing or retailing consortia, industrial parks, technology transfer guidelines, vocational educational programmes, fashion institutes, quality standards enforcement procedures, and consultancy agencies. The organisational form of inter-firm institutions may be private, public or quasi-public. Their purpose is to manage and nurture collective services so that the famed free-rider effect does not erode the requisite co-operation of world-class productive organisations.

An example: flexible specialisation and the Jamaican woodworking industry

Success at industrial policy, like the building of business enterprises or competitive athletic teams, demands more than good analysis and technique: it is a social process that requires involvement, commitment, experience and teamwork. The approach can be illustrated with a brief description of the first steps in an ongoing effort to restructure the Jamaican woodworking industry.

Sector analysis
A Jamaican woodworking sector analysis informed by plant visits to 20 firms revealed that the Jamaican furniture industry suffers from a low level of productivity for every productive input. Output per direct labour is about J$60–75,000 which, given 50% material costs and a 20% overhead charge, leaves only J$18–22,500 (US$2,300–2,850) annual income per worker, a level roughly one-tenth that of a US furniture worker.

Working capital productivity is extremely low, with work-in-process turns of two being commonplace. One of the most efficient Jamaican furniture firms (certainly one of the few with detailed factor cost accounts) has an interest charge of nearly 80% of its wage bill. This is because of, first, a work-in-process total of over one-half annual sales; second, a 36% interest charge on an overdraft facility that matches the work-in-process magnitude (this company is exceptional in that it has been able to receive European finance at 11.5% on highly collateralised debt); and, third, the slow pace of pre- and post-factory material flow caused by an inefficient customs and transportation infrastructure.

Fixed capital productivity is also low. The problem here is not the existence of excess capacity. Rather it is the poor working performance of machines and tools that are not properly maintained, that lack accessories, that are being used for purposes other than that for which they were designed. It is common, for example, to find tenons being made with boring machines; to find workers wrestling with 6 foot clamps where a 6 inch clamp would do the job more effectively; to find a bottleneck at sanding because sanding is being done laboriously by hand *after* assembly instead of with the aid of a simple machine *before* assembly.

Organisational productivity is low because of the lack of specialisation. Consequently, most firms seek to make a wide range of products in the same plant, making it virtually impossible to standardise or modularize anywhere along the product chain. The lack of specialisation contributes to poor quality, as no one firm develops a distinctive competence in one or a limited number of activities such as turning, finishing or veneering. Instead of developing an array of machines capable of producing many variations of specialist activities to high degrees of accuracy, each company has the same range of machines none of which is capable of achieving high degrees of accuracy. The spontaneous adjustment to apparent market opportunities has resulted not in specialisation and co-ordination but imitation and excess capacity.

Establishing a restructuring vision
The sector analysis should feed into a vision that can guide restructuring efforts. The vision must emerge from the international competitor analysis specific to the sector. In the case of the Jamaican woodworking industry, a flexible specialisation vision is being elaborated. The goal is to increase the rate of throughput; only with greater throughput can incomes increase.

The primary barrier to increased throughput in most companies was identified as the limited application of the three production principles of interchangeability (standardisation), flow and flexibility. Interchangeability demands that machines and procedures be established that can produce the same unit to narrow tolerance limits so that the output can be assembled without being handfitted. Interchangeability is a prerequisite to increasing the rate of throughput for any one part or product. Flexibility demands that set-ups on the machines take minutes as opposed to hours but without compromising either interchangeability or (multiple product) flow time.

While idle machines are considered a sin according to the postulates of mass production, wasteful production is the no-no for flexible specialisation. Under mass production, output per machine was an index of productivity. Not so under flexible specialisation, where it is far better to have idle machines than machines producing ill-suited or unwanted products. The goal is to increase not the productivity of machines but the rate of throughput. Machine or labour activity that produces to inventory or that does not increase the flow out of the factory gate is useless activity.

Application of flexible specialisation methods can be illustrated by a comparison of the unproductive methods that two companies now use to make drawers and panel doors with specialised, flexible and cellular production arrangements. Currently, all three principles are violated. The first problem is that the same machines are used for both products. The way ahead is to set up separate product lines, one for drawers and the other for doors.

Drawers can be cut and assembled in less than 1 minute using three simple, heavy-duty, precision-cutting, non-electronic router machines, which together can make corner cuts, bottom grooves and mortise and tenon joints.[5] Together the three routers, run on independent 3 hp motors and equipped with cutters and clip-on, colour-coded guide fences and plates, can do all the operations required to make and assemble drawers in a manner that is solid, high quality and quick. Changeovers to drawers of different depths of cut can be made in 10 seconds. One machine expert quoted a price of $1,500 for such a three-machine configuration. It can be easily demonstrated that the construction method proposed here will substantially increase quality. The drawer is firm without nails or clamps. With glue it will provide a solid drawer for years of normal use.

A similar machine specialisation arrangement can be established for shaping panel doors. Small-scale but durable machines designed for short set-up times without electronics are available at low prices here as well.

The economical use of these machines does not depend upon their utilisation rates *unless* the making of drawers or panel doors is the bottleneck which limits throughput. Whether or not they should be operated depends upon the relationship between throughput and operating expenses. If they do not increase throughput, don't run them, because they will only add to operating expenses.[6] The same applies to labour once piece-rates are abandoned.

Under flexible specialisation labour, not machines, is the fixed factor of production. Labour is also the main source of flexibility in the wood processing industry, unlike processes that can work with liquid materials.[7] For these reasons, it is important to utilise labour effectively. The key to effective utilisation of labour is to make it multi-skilled so that the worker can do set-ups and maintenance as well as operate a machine, and so that he/she can operate multiple machines. In our example, if the worker can shift from producing drawers to doors then the goal of increasing throughput can be realised. For then the whole product or range of products can be produced to demand and not to stock. The result will be shorter and more dependable lead times and lower working capital requirements.

Under flexible specialisation, labour produces more but does not work harder. Present methods demand much harder work, particularly in hand sanding, fitting and assembling, than is required with properly functioning machines. Skills are not less but they are different: instead of being a wizard at fitting irregular drawers into irregular spaces, the worker must be able to read routing sheets and set up machines to do a variety of operations on a range of products.

Making the transition to flexible specialisation methods will require new route sheets defining the methods and machines to be used for every activity. It will also require the rearrangement of machinery, which will actually reduce the space required. A precondition to establishing the new methods is that workers do not fear that jobs will be lost. It is for this reason that the owner/manager needs a problem-solving as opposed to a labour speed-up mentality, which is not compatible with making the transition to flexible specialisation production methods.

Making the transition requires the technical skills of a machine engineer. Their job is to redefine how the products are produced consistently with the principles of interchangeability flow and flexibility, to lay out machines according to the new principles, to develop route sheets for each product, and to demonstrate how to carry out the new methods to the workers involved. The provision of such targeted technical services to small firms by an industrial policy agency is an example of a 'real' service.[8] In conjunction, the training departments within the appropriate governmental and educational institutions can be called upon to conduct group training sessions on the new methods. And before and after practices should be video-recorded so that the transition can be demonstrated in other Jamaican plants.

Workshops and pilot projects

The next step is to conduct workshops on the new production methods which include several individuals from each participating firm. The purpose of the workshop is twofold: to develop a better understanding of the principles of production and organisation and to go back to the companies and develop a pilot project. The idea of the pilot project is to illustrate one theme, which in turn captures a key element in the flexible specialisation vision. For example, a team may illustrate how the proper construction and care of jigs can increase standardisation, reduce hand fitting and increase the rate of material flow. Or a team may demonstrate how reducing set-up times in the cutting or machining department reduces scheduling difficulties in the finishing department and, ultimately, delivery times.

Developing action plans

As individuals in the various enterprises become more familiar with the new principles of production and organisation they will be better equipped to construct performance criteria which contrast their factories with the benchmark, or world-class plants. The refinement of action plans will also serve to identify more precisely what resources are needed to make the transition. At this point the common services that are most critical to success will be clearer. This, in turn, will enable the industrial policy-making agency to redefine its instruments on the basis of real needs. Success will depend upon the state making the transition to flexible special-isation as much as the business enterprises.

The establishment of action plans cannot be achieved by turning to organisational blueprints. The flexible specialisation vision is about, in part, seeking market niches and developing unique competences to satisfy them. For example, a number of Jamaican

companies seek to combine skills with the new principles of
production in ways that will allow them to offer products that cannot
be reproduced by machines alone.

Conclusions

Industrial enterprises, particularly in the Third World and Eastern
Europe, are finding severe competitive pressures not only in efforts
to export but simply to satisfy home demand. At the same time the
globalisation of consumption has put increased pressures on
imports from the regions of the world with enterprises that can
produce at high quality and low cost. Economic growth of the
importing regions is constrained by the squeeze on foreign exchange. In the case of Jamaica, huge foreign capital inflows have
only exacerbated the problem.

The claim of this paper is that traditional industrial development
visions of the right and the left have failed to promote industrial
development in part because the economic theories that have guided
both visions have no conceptual space for production or industrial
policy. The aim of the paper has been to establish an alternative,
production-led vision and to illustrate how an associated concept of
industrial policy can promote industrial development and reduce
the risk that implicit industrial policies will continue to thwart the
internal development of production capabilities in Jamaica.

Notes

I wish to thank Cristian Gillen, Country Director of the United Nations Industrial
Development Organization for Jamaica, with whom most of the ideas in this paper
have been discussed and many have been jointly developed.

1   This first section draws heavily on Levitt (1990).
2   This section is a condensed version of arguments that are made more fully in
Best (1990).
3   A prime example is Lenin's admiration for Henry Ford and Frederick Taylor
which, based on the mistaken view that mass production was about economies of
size, figured in the identification of modernism with giant factories throughout the
Soviet Union and Eastern Europe. See Murray (n.d.).
4   Taiichi Ohno is credited with the creation of the JIT system. See Ohno (1988).
5   This example was worked out in consultation with three Jamaican furniture
companies and Joel Suris, a woodworking technical consultant.
6   The relationship between throughput, operating expenses and inventory is
elaborated in Goldratt and Fox (1987).
7   Dieter Haas, a leading German furniture consultant for many years, makes the
point as follows: 'For the majority of business firms, terms such as all-automation or

CIM/CAM/CAI etc. will remain marketing slogans of the manufacturers of electronic appliances and computers. However in the furniture industry there will not be the complete automatic solution in the foreseeable future. The variety in design and constructive [*sic.*] possibilities, as well as dynamics of change, set limits' (n.d.).

8 For more examples of real services see Brusco (1982), and Bianchi and Bellini (1991); a summary can also be found in Best (1990).

References

Best, Michael (1990), *The New Competition, Institutions of Industrial Restructuring*, Cambridge, MA: Harvard University Press, and Cambridge: Polity Press.

Bianchi, Patrizio and Bellini, Nicola (1991), 'Public policies for local networks of innovators', *Research Policy*, No. 4 (*forthcoming*).

Brusco, Sebastiano (1982), 'The Emilian model', *Cambridge Journal of Economics*, 6, 167–84.

Levitt, Kari Polanyi (1990), 'The origins and consequences of Jamacia's debt crisis, 1970–1990', Consortium Graduate School of Social Sciences, Mona, Jamaica.

Goldratt, Eli and Fox, Robert (1987), 'Revolutionizing the factory floor', *Management Accounting*, May, 18–22.

Haas, Dieter (n.d.), 'Investments with regard to material flow acceleration', Unternehmensberatung Gerhard Schuler, Germany.

Murray, Robin (n.d.), 'Fordism and socialist development', Institute for Development Studies, Sussex University.

Ohno, Taiichi (1988), *Toyota Production System*, Cambridge, MA: Productivity Press.

Piore, Michael and Sabel, Charles F. (1984), *The Second Industrial Divide*, New York: Basic Books.

What Henry did, or the relevance of Highland Park

What Henry Ford said throughout his life was resolutely anti-intellectual. He denied theories of business administration, dismissed history as bunk and, if industrial policy had been invented for his time, Henry would no doubt have condemned it as pernicious interference. What Henry Ford did for nearly 20 years was build the Model T at Highland Park. His manufacturing practice provides rich material for a practical intellectualism which aims to understand the activity of mass manufacturing and the limits of industrial policy intervention.

The success of Ford with the newly introduced Model T between 1909 and 1916 is a brilliant example of cost-reducing market-extending mass manufacture. In these years, a new mass market for a 'people's car' was created; the company which shipped 14,000 Model Ts in 1909 shipped 585,000 Ts in 1916. Demand was stimulated by Ford's policy of dramatic price cuts; an open Model T tourer which cost $950 (fully equipped) in 1909 cost just $360 in 1916. The policy of price cuts was underwritten by successful manufacturing cost reduction which allowed Ford to maintain his profit margins; in 1916 Ford cleared more than $100 of profit on a $360 car and the profit margin of 31% was higher than it had ever been.

If no one can deny the achievement, social scientists now believe that Ford's activities have a limited relevance for today. Ford and the T supposedly represent an obsolete model of mass production, using Taylorism and dedicated equipment to produce a run of 15 million Ts in 'any colour you like so long as it is black'. Recent historical accounts of Ford by Hounshell (1984) and Lewchuk (1987) qualify the stereotype of Taylorism and dedicated equipment but otherwise reinforce the traditional view by presenting the moving assembly line as Ford's central innovation; for Hounshell mature mass production is constituted by the addition of the line, which Lewchuk sees as an efficacious way of controlling labour.

Our own research on Ford challenges the stereotype of mass production and revises the historical orthodoxy about the moving line. This work is fully reported in an article in *Work Employment and Society* (Williams *et al.*, 1992) which includes references to archive sources. In this essay we aim to summarise our revisionist results and to show how they re-establish Ford as our contemporary. We will drive home that second point by cross-reference from veteran Ford to contemporary Japan, which leads mass manufacturing now as the Americans did before 1914. Of course, if Ford is our contemporary he is so in a particular way: because it is impossible to talk to Henry and pointless to read his (largely ghostwritten) texts, it is essential to examine and re-evaluate his manufacturing practice. In the first half of our paper we take up this task before arguing the relevance of Ford in the second half of our paper.

What Henry did

The Highland Park factory, which opened in 1909, was a kind of experiment which illuminated the possibilities of mass manufacturing. This experiment can be reconstructed because Highland Park is the best-documented manufacturing site of the twentieth century. The sources include an extensive secondary literature (e.g. Arnold and Faurote, 1915), an archive of primary sources which features photographs and oral reminiscences as well as the company records, and the semi-derelict factory building. These sources can teach us much if they are set in the context of a general understanding of the activity of manufacturing and especially of multi-process manufacturing. Only after Ford has been set in this framework is it possible to consider how Ford before 1916 (and the Japanese after 1960) exploited the levers of dynamic cost reduction.

The activity of manufacturing is physically about the conversion of materials and financially about adding value. The general problem of the activity is that conversion usually requires a substantial labour input and adding value therefore incurs substantial labour costs. In a typical American or British manufacturing firm now, labour accounts for 70% of value added

(Williams *et al.*, 1989). As long as this is so, it is difficult to sell the manufactured product cheaply. So cost reduction in manufacturing almost always means taking labour time and labour cost out of the product.

Highland Park is a classic case of taking labour out. Ford started with, and maintained, a very lean conversion operation; labour's share of value added averaged 31% between 1909 and 1916. Ford also bought in most of the car when T production began; in 1910 the T cost less than $750 to make and $590 of that was bought-in components. Ford's competitors and suppliers ran much less lean operations; in 1904 and 1908, labour's share of manufacturing value added was around 50% in Michigan State, as in the United States as a whole.

Ford was therefore able to secure dramatic cost reductions by building more of the car in-house; it was quite usual to halve the cost of components whose production was brought in-house. The miracle of Highland Park was that, as purchases fell to half the value of the car and Ford built more of each T, so total labour hours dropped out of the car; as Table 6.1 below shows, between 1910 and 1916, total labour hours per T dropped from 400 to 134. In the whole history of mechanical engineering, probably no one has ever taken labour out so rapidly. And if we next ask how Ford did this, we must begin by considering the specific characteristics of multi-process manufacturing.

Mass manufacturing means volume runs of single products and product families in mechanical, electrical and electronic engineering. Most of this mass manufacturing is multi-process manufacturing because there are many conversion steps involving fabrication and assembly. Multi-process mass manufacture of complex products like cars, washing machines or video-cassette recorders is organisationally the most difficult kind of manufacturing. Its characteristic problem is internal disintegration of production as gaps of space and time open up within and between processes. Whenever these gaps open up, direct labour cannot be used continuously; labour time is wasted on walking or waiting when work is not to hand because the workpieces are piled elsewhere, being clamped up or whatever. In all the gaps, work in progress (wip) accumulates and that costs more money because, at least where the work in progress is bulky, indirect labour is required to process and handle it.

Ford was engaged in the multi-process manufacture of a complex, relatively heavy mechanical engineering product. By 1915, Ford was making around 5,000 separately numbered T parts in-house. The fabrication and assembly of these parts (plus a similar number of bought-in components) required hundreds of thousands of separate processes. One simple low-tech component like the pressed steel sump required no fewer than 78 separate fabrication operations. The other complication was weight when each open T weighed 1,200 lb. By 1914, when the company was making 1,000 cars a day, Ford was shipping 625 tons of metal out the door each day and that weight had to be shifted many times in production.

Ford's achievement was to reduce internal disintegration and realise the ideal of production as continuous flow. The low level of wip and the favourable ratio of indirect to direct workers are the best indicators of the company's success. Highland Park ran on two–three days' stocks including raw materials and major bought-in components like chassis frames; there was certainly less than two days' wip between the processes and virtually none within the processes, so the Ford wip/turnover ratio was probably around 1:200. The ratio of indirect: direct wages payments was around 2.5:1. As we will demonstrate below, Ford's performance on these two criteria is very much stronger than that of modern American or British manufacturing and stands comparison with modern Japanese manufacturing.

The parallel between Highland Park and later Japanese achievement is quite uncanny. Japanese success in tradable goods is based on their expertise in multi-process manufacture of cars and electronics. As with Ford, the basis of Japanese success is their ability to build a product with fewer labour hours; in cars, Japanese firms can build a comparable product with half the labour hours of a Western firm (Womack *et al.*, 1990). And again the evidence shows that the Japanese run internally integrated manufacturing operations with little wip and few indirects. At the leading edge, Toyota runs with a wip/turnover ratio of 1:230. And the ratio of indirects to directs in Japanese manufacturing as a whole is around 4:1 compared with 8:1 in modern American manufacturing.

After making these general points, we can now turn to examining how Ford achieved its remarkable performance. Between 1909 and 1916, the Ford company found and exploited three key levers of cost reduction: design, component supply and reorganisation of production. This process of discovery was the result of exploratory behaviour in a flat, informal and task-centred manufacturing organisation which rejected existing forms of management control like Taylorism and cost accounting. Sorensen (1957, p. 128), who was one of the prime movers in this process, afterwards described the Ford company of this period as 'an organisation which was continually experimenting and improvising to get better production'.

The resourcefulness and intelligence of Ford's improvisation is confirmed by the way in which the Japanese have subsequently exploited the same levers of cost reduction. Perhaps that is not surprising because, as long as the activity of multi-process manufacture remains the same, then the points of intervention will be very similar. But if the problems are basically the same, it is understandable that latecomers, operating in different circumstances, will come up with new solutions to old problems. Regrettably, academics, with a limited understanding of manufacturing, will then present the new solution as a paradigm of production which is essentially different from, and antithetical to, veteran Ford.

Design for low-cost manufacture is important because it can create a new model which will be inherently cheap(er) to manufacture. And design always determines the initial cost platform which 'Kaizen' (continuous improvement) tries to reduce once production begins. The importance of design and development was appreciated by Ford, whose aim was to design a car that was light yet strong. The two contradictory qualities were reconciled through careful choice of materials; pressed steel covers and cases were used in the power train, vanadium alloy steel was specified for stressed parts of the engine and chassis, while every metal component in the car was heat treated for strength. The result was a 20 hp, 1200 lb car which Ford advertised as 'the equal of a 30 hp, 2000 lb car'. In manufacturing terms, the benefit of lower weight was a roughly proportional reduction in manufacturing cost.

The Japanese share Ford's preoccupation with design, particularly in electronics, where the integrated circuit has created opportunities to put complex assemblies (like FM tuners) into a single chip. At Sony TV in 1990 (Williams *et al.*, 1991), the managers insisted that reduction in number of components remained a major design aim in television. More generally, our interviews with senior managers in Japanese electronic and car companies (Williams *et al.*, 1991) demonstrated how the Japanese credit new model design on a two–five year cycle with the same importance as Western firms now give to fixed capital investments; within the problematic of Japanese manufacturing, design is the decisive moment at which resources are committed and cost parameters are set.

The main change over the past 80 years since the T has been a shift from artisan design to large-scale development. Design and development (D & D) has become an expensive large-scale activity which requires teamwork, systems and organisation, so that companies like Nissan operate with elaborate systems for the control of development expenditure. In this context, the importance of D & D is re-doubled because D & D cost is directly important in its own right as well as indirectly through its influence on production cost level. Productively inferior Japanese firms, like Nissan, often try to find competitive advantage through faster, cheaper development (Williams *et al.*, 1991).

The cost-reducing design potential of the T could not be realised as long as Ford bought in most of the car. In 1909 the T's springs, chassis frames, wheels, finished bodies, soft tops and even some of the engines represented several tiers of inefficient embodied supplier labour and conversion profit. As a rule of thumb, at any given level of production, Ford could make a component in-house for half of what it cost to buy in. By 1914 Ford was manufacturing and assembling the complete engine and gearbox of the T for just $6 more than it cost to buy in a lightweight open touring body. Ford had a powerful incentive to displace suppliers and bring component production in-house.

The issue of component cost reduction remains central in late twentieth-century mass manufacturing. In Britain or America now, bought-in components typically account for half the value of the finished product; while in Japan the bought-in element can account for as much as 75%. The Japanese percentage is higher because their majors choose not to displace inefficient suppliers but to improve their efficiency. Ford was never interested in helping suppliers because his suppliers were never organised (in the Japanese style) into a captive network whose profitability could be policed. And Ford therefore never developed formalised, transferable manufacturing techniques like 'Kanban' which could be applied in supplier factories. For this reason, Ford's productive capability was never an easily diffused 'innovation'; indeed, few observers (then or since) have understood how and why productive reorganisation allowed Ford to manufacture so cheaply.

Reorganisation of production is the main lever of in-house cost reduction once a model has been put into production. In multi-process manufacture, changes in layout can improve workflow at little or no capital cost. Flow improvement takes labour cost out by closing the gaps of space and time so that direct labour works continuously and unneccessary indirects are dispensed with. If the possibility of such improvements is not recognised in modern social science, it was an obsession at Ford Motor Company where taking labour out was explicit policy. In 1912 the company's house magazine insisted that 'every extra motion, every trivial waste of time on the part of any workman must be eliminated'; senior engineers argued that all the trucking labour employed in materials handling was wasted because it was non-productive.

Ford's labour cost reduction was successful because the company relentlessly closed up the gaps through three distinct kinds of productive intervention: mechanised transfer, short travel layouts and rapid cycle set-up. All the historical accounts of Ford since Nevins (1954) privilege the moving assembly line (mal). But, for a variety of reasons, the mal is not the secret of Ford's success. The mal was introduced relatively late in the day after spring 1913 when, as Table 6.1 shows, more than half of the total reduction in labour hours had already been achieved. And the mal was only one device in a whole battery of mechanical handling devices at Highland Park; in 1915 the 1.5 miles of conveyor, mainly in chassis assembly and trim, was complemented by 1.75 miles of overhead monorail in the machine shop and extensive delivery of raw material by overhead crane.

It is equally important to realise that Ford's philosophy was wherever possible to eliminate (rather than mechanise) handling by designing short travel layouts which minimised wip. The engine block, which originally travelled 4,000 feet between operations, finally travelled only 334 feet. This kind of spectacular reduction in travel distance was achieved by layout change, after production had started up in 1909, through careful attention to sequence of shops, position of machines and inter-process transfer. In our view these productive interventions were the crucial dynamic behind Ford's cost reduction.

Table 6.1 *Ford Ts per man year and man hours per T*

	Cars per man year	Labour hours per car
1909	8.4	357
1910	7.5	400
1911	13.5	222
1912	12.0	250
1913	13.9	216
1914	18.8	127
1915	19.5	123
1916	17.9	134

Source: Ford archive.

By 1912, the shops in Highland Park were laid out on a west to east axis along which wip travelled to final assembly; in the multi-storey buildings, components and sub-assemblies travelled down to ground-floor assembly. Within the shops, Ford's practice was to put machines close together and in order of use; this principle was applied not only in the main machine shop but also in other departments where annealing furnaces and aluminium foundries were fitted in between other processes. When the machines had been jammed close together and in order of use, it was possible to introduce simple, re-usable inter-process transfer devices like roller beds and gravity slides made of pipe and angle iron.

If layout improvement eliminated unnecessary indirect labour, the utilisation of direct labour was improved by careful attention to rapid cycle set-up. In the machining of engine and gearbox, one of the key limits on throughput was the amount of unproductive time which was wasted on clamping the workpieces at each process stage. Ford engineers reduced cycle set-up by developing quick-acting 'one-touch' clamps and gravity location as well as increasingly sophisticated fixtures which allowed several cuts on more than one workpiece for each clamping. Changeover was not a problem for Ford because the company produced a periodically updated and restyled family of five or six differently bodied Ts rather than a range of differently sized cars.

When Japanese firms like Toyota and Nissan (re)entered car production after World War II, their mission was to supply a small domestic market which required variety (Cusumano, 1985). They achieved rapid changeover by much the same means and with the same enthusiasm that Ford brought to cycle set-up. More generally, Japanese manufacturing practice recovers and resumes Ford's old preoccupation with continuous reorganisation of production to take labour out. Significantly, the preoccupation with labour rather than machine utilisation is equally explicit; Toyota's slogan of 'machines rather than men must wait' is prefigured in Ford's machine shop practice. Similar techniques of low-cost reorganisation are equally prominent in both cases; the Japanese, like Ford, jam the machines together with simple inter-process transfer devices. The main difference here is that the Japanese invented a concept which describes what they do (and Henry did) as 'Kaizen', or a step towards improvement.

The relevance of Highland Park

The story of Highland Park and the parallel with Japan cannot be reconciled with the doxa that veteran Ford represents an obsolete form of mass production: the Japanese achievement is best interpreted as a rediscovery and resumption under different circumstances. If we are concerned more positively to re-establish the relevance of Ford for today, it is probably best to concentrate on two implications of Highland Park: first, for existing discursive misunderstandings of the activity of manufacturing; and secondly, for existing political misunderstandings of the role and scope of intervention through instruments such as industrial policy.

Before we began our research on Highland Park, we had already framed the hypothesis that established academic discourses mis-represent the activity of manufacturing. We have elsewhere detailed the misunderstandings of management accounting and explained how the ineffectual Western problematic of financial control cannot be reconciled with the practice of Japanese manufacturing man-agement which exploits the levers of cost reduction (Williams *et al.*, 1991). At this point we can extend the critique by contrasting Ford's masterly practice of productive intervention with the misunder-standings of managerial economics and strategy, as represented in typical American and British textbooks which expound these discourses.

Strategy texts do occasionally notice design to cost (e.g. Rowe *et al.*, 1989, p. 211), but the importance of doing more with less before production does not figure in managerial economics. Here, pre-production is discussed only in terms of 'research and development' (e.g. Davies, 1991, pp. 25–6) on the assumption that innovation requires a strategic commitment of extra resources. Worse still, neither discourse provides the conceptual tools for understanding production. The internal complexities of multi-process production are recognised only in the form of the division of labour, which is naively assumed to be wholly beneficial (Davies, 1991, p. 137). Both economics and strategy operate in a kind of input/output problematic where the attention is focused on either side of the production process rather than on what goes on inside.

Orthodox production function analysis explicitly assumes that, with given inputs of labour and fixed capital, the productive result is always the same, so that it is possible 'to develop a mathematical model that can be used to predict the output that can be obtained from any mix of inputs' (Seo, 1991, p. 326). In strategy, the same assumption is implicit in the matrix analysis of product portfolios (e.g. Rowe *et al.*, 1989, pp. 132–5; Johnson and Scholes, 1989, pp. 104–6) where the star, dog, cash cow and question mark products all have fixed pre-given patterns of profit and cash flow which can be read off market share and market growth. The converse of this assumption is the idea that semi-automatic benefits can be obtained by increasing output volume or varying the input mix. In orthodox economics, increasing the output volume allows the firm to realise technical economies of scale (Davies, 1991, pp. 136–7; Seo, 1991, p. 364), just as in strategy cumulative volume moves firms down the experience curve (Rowe *et al.*, 1989, pp. 130–2; Johnson and Scholes, 1989, pp. 101–4). Input mix is classically conceived in terms of increasing the quantity of fixed capital input; the work of Porter here serves as bridge between economics and strategy because Porter takes an orthodox view of the benefits of fixed capital investment. More recently, increasing the quality of the labour input through training has been a centrist enthusiasm in Britain.

Highland Park is a brilliant refutation of these simplicities which shows how the academic discourses misrepresent the key causal relations behind cost reduction. Ford did apply increased division of labour in assembly and piled investment into the machine shop so that investment per worker doubled from $870 to $1,606 between

1909 and 1916. But, without productive reorganisation, the sub-division of assembly labour tasks would have brought productivity loss as well as gain. And in the machine shop Ford could not buy in labour saving because he was buying in standard machine tools whose manufacturers envisaged one skilled operative and backup trucking for each machine. The real dynamic was the endless layout change which took out labour time and cost as well as wip (or working capital); and did so at minimal expense through transfer devices like gravity slides or face-to-face layouts which allowed one worker to tend two machines. The gap between what Ford and his suppliers could do suggests that this kind of 'more for less' innovation was an organisational capability rather than a discrete, easily diffused technique.

The lesson of Ford is that, in multi-process manufacture, it's not what you have but how you use it through productive reorganis-ation. If this basic point is invisible in economics or strategy, it has been further obfuscated by the recent enthusiasm for mass produc-tion and its opposite (flexible specialisation, post-Fordism, etc.) as concepts for understanding manufacturing. Under strong criticism, these concepts have been defended as either descriptive historical generalisations or analytic ideal types which act as a research heuristic (see Hirst and Zeitlin, 1991). In our view, these concepts cannot fulfil either function.

If mass production is a historical generalisation, it is a bad one because it encourages us to understand the present as a break with a mythical past. Emilia Romagna or Japan are represented as the escape of manufacturing from a 50-year period up to 1960 when product changeover was slow because dedicated equipment and unskilled workers could only produce long runs. This periodisation confuses and conflates the last degenerate phase of American mass manufacturing after 1950 with what came before in America and was developed elsewhere in Europe (see Woollard, 1954). And, in this respect, the story of Highland Park is exemplary because this was a flexible factory whose variable layouts, re-usable equipment and malleable workforce easily changed over to war production in 1917–18 (Bryan, 1990). Ford's decision to develop the T, rather than introduce new models, was a matter of marketing choice rather than productive necessity.

The ideal-type defence of the concept of mass production can conjure away embarrassing empirical discrepancies but it cannot turn mass production into an adequate research heuristic. The concept of mass production (and its opposite) does not identify the levers of dynamic cost reduction through regular product (re)design and continuous process improvement. The issues of layout, work-flow and labour content barely figure at all because mass production conserves most of the input/output assumptions of orthodox economics. The main add-on complication is market demand, whose increasing sophistication disrupts the otherwise productively stable system of mass production. That adds a dubious supplementary assumption without confronting the weakness of the basic concept of production. As our account of Highland Park shows, it is intellectually possible and necessary to start with a different and more realistic concept of the activity of manufacturing.

If we turn now to policy issues, these arise because, if mass manufacturing is in principle conceptually easy to understand, in practice it is very difficult to master. As a result, there are large and persistent differences in national manufacturing capability. These differences in capability are encapsulated in the wip/turnover ratio because the existence of wip is an infallible indicator of dislocation and disintegration of workflow. Table 6.2 considers four advanced country manufacturing sectors and expresses wip as weeks of stock cover: a wip/turnover ratio of 1:26 equals two weeks' stocks.

Table 6.2 *Manufacturing wip/turnover in Germany, Japan, UK and USA manufacturing, 1989*

	Work in progress : turnover ratio	Sales cover No. of weeks
Germany	1 : 25	2.04
Japan	1 : 48	1.08
UK	1 : 7	7.72
USA	1 : 19	2.69

Source: Datastream.

The Japanese are way out in front with a wip/turnover ratio which is roughly twice as good as in the USA or Germany. While the British are way behind because their factories contain nearly eight weeks' wip, compared with two weeks in the USA and Germany or one week in Japan.

We do not wish to substitute national stereotypes for the productive stereotypes which we have criticised and therefore it is important to emphasise that large Japanese manufacturers are not all uniformly excellent. The aggregate superiority of Japanese manufacturing is above all due to the success of a few large car companies like Toyota, Honda and Mazda, which operate with wip/turnover ratios around 1 : 200 just like Ford at Highland Park; the 1 : 20 ratios at GM or Ford today measure America's subsequent deterioration. But several large Japanese electrical and electronic companies, like NEC and Hitachi, have distinctly mediocre wip/turnover performance; while, focused American companies like Caterpillar or Black and Decker can match or beat their Japanese competitors. That is no consolation for the British because 'hollowing out' leaves Britain with few national champions and no large British-owned manufacturing company performs well on wip/turnover criteria.

For a small, unsuccessful manufacturing country like Britain, this observed inferiority in manufacturing performance raises three sets of policy issues: first, what forms of enterprises and relations between enterprises should be encouraged; secondly, should policy intervention be at the strategic or operational level; and, thirdly, should intervention be geared to improving the capability of indigenous firms or bringing in outsiders? On all three issues, the story of Highland Park provides a critical historical perspective on currently fashionable panaceas.

On forms of enterprise, the historically illiterate always take one contemporary model of success and try to generalise it as a universal recipe. Thus some would argue that Britain needs to be re-made in the image of Emilia Romagna while others would argue that it needs to Japanise. The story of Ford is a nice antidote to this kind of prescriptive universalism because it shows how naive it is to suppose that all can succeed by supplying a specific market in the same way. Manufacturing supply never creates its own demand to the extent of abolishing market limitations; even the Ford Company faltered after 1923 as Chevrolet became a major player in the cheap car market. Furthermore, successful manufacturers do not adopt but adapt their practice to local circumstances; while Ford built success by cutting out suppliers, his Japanese successors built their industrial system on a foundation of small and medium suppliers. The implication is that good production engineering is compatible with a wide variety of institutional and organisational structures.

If that conclusion seems weakly permissive, maybe we could add a negative point about the m-form organisation which was invented in America in the 1920s and imported into Britain in the 1960s (Channon, 1973). M-form firms depend on strategy and financial control. In our view, such firms are very unlikely to generate a commitment to continuous manufacturing improvement because their centres of decision-making are too remote from production. The depressing implication is that British manufacturing is a chronic case which will not easily respond to any policy treatment. It is certainly difficult to envisage industrial policy intervention succeeding if it is confined to the strategic level as the Industrial Strategy Group (1989) propose.

This kind of industrial policy proposal accommodates and reflects the ideological pretensions of the discourse of strategy and the dominant organisational form of British big business. It is, however, unlikely to lead to any regeneration of manufacturing if, as we have argued, there is a general deficiency of operational capability. If they operate in exposed activities, incompetent firms (private or state-owned) cannot deliver any promises they make about manufacturing. And government has little leverage over productively incompetent firms which adapt pathologically and retreat from contested manufacturing into sheltered activites like dealing and services. As a result, Britain has an increasingly 'hollowed out' manufacturing sector, which may generate profits and cash flow but cannot generate value added and employment (Williams *et al.*, 1990).

Hanson shows how financial engineering can be used as a substitute for production engineering: the low-tech businesses of bricks, batteries and tobacco are only a secondary source of cash and a cover for the primary activity of buying and selling companies (Adcroft, 1991). The Hanson and ICI affair shows how old-fashioned productionist companies can now be forced into defensive restructuring, which is a euphemism for selling assets and sacking workers to raise profitability. It is difficult to tighten the regulatory constraints on financial engineering as long as companies have the option of leaving for America through acquisition. And, if financial engineering cannot be curbed, that greatly complicates any initiative to improve operational capability through management education. In Britain, as in America, business education has expanded by meeting the growing demand for financial expertise, and productive intervention has been evicted from the management syllabus (Armstrong, 1987).

If the performance of indigenous manufacturing firms cannot easily be improved, the locational decisions of world-leading manufacturers are of crucial importance because much depends on bringing in outsiders. These leaders will all be 'transnational companies' but their motives and behaviour will vary according to circumstance and the nationality of the parent company. For Ford and his less capable American successors, overseas manufacture was initially a way of tapping protected high-income markets and subsequently a way of exploiting low-wage production, which is especially attractive to firms that cannot take labour hours out. By 1916, Ford already had full manufacturing plants in operation in Canada and Britain.

Under relatively free trade, Japanese (and German) manufacturing leaders can now stay at home and send direct exports to their high-income markets. Thus, the Japanese do not have a significant manufacturing presence in America or Britain; manufacturing employment in Japanese-owned factories totals 85,000 in the United States and 25,000 in the United Kingdom. Japanese-owned warehouses are much more important than factories; in 1988, for example, the wholesale turnover of Japanese manufacturing firms in America was more than 10 times larger than their manufacturing turnover. Token manufacturing in the advanced countries is used as a way of defending exports from Japan which maintain domestic value added and employment. Within the EC, West German firms have an equally strong preference for export rather than relocation; the old FRG exported 50% of its manufacturing output and claimed a 38% share of EC12 manufacturing ouput, although its share of EC12 population was only 18% (Cutler *et al.*, 1989).

If mass production had been superseded by new principles of production and consumption, it would be easy to be optimistic about the potential of industrial policy, which could assist as grave-digger of the old order and midwife of the new order. A de-mythologised account of what Henry did and a brief reflection on the relevance of Highland Park suggest that the task of policy is by no means that straightforward. The reconceptualisation of the activity of manufacturing needs to be developed further before it creates the intellectual space for a new kind of industrial policy that does not yet exist.

References

Adcroft, A. (1991), 'Hanson and ICI: the consequences of financial engineering', East London Polytechnic Business Paper.

Armstrong, P. (1987), 'The abandonment of productive intervention in management teaching syllabi', University of Warwick Papers in Industrial Relations.

Arnold, H. L. and Faurote, F. (1915), *Ford Methods and Ford Shops*, New York: Engineering Magazine Company.

Bryan, F. R. (1990), *Beyond the Model T*, Detroit: Wayne State University Press.

Channon, D. F. (1973), *The Strategy and Structure of British Enterprise*, Basingstoke: Macmillan.

Cusumano, M. A. (1985), *The Japanese Automobile Industry*, Cambridge, MA: Harvard University Press.

Cutler, T. *et al.* (1989), *1992 – The Struggle for Europe*, Oxford: Berg.

Davies, H. (1991), *Managerial Economics*, 2nd ed, London: Pitman.

Hirst, P. and Zeitlin, J. (1991), 'Flexible specialisation versus post-Fordism' *Economy and Society*, 20(1), February, 1–30.

Hounshell, D. (1984), *From the American System to Mass Production*, Baltimore, MD: Johns Hopkins.

Industrial Strategy Group (1989), *Beyond the Policy Review*, Edinburgh: Industrial Strategy Group.

Johnson, G. and Scholes, K. (1989), *Exploring Corporate Strategy*, London: Prentice Hall.

Lewchuk, W. (1987), *American Technology and the British Vehicle Industry*, Cambridge: Cambridge University Press.

Nevins, A. (1954), *Ford: The Times, The Man, The Company*, New York: Scribner.

Rowe, A. J., Mason, R. O., Dickel, K. E. and Snyder, N. H. (1989), *Strategic Management*, 3rd edn, Reading, MA: Addison Wesley.

Seo, K. K. (1991), *Managerial Economics*, Homewood, IL: Irwin.

Sorensen, C. E. (1957), *Forty Years with Ford*, London: Cape.

Williams, K., Williams, J. and Haslam, C. (1989), 'Do labour costs really matter?' *Work Employment and Society*, 3(3), September, 281–305.

Williams, K., Williams, J. and Haslam, C. (1990), 'The hollowing out of British manufacturing and its implications for policy', *Economy and Society*, 19(4), November, 456–90.

Williams, K., Haslam, C. and Williams, J., with Abe, M., Aida, T. and Mitsui, I. (1991), 'Management accounting: the Western problematic against the Japanese application', mimeo, forthcoming in *Accounting, Auditing and Accountability*.

Williams, K., Haslam, C. and Williams, J. (1992), 'Ford versus Fordism, the beginning of mass production' *Work, Employment and Society*.

Womack, J., Jones, D. and Roos, D. (1990), *The Machine that Changed the World*, New York: Rawson Associates.

Woollard, F. G. (1954), *Principles of Mass and Flow Production*, London: Iliffe.

Just-in-time and the costs of complexity

Introduction

Flexible production
In recent years business consultants (for instance, Hall 1983, Monden, 1983, and Schonberger, 1982) and industrial engineers (see Shingo, 1989) have proclaimed the virtues of a Japanese (or, more properly, Toyotan) system of product management and production organisation. The theme has been taken up in the form of attempted (or purported) imitation on the part of Western manufacturers of new 'best practice' methods (see Oliver and Wilkinson, 1988). And these methods have become inextricably linked to contemporary discussion of the parameters of 'flexibility' in production. This is reflected in the current state of much of the academic literature within the social sciences (see Wood, 1989).

But what is meant by 'flexible production'? The precise meaning to be attached to the phrase is not always clear. In this paper we are concerned with 'flexible production' where it is taken to denote a manufacturer's ability to respond with speed and efficiency to a perceived change in customer demand for the product on offer. It is the terms of this definition, i.e. the 'product' on offer and the contextual meaning of 'speed' and 'efficiency', which constitute the substance of this paper. This is developed through an analysis of the just-in-time (JIT) method of parts movement and inventory control, an integral part of the 'best practice' literature, and its relationship to flexibility.

Just-in-time production
JIT systems have often been summarised in the notion that 'the correct part should arrive in the correct place at the correct time'. As

a statement of practical purpose this formulation is clearly rhetorical rather than analytical (in as much as any system of planning material requirements satisfies these criteria provided it functions adequately). But it is intended to emphasise JIT delivery as a means of controlling the pace and content of the flow of component parts and work-in-progress to and between production processes, in a way which differs from 'traditional' methods.

Put this way, the JIT supply concept pertains to the achievement of a 'smoothed' flow of parts to the point of parts use (e.g. components to an assembly line) in a 'minimal' inventory context.[1] However, most social scientists, and some operations research specialists, have been preoccupied with a supposed relationship between JIT parts delivery and 'flexible production'. This has resulted in an extension of the initial summary statement of JIT to encompass 'delivery of the correct product to the correct person at the correct time', stressing a link between adoption of a JIT supply strategy and producers' capacities to respond to changes in final demand.

This paper identifies some of the difficulties faced in attempting to define a 'flexible' production system adequately, and critically examines the purported relationship between a firm's 'capacity to respond' and maintenance of a JIT parts regime. It argues that the need to forecast demand on a complex product constitutes the main barrier to achieving reliable delivery dates in response to customers' orders. Moreover, adoption of JIT parts provision *per se* does not solve this difficulty. On the other hand, JIT parts supply does bring with it a need for organisational discipline, which imposes it own constraints on the production process. These constraints include a low tolerance for complexity in the product environment, which comes to impose a cost on the system which is not readily tolerated. The need to reduce complexity, a precondition for an acceptable JIT strategy, would seem to eliminate one obstacle to achieving a component of flexible production by delimiting the feasible content of that flexibility.

Case study material

This argument is evolved from case work conducted in the UK at Rover's Longbridge plant. As such it does not proceed deductively from basic principles but is inferred from experience on the 'R8' line at the Longbridge facility, where an 'aggressive' JIT scheme for parts delivery has been in operation since the platform launch in 1989.[2]

The conception of JIT parts delivery which is developed in this paper is that it is most pertinently described in terms of a difficult and restrictive exercise in 'organisational logistics'. The intrinsic difficulty of this exercise underpins a basic incompatibility between a high level of product complexity and JIT parts delivery. The contextual meaning of product 'complexity' is developed as the paper proceeds. But in effect it is argued that reduced product complexity (corresponding to traditional notions of 'marketed variety') permits an enhanced demand forecast within a restricted product environment. The curtailment of permissible variety thereby enables a more reliably rapid delivery response to customer orders.[3]

The paper proceeds in essentially two parts. In the next section we develop the nature of demand forecasting and its relationship to complexity. Following this we explore in more detail the daily operational requirements of a JIT system. There are two pitfalls to avoid in interpreting the recorded findings. Complexity has become a major issue within Rover. But at the same time it is important to distinguish the manner in which this issue has come to the fore inside the company from the basic principles involved. And, closely related to this, if these principles are in some degree generalisable to the Japanese experience, then there is no need to imagine that the surrounding circumstances have been in any way similar.

Forecasting complexity

The need for forecasting

Forecasting is inevitable where there is a combination of a strong seasonal demand (the result of UK August registration) and a limited productive capacity, and where suppliers' lead times are positive. Both conditions undoubtedly pertain to the R8. If forecasts were perfect, then from the point of view of achieving an 'instant' delivery response to customer orders the product could be treated as though it were in 'free supply'. In effect cars would be built to correct volume specifications in advance of order placements and distributed accordingly across the dealer network. The temporal separation of production and demand would reflect capacity constraints, and the notice on material requirements given to suppliers in advance of production would reflect suppliers' lead times.

When forecasting is imperfect, lead times which are positive (and variable) separate customers' orders from deliveries. If cars matching individual customer specification have been built but distributed incorrectly across stock holdings, then lags will be incurred while transfers between dealers are negotiated and shipments from parent stock arranged. On the other hand, if a car matching an order specification is yet to be built, lags will be incurred in the form of the manufacturer's own lead time. In part this will depend on whether a matching vehicle will soon be produced according to the original forecast. But where the variance in orders specified is large, and the deviance of market demand from forecast substantial, severe 'queuing' problems will occur. The ability to accommodate all customers quickly in an imperfect forecasting situation will then depend on the severity of those restrictions on the immediate employment of capacity which provided us originally with the rationale for forecasting, i.e. scheduling constraints and suppliers' lead times.

Forecasting and just-in-time

Scheduling constraints on the R8 take two basic forms. The first concerns the limits on total volumes which can be produced as a result of the peak demand cycle in UK car manufacture. This is unavoidable. Within these ceilings, however, a second constraint operates in the form of restrictions on the type of car which can be produced at a point in time (in the sense of production to a detailed specification). This is a consequence of maintenance of a JIT parts policy and of the batching rules governing the composition of car production schedules on the R8.

We discuss batching further below. To understand the role played by JIT supply in restricting content of production consider the situation where a sufficiently large stock of parts is held, creating a short-term situation of 'parts in free supply'. Suppliers' lead times would still have to be accommodated in the form of advance orders to maintain stock, but the problem posed from the viewpoint of immediate production needs would not be severe. With a JIT policy in place around the R8, however, involving a non-reliance on substantial parts stocks, the problem posed by lead times in the context of immediate production possibilities is much more difficult.

When market demand departs from the initial forecast, the ability to accommodate this fluctuation now turns on the question of how rigidly parts suppliers adhere to initial forecasts. To make a proper assessment in this respect, however, it is necessary first to understand the process generating parts orders in the R8.

Generating parts requirements
Each forecast made for a particular specification of car can be most usefully thought of as a forecast made on a required set of parts. The process which generates orders to suppliers for parts on the R8 is based on a long-term forecast made on final production needs. This takes the form of a procurement programme issued to suppliers each month as a supply schedule compiled on the basis of a final sales forecast over a six-month period. These forecasts encompass total car volumes expected to sell in each month of that period, the mix of derivatives within those volumes and the expected option 'takes' in each instance. The procurement programme itself is derived from sales forecasts in a way which smoothes capacity utilisation against seasonal demand through planned adjustments in car stock.

The monthly supply schedule can be thought of as reflecting the contents of a 'pipeline' carrying a sequence of forecasted vehicles closer to the point of actual scheduling for production, each vehicle taking an average of six months to traverse the full distance. This is shown schematically in Figure 7.1. The supply schedule informs each supplier of Rover's requirements for each month of that six-month period. Compilation of the procurement programme proceeds on a rolling basis, the last five months' forecast of the first month's issue becoming the first five months' forecast of the second month's issue. The actual 'call off' to suppliers for parts occurs close to the point of actual production. On a weekly basis, cars at the end of the pipeline are selected into a final build programme (called the 'Selected Order Bank') for actual production. This Order Bank covers two weeks' production (the second week of the first week's Bank becomes the first week of the second week's Bank) and provides a rigid schedule for immediate production, as well as generating the final 'call' on parts from suppliers (see below).

How flexible is this system? Some limited flexibility is permitted within the plan driving the procurement process, in the form of revisions to earlier forecasts when subsequent monthly schedules

FIRST FORECAST .. SELECTED ORDER BANK... BUILD
(6 months out) (two weeks out)
Suppliers plan .... Confirmation of ....Parts
ahead requirements use

Figure 7.1 *Order bank pipeline for R8*

are issued to suppliers. In effect, however, the schedule gives a fairly firm commitment to suppliers on parts orders, in the form of a six months' lead time allowance. But to fully understand the form which the rigidity indicated here takes it is first necessary to understand the 'batching' procedure employed in scheduling final production.

Building to batch
Vehicles going down the R8 track should be produced in sequence according to the instructions contained in the final build programme. This sequence, however, is not 'random', in the sense that cars of differing specification can be scheduled in for production in any order, but conforms instead to a system of 'batch-building'. It is this system of building to batch which provides the governing framework for production scheduling. And when sales forecasts are made six months out on future production requirements, those forecasts must be 'submitted' into the far end of the 'pipeline' in a manner satisfying the batching criteria. These criteria constitute rules based on the derivative features, options content and sales destination of individual cars which serve to group those cars into batches.

Several factors drive the build to batch programme employed on the R8, chief amongst which is the JIT policy for parts delivery. In addition to the effort which would always be invoked to co-ordinate and control a precise build sequence for a complex product, production on the R8 is carried out under the constraint of holding a minimum inventory of parts. Not only does this accentuate the problems posed by an inaccurate forecast, as we noted above, but it also means that parts delivered must match production requirements very exactly within a tightly scheduled time frame (in terms of Figure 7.1, parts provided for use must match parts required for build). Sorting individually sequenced cars into identifiable batches has the effect of easing some of the difficulties involved in attaining this degree of process and parts movement control, since it is easier to target parts movement against a batch than against a single sequenced vehicle. We can think of this as the 'logistical' dimension of JIT production, with batch-building making a contribution towards a partial solution.

JIT constraints and flexible production

We can now also begin to appreciate the contribution made by adoption of JIT delivery of parts to R8 production in terms of the 'flexibility' of the system. We noted at the outset of this section that if a car ordered by a customer does not match those in stock then a delay must be incurred while the car is produced. And we also noted that, if the deviance of the market forecast from the market needs is substantial, then a 'queue' of unsatisfied orders might be the result. If there are no parts constraints to limit production, i.e. if parts are held in sufficient stock to meet immediate needs, then this backlog of orders is solely the result of technical and volume limits on productive capacity. On the other hand, if parts are delivered just-in-time, then the degree to which suppliers' forecasts are binding also becomes a limiting factor.

While the forecasting system as a whole is fairly rigid, there is scope within the programme to bring forward or delay the deployment of parts which have been scheduled for use. This is a finite possibility, but it is not too misleading to think of it in terms of a commitment to suppliers to use all parts scheduled for use, in a particular month, on average. Therefore if a random build sequence were permitted in the final production schedule, i.e. if cars could be scheduled for production in any order desired within the confines of the monthly parts commitment, the queuing problem might not be too severe. But since vehicles can be built only if they conform to a complete batch scheduled for production, the problem is made that much worse. And as we note in the next section, the discipline required to make JIT delivery workable precludes any wholescale movement of batches out of their scheduled position in the final production sequence.

To conclude this section we might say that the sorting of individually sequenced cars into identifiable batches has the effect of easing some of the logistical difficulties involved in running JIT parts delivery by paradoxically increasing the rigidities already inherent in the production scheduling process. But before moving on to the next section we must return to the initial theme of 'complexity' to develop further the arguments made in the introduction to this paper.

Forecasting complexity

In the introduction we stated that the need to anticipate the market through generating forecasts on a 'complex' product was the major obstacle to achieving 'flexibility' as we defined the term. We also noted that adoption of JIT production does not constitute a means to a solution. The reasons for this conclusion have been developed above. But what do we mean by 'complexity' and what is its relationship to 'marketed variety', i.e. those variants of the product which form the basis of a producer's marketing strategy?

Traditionally cars in the UK have been marketed and sold as 'badged' derivatives, for instance a 214Si or a 220Gti from the R8 platform. Each derivative will include its own features, though different cars under a common badge may have different core characteristics. In addition to this choice between and within 'derivatives', the customer may also choose from a number of 'options' (power aided steering, air conditioning, etc.) in each instance, as well as from a range of interior and exterior colours.

The total number of permutations here is very large, and we might think of it in terms of 'marketed' variety. There can be little doubt that forecasts will prove inaccurate where there are as many permutations to the product as there are on the R8. While forecasts have proved tolerable on the mix of basic derivatives, and even on the uptake of individual derivative options, matching particular option combinations to colours has proved impossible. As a result of this complexity, forecasts have thus proved an imperfect way of gauging market needs. The cost of complexity in this respect has been the need to hold a large stock of vehicles (an expensive option) yet none the less accept a variable lead time on customer orders simply because all permutations could not be covered.

From the viewpoint of production, however, this variation does not capture fully the parts variance involved in changing from one 'derivative type – option – colour combination' to another. A seemingly small change in terms of the marketed product may have an implication for parts requirements which is very substantial but 'invisible' from the viewpoint of the final purchaser. We might think of this in terms of 'produced' complexity. Not every potential variation in marketable attributes has a large parts implication, but in the context of the design and engineering history of car manufacture at Rover the cost of 'marketed' variety in terms of 'produced' complexity is very high indeed. This is particularly true in the case of the R8, which has a very high number of base derivatives.

It is this level of complexity that makes the logistics of JIT delivery so difficult to manage effectively. Each specification of each part type has to be monitored against production needs, no matter how low the use of that part is. We look more closely at some of the operating difficulties of JIT production in the next section, but it is this level of complexity, inextricably linked to the complexity described above, that has initially driven the impetus to bring it down within Rover.

Practising just-in-time

Maintaining build integrity
Provided that the production environment is sufficiently well controlled, the system as a whole functions in the manner depicted in Figure 7.2. The manufacturing lead time on the final assembly operations from construction of body-in-white (BIW) to car-off-assembly is under 30 hours. If everything goes to plan the batch of vehicles (for instance, a batch of 30, 5-door right-hand drive GSi's) moves from framing through paint into trim and assembly. In the last stages suppliers' component parts arrive just-in-time at track-side to coincide with the arrival of the GSi's. There is a perfect match between parts required and parts available. At the same time the 'balance' of jobs involving high work content and low work content jobs is calculated with the overall sequence of batched vehicles in mind.

The system will function in this way only if the flow of parts to trackside is maintained and correctly synchronised with the planned build sequence, and if the 'integrity' of this sequence itself is maintained. The concept of 'build integrity' is a key to understanding the difficulties of running a JIT parts regime.

Suppose for the moment that a failure to maintain build integrity arises at the body framing stage. On the one hand, a quality problem in framing itself might lead to the withdrawal of a vehicle from its batch and placement in a rectification bay. In this event the vehicle

Stage	BIW	Paint	Trim/assembly
Batch size	Intitial batch (e.g. 30 GSi's)	Takes up batch	Batch breaks into sub-batches
Outcome			Components delivered JIT match needs Line balance preserved

Figure 7.2   *R8 batch production: maintaining build integrity*

Stage	BIW	Paint	Trim/final assembly
Problem and effect	Quality problem (delete car) Ageing batch (delete batch)	Batch disintegration Altered sequence of batches	Resultant break in line balance & Build up in semi-depleted pallets

Figure 7.3   *R8 batch production: losing build integrity*

passes through what in effect is a finite control loop which reinserts the vehicle into the main production sequence after rectification. This depletes by one the original batch as it enters the paint shop. At the same time, if the deleted vehicle re-enters the sequence as a 'foreign' derivative into another batch, this disrupts that batch formation. If this process is repeated on any significant scale there is a departure from the planned build sequence with a disintegration of 'batch integrity' (see Figure 7.3).

On the other hand, the 'ageing' of a batch, where an entire batch is delayed from being framed in the body shop, may displace a large number of other batches from their place in the planned build sequence. In either case the disruption to the planned flow causes severe control problems further down the system. The unplanned variance from the original build sequence means that the 'balance' of work tasks on the trim and assembly lines is disrupted. At the same time there is a visible accumulation of semi-depleted pallets by trackside.

To overcome these problems, management at Rover have concentrated on honing the reliability of the sequence and on increasing the ability of the JIT delivery systems to adapt to a breakdown in the integrity of the sequence. We now turn to look at a concrete example of the latter instance, in order both to demonstrate more thoroughly the sort of efforts taken to effect process and parts movement control, and to fill out in more detail the actual means of delivery employed in the JIT system on the R8 line.

Mapping parts movement
For JIT delivery itself a number of methods are used on the R8. Table 7.1 gives an approximate breakdown of the importance of each type of delivery. The two basic divisions are between those parts delivered just-in-time to their factory fit-points and those sent through more conventional stock routes. This latter category of parts is grouped under 'conventional and small fit parts', and for the most part these are held in stock on sites adjacent to the trim and assembly tracks at Longbridge. These items are considered intrinsically unsuited to JIT delivery, consisting in the main of low value added, high volume turnover parts (sometimes with a high wastage content, as in the case of fasteners). Parts falling into the category of JIT delivery are entered under different headings according to the twin criteria of 'bulkiness' and 'complexity'.

Table 7.1   *Delivery methods to R8*

Type of delivery	*% of parts*
JIT method:	
Timed delivery schedule (TDS)	44
and sequenced delivery	
Kanban (LDC)	30
Other method:	
Conventional/small fit parts	16

Source: Rover.

Parts deemed suitable for JIT delivery but lacking a significant 'pallet factor' are delivered by firms on a regular (several times a week) or semi-regular basis to a distribution centre located close to the Longbridge plant. The small 'pallet' (or container) factor is a reference to the economies to be had from consolidating different parts due for delivery trackside into a single vehicle load before final movement. In this way a frequent small lot delivery of parts trackside does not result in an underutilisation of trucking capacity. Prior to consolidation for final delivery these parts are delivered individually in greater bulk to the Longbridge Distribution Centre (LDC) on a less frequent basis. The 'Kanban' in this instance refers to a trackside small stock repletion system which 'pulls' in parts from the LDC through an electronic message activated by the emptying of the first container of a two-bin system. By this means (labelled) parts are 'called' in to their respective trackside fit-points several times per shift, after consolidation into a single vehicle load.

The timed delivery schedule (TDS) system involves direct parts delivery from suppliers to the Longbridge assembly plant according to a predetermined time slot. These parts are sufficiently bulky to possess a significant 'pallet factor', i.e. to require at least one full vehicle load per shift to meet production needs. This negates the need for prior load consolidation at the LDC, though in most cases parts are routed through local warehouse or distribution centres to minimise the distance travelled in the final JIT delivery.

Lastly, sequenced deliveries consist of high-level complex sub-assemblies possessed both of bulk and a marked individual variance. The lack of homogeneity of these parts together with their bulk means that derivative members of each parts 'family' are packaged individually into containers to be carried trackside in reverse sequence to the order of their final use. These sub-assemblies are then 'called' in from suppliers by electronic signal shortly before fitting during car assembly, once again via holding points in strategically placed warehouse and distribution centres.

Both TDS deliveries and the LDC Kanban system are particularly susceptible to the type of disruption caused by a failure to maintain integrity. Parts brought in in TDS deliveries are only partially exhausted within their targeted time slots as the vehicles belonging to their planned batches arrive out of sequence. In the Kanban system the automatic trigger is activated for shortfalls in some parts only, while other parts accumulate, a consequence of a delivery system based on consolidation across different part types combined with a breakdown in the planned mix of car derivatives within the sequence. A new consolidated delivery brings parts of each type indiscriminately. In both cases trackside congestion results.

This problem does not arise in the case of sequenced deliveries. The actual 'call' on sub-assemblies is originally made automatically as framed bodies come off of the framing lines and move past the monitoring point. This meant that each vehicle 'sends' a message for its 'own' sub-assembly only as it passes from the BIW stage. The lack of any pallet factor means that each sub-assembly can be loaded individually in its own container and carried trackside.

To appreciate the 'push' basis for each of these JIT methods it is important to bear in mind the forecasting system underpinning each of the operations. The limited stocks of each part located in warehouse and distribution centres around Longbridge (for reasons of reliability and economy in final transport) are based on initial 'orders' made up to six months prior to JIT delivery. Whilst the Kanban and sequenced delivery methods operate on a 'pull' basis in the most short-term operational sense, this is a reflection of the intrinsic character of the parts themselves in terms of pallet factor and complexity rather than a result of the basic forecasting system.

Conclusion

This paper can be summarised in the following way. The application of a regime of just-in-time parts movement and inventory control to auto production brings a new level of difficulty to the questions of logistical organisation and process control. This is accommodated in the use of 'batching' and a tight time sequencing of component parts to trackside. At the same time, this puts pressure on the potential responsiveness of 'just-in-time' production to customer demand. The link between JIT and 'flexible production' is to this extent clarified: the flexible production goal can be reached only through accommodating the constraints placed on its scope by the JIT system of supply scheduling.

Notes

1   Part of this paper's intent is to establish the point that different part types have different needs, in terms of modes of delivery, if JIT supply is to meet basic criteria of economy and efficiency. It is concerned primarily with JIT delivery as it relates to the parts flow from car component manufacturers to Rover's Longbridge assembly tracks. In this context we avoid a separate discussion of JIT delivery of parts

produced in-house or on site. There are, however, some general features of the JIT philosophy worth noting.

The first point is that 'small lot' parts delivery *per se* involves an apparent extension of the flow-line principle of production, as exemplified in the assembly stages of car manufacture, backwards into component supply. This, in itself, is not inconsistent with the maintenance of finite stocks of parts bought out, provided that the absolute level of stock for each part is not permitted to increase or decrease substantially. This requirement is satisfied by the regular 'topping up' of stock made possible by frequent delivery. The principle here is analogous to the planned maintenance of a finite intermediate buffer between successive stages in a continuous assembly process. In JIT delivery this stock is 'minimised' in order to economise on floorspace and to (potentially) achieve savings in costs of capital. As a 'minimisation' problem where constraints operate the 'optimum' level of stock depends on the part in question and the environment in which it is produced.

The second point is that there are limits to the extent to which this 'appearance' can meaningfully correspond to reality. In a 'traditional' production context stocks are held of component parts in order to make allowance for the composition, extent and periodicity of demands made upon suppliers' capacities by the parent company, suppliers' lead times and geographical dispersion, and the general prevalence of uncertainty. None of these features of the production environment disappear simply by merit of the fact that a policy of JIT delivery has been adopted. They exist as real problems which cost time and resources to overcome. This paper demonstrates some of the directions taken in making these efforts in the case of JIT production at Rover. It is important to appreciate that these are costly, time-consuming exercises which arise from pragmatic necessity and not from a 'deficiency' in management skill or understanding.

2   The R8 platform consists of models in the R200 and R400 ranges, produced in a combined build programme with the Honda Concerto series at the Longbridge facility.

3   It would be tempting to describe low complexity as a 'sufficient' condition for production which is 'restricted and flexible' and a 'necessary' condition for a JIT parts service. But this sort of temptation is probably best ignored if an unduly mechanistic formulation is also to be avoided.

Bibliography

Hall, R. (1983), *Zero Inventory*, Homewood, IL: Dow Jones–Irwin.

Monden, Y. (1983), *Toyota Production System*, Industrial Engineering and Management Press (Institute of Industrial Engineers).

Oliver, N. and Wilkinson B, (1988), *The Japanisation of British Industry*, Oxford: Basil Blackwell.

Schonberger, R. J. (1982), *Japanese Manufacturing Techniques*, New York, Free Press/Collier Macmillan.

Shingo, S. (1989), *A Study of the Toyota Production System*, Productivity Press.

Wood, S. (ed.) (1989), *The Transformation of Work*, London: Unwin Hyman.

PART III
THE THIRD WORLD

Industrial policy in the Third World in the 1990s
Alternative perspectives

Introduction

Although in the post-World War II period as a whole, developing countries have made substantial economic and industrial progress, during the last decade many of them, particularly in Latin America and Africa, have been in an acute economic crisis.[1] As a consequence, these countries have been obliged to go to the Bretton Woods institutions for economic assistance for stabilisation and structural adjustment. Such assistance has, however, normally only been forthcoming subject to conditionality, both short term and long term. Implicit in this conditionality is a specific approach to and a philosophy of industrial policy. This paper will first elucidate the World Bank/IMF approach to industrial policy issues in the Third World (see also Chapter 5). Secondly it will provide a critique of these concepts and argue that, if implemented, in many developing countries such an industrial policy would in general do more harm than good. Thirdly, the paper will outline an alternative framework for industrial policy in the South which in the author's view is more appropriate for the economic circumstances of the 1990s and beyond. The paper concludes by drawing some lessons for industrial policy from the actual experience of industrialisation in the developing countries during the last four decades.

Industrial policy in the South: the orthodox perspective

The balance of payments difficulties and the serious foreign exchange constraints faced by the developing countries in the 1980s have forced a very large number of them to turn to the IMF and the World Bank. These two international institutions[2] have imposed increasingly severe and detailed conditions with respect to the economic and industrial policy of developing countries that wish to obtain funds from them. Avramovic (1988, pp. 1–2) sums up the current situation as consisting of four layers of conditionality:

(a) Demand conditionality pioneered by the IMF through their monetary approach to the balance of payments. This focuses on cutting spending, primarily that of the government, currency devaluation, raising interest rates, and trade liberalization. There are now also elements of supply conditionality, mainly in eliminating price controls.

(b) Supply conditionality, pioneered by the World Bank, originally focused on project (or micro) formulation and implementation, and dealing with pricing of products and services to be sold by the project, and its management. This was then extended to cover sectors, and now, with 'structural adjustment lending' to the entire economy. The centre of attention is the investment program, system of incentives, pricing, financial liberalization, and trade liberalization.

(c) 'Growth' conditionality, in application during the last year or so, focused on giving a free hand and incentives to the private sector of the economy, including 'privatization' of government-owned enterprises as much as possible, rationalization of the rest, promotion of foreign direct investment, and again, trade liberalization.

(d) Cumulative total of (a), (b) and (c), called 'cross-conditionality', where lending decisions of each agency depend on the borrower having met the loan conditions of some other agency. This is now in increasing use, and it involves private as well as official lenders. The breakdown in arrangements between a borrowing country and any one of these agencies – in particular the IMF and The World Bank – can have a 'domino effect' in relation with all other agencies. The situation is still fluid: the number of instances of 'cross-conditionality' is increasing, but it is not yet clear how firmly committed to coordinated action individual lenders feel they are.

Many of the above measures are highly controversial and there is a large literature on the efficacy and the validity of the specific parts of such programmes, e.g. currency devaluations, rise in real interest rates, monetary and fiscal targets.[3] However, in the context of this paper, this conditionality also reveals a particular approach to industrial policy. Central to this perspective are two elements:

(1) An increase in the role of free markets and private enterprise as far as possible and a diminution in that of the state; hence measures such as privatisation, deregulation, financial liberalisation, changes in taxation and other incentive systems.

(2) A closer integration with the world economy; hence the emphasis on export promotion, import liberalisation, bringing domestic prices in line with world market prices through changes in the exchange rate, promotion of foreign investment.

Denying any philosophical or ideological proclivities, the IMF and the World Bank, as well as many mainstream economists, argue that they favour such a policy programme because of its empirical validity and its proven record in promoting fast and 'efficient' economic growth. Thus De La Rosiere (the former managing director of the IMF): 'Advocacy of these policies is not a matter of theology. It is instead grounded in the lessons of actual country experience' (1986, p. 308).[4] Similarly, Balassa *et al.* (1986, p. 124) suggest: 'The essential factor that gave impetus . . . to the severity of the economic and social crisis of the 1980s was the pervasive and rapidly expanding role of the state in most of Latin America' (Quoted in Fishlow, 1991). It is argued that, quite apart from international economic factors, the inappropriate policies of import substitution and inward orientation, excessive regulation of private enterprise leading *inter alia* to resource misallocation, rent seeking and corruption, the large role of the state-controlled enterprises, which are invariably poorly managed, have all greatly contributed to industrial failure in many countries in the Third World. A very important place is accorded in this thesis to the contrasting industrial success of the East Asian newly industrialising countries (NICs) in the last decade. It is suggested that the far superior industrial performance of these countries, relative to those in Latin America and Africa, provides a practical demonstration of the desirability of outward and more market-oriented economic policies.

A critique of the Bretton Woods approach: the East Asian experience

Both the theoretical arguments and the empirical evidence bearing on the above issues are far more complex than is recognised in the orthodox analysis. To begin with, on closer examination, even the East Asian experience does not in fact lend much support to the IMF/World Bank views on how successful economic development can best be achieved. Sachs (1987, pp. 295–6) presents an instructive fable which is worth repeating at some length:

> Let us begin with a country example. Country 'X' pegged its currency to the dollar in 1950, and kept the nominal parity absolutely fixed for more than twenty years. During the first 15 years of this period (until 1964), foreign exchange was strictly rationed by a government agency, and the currency was always overvalued. Purchasing power parity calculations using home and US consumer price indices show a 60% real appreciation in the 20-year period. A Foreign Exchange and Foreign Trade Control Law of 1949 required that exporters remit all earnings to the government within ten days, making the government the only legal source of foreign exchange, a privilege jealously guarded by the bureaucrats in charge of foreign exchange rationing. No explicit rules governed the distribution of foreign exchange. Bureaucrats allocated foreign exchange to favoured sectors and clearly gave attention to particular firms that they were interested in nurturing. Government bureaucrats often retired to those firms at the end of their official careers. Rationing was so tight that private individuals were not allowed any foreign exchange for tourism abroad between 1950 and 1964.
>
> Domestic capital markets were highly regulated and completely shut off from world capital markets. The government was the only sector with access to international borrowing and lending. Foreign direct investment was heavily circumscribed, with majority ownership by foreign firms both legally and administratively barred. During the early to mid-1950s, about a third of external funds for industrial investment originated in loans from government financial institutions, at preferential rates that varied across firms and industries. These state financial institutions remained an important source of cheap financing until the 1960s.

Sachs goes on to observe:

> The country in question, as will be familiar to many, is Japan. But the description sounds like many countries in Latin America, complete with overvalued exchange rates, foreign exchange rationing, restrictions on foreign direct investment, government allocation of credit, and so on. Moreover, this policy framework was in place for much of the 'rapid growth period' in Japan (conventionally dated as 1955–73), which may arguably be the most remarkable two decades of a country's economic

development in world history. I begin with this example to urge on the reader a humble and inductive state of mind regarding growth-oriented adjustment. The policies of 'outward orientation' in Japan, and in East Asia generally, have not been modeled on a free market approach as is frequently asserted.

As for the East Asia NICs, there is a large body of evidence which shows that, in countries like Taiwan and South Korea, the state has played a large and highly interventionist role. In relation to South Korea, Amsden (1989) draws attention *inter alia* to the following crucial aspects of the government's 'supply side' policy:

   (i) the use of long-term credit at negative real interest rates to foster particular industries;
 (ii) 'heavy' subsidisation and the 'coercion' of exports;
(iii) strict control over multinational investment and foreign equity ownership of Korean industry;
(iv) a highly active state technology policy.

With respect to Taiwan, Sachs (1987) points out that the country is more heavily dependent on state-owned industry than is probably any country in Latin America, with the possible exception of Venezuela. This point is discussed further below.

Public enterprises

Turning from the general role of the state in promoting and regulating industrial development to the specific case of state-owned enterprises, the IMF/World Bank industrial policy proposals favouring the privatisation of such industrial and commercial enterprises are not based either on sound analytical reasoning or on systematic evidence. It is often claimed by World Bank publications[5] that the public enterprise sector in the developing countries is inefficient and over-extended and that in general state enterprises perform very poorly. This claim does not, however, stand up to serious examination.

The question of the economic efficiency of public sector enterprises in developing countries has been considered at length both at a theoretical level and empirically in a recent paper, Chang and Singh (forthcoming). They suggest that there are very good

economic reasons for developing countries to wish to establish
public enterprises: incomplete markets, externalities, the lack of
entrepreneurship, the enhanced capacity of the government to co-
ordinate investment decisions at a microeconomic level, the ability
of the government to have a longer time horizon than the private
sector enterprises, which may be subject to 'short-term' goals
dictated by the workings of the stock market.[6] Using the results of
new developments in the theory of the firm and the theory of
industrial organisation (e.g. agency theory), Chang and Singh go on
to point out that there is no theoretical basis for the belief that the
public enterprises should necessarily perform less efficiently at the
microeconomic level than the similar large management-controlled
private enterprises operating in oligopolistic markets and subject to
the imperfect, if not infrequently perverse, discipline of the real
world stock markets. They note that there is a growing consensus
among the scholars in this field that, as far as enterprise performance is concerned, it is not ownership *per se* which is the critical
variable, but rather the nature of the competitive environment in
which enterprises, whether public or private, operate.[7]

Turning to empirical evidence, Chang and Singh suggest that the
allegation that public enterprises (PEs) are invariably 'inefficient' or
that in general they perform badly cannot survive even an
elementary examination of facts. Briefly, first, it should be appreciated that public enterprises are ubiquitous in mixed economies
throughout the world – they have not simply been confined to left-
wing regimes or poorly performing countries. In view of the
differences in definition of what constitutes a PE and a variety of
other statistical problems, it is difficult to obtain data on an
internationally comparable basis of the relative size of PE sectors in
different economies (for a discussion of this point, see Short, 1984).
Nevertheless, the best available information from the IMF suggests
that, excluding centrally planned economies, in the mid-1970s PEs
in the developing countries accounted on average for 8.6% of GDP
and 27% of total gross fixed capital formation. More importantly,
information on the size of the PE sector for the individual
developing countries indicates that PEs play a significant role in the
highly successful East Asian economies of Taiwan and South
Korea. In fact the PE sector in these countries is at least as large, if
not larger, than in the leading Latin American economies of
Argentina, Brazil and Mexico. Taiwan, hardly a 'socialist' regime,

has one of the biggest public enterprise sectors among the developing mixed economies; the PEs contributed a third of gross fixed capital formation throughout the years 1950 to 1975 in that country, a period which witnessed its most spectacular economic and industrial growth. In Africa, PEs have played almost as large a role in the marked-oriented (and often regarded as successful) economies of Ivory Coast and Kenya as they have done in 'socialist' Tanzania. Jones and Mason (1982) suggest that, although ideology does have an influence, there are very important structural factors which can account for the relative size of the PE sector in the developing countries.

Secondly, Kirkpatrick (1986) has examined the relationship between the size of the PE sector, per capita GDP and the rate of growth of GDP between 1961 and 1981 for a sample of 23 less developed countries (LDCs) in Asia, Africa and Latin America. He found little relationship between these variables. If PEs always performed poorly, other things being equal, one would expect a negative correlation between the size of the PE sector in a country and its economic performance. However, the observed correlation coefficients are very small and statistically insignificant and do not always have the correct sign. Clearly at the very least the notion that the PE sector is inimical to economic growth fails to be confirmed by an analysis at the aggregate level.

Thirdly, as it happens, the most efficient steel company in the world is the giant Korean enterprise Posco (Pohang Steel Company). Posco is state-owned; it produced 467 tons of crude steel per person in 1986 compared with an average of 327 tons for Japan's five biggest steel producers. Posco's efficiency advantage is passed on to its Korean customers. It charges its domestic steel consumers $320 per ton – far less than American or Japanese car-makers, who (according to Posco) pay $540 and $430 respectively (see *The Economist*, 14 May 1988; also see Amsden, 1989, pp. 298–9). Although Posco is by no means typical of the public enterprises in developing countries, evidence suggests that it is not a total exception either. In general, on the basis of a comprehensive review of empirical studies for developing mixed economy countries, Chang and Singh conclude that, if one controls for the influence of variables such as age, size and industry, and if more appropriate criteria for measuring enterprise efficiency are employed rather than just private profitability, there is little reason to castigate public enterprises and to advocate large-scale privatisation. This is not to say that public enterprise performance should not or cannot be improved. This point is taken up further below.

Import liberalisation and export promotion

Next consider the IMF/World Bank policy measures with respect to closer integration with the world economy. In addition to the promotion of foreign private investment, these proposals involve both import liberalisation and export promotion. Import liberal-isation is supposed to make the domestic economy much more efficient as well as promote exports. However, both common sense and economic theory tell us that competition can be a spur to efficiency but it can also kill domestic industry. If domestic industry is in a weak state because of inadequate investment (as is the case in many developing countries today on account of their economic crisis during the last decade), precipitate import liberalisation is likely to lead to deindustrialisation. Moreover, in the short to medium term, such liberalisation may also worsen the balance of payments, thus defeating the objectives of a stabilisation pro-gramme. Balassa *et al.* (1986) have proposed for the Latin American economies that they should adopt a flat-rate tariff of 10–20% over a five-year period. Such a draconian programme of import liberalis-ation was never adopted by Taiwan, South Korea and Japan in the course of their highly successful industrialisation. Evidence sug-gests that in these countries import liberalisation was implemented only after the successful export promotion had been achieved; furthermore, it was closely tailored to the strength of domestic industry.[8]

Advocacy of export promotion for the severely foreign exchange constrained economies of the South may appear non-controversial. There are however two issues which need further reflection: first, the method of promoting exports; and second, the alternative of efficient import substitution. The World Bank puts primary em-phasis on changes in the exchange rates as the main instrument for promoting exports. However, leaving aside the question of the efficacy of a devaluation for this purpose in normal times,[9] for the developing countries in the midst of an economic crisis such a blunt weapon has the enormous disadvantage that it is likely to conflict with the requirements of stabilisation of the economy. Stabilisation may, for example, need a confidence-building measure of a stable exchange rate rather than a fall in the exchange rate, which is inflationary. Export promotion in these circumstances may be better achieved by selective subsidies or the targeting of particular industries or firms by the government, as indeed was practised in the past by both Japan and South Korea. However, such non-market methods are not approved of by the Bretton Woods institutions.

Turning to the second point, when the world economy and world manufacturing trade are growing relatively slowly (see further below) and when there is increasing protectionism in the advanced countries in relation to Third World exports,[10] there is a fallacy of composition in the view that all developing countries, including important new entrants such as China, can achieve a sufficiently high rate of expansion of manufactured exports so as to be able to resume their long-term trend rates of overall economic growth.[11] In these circumstances, as Singer (1988) notes: 'efficient import substitution may be as good if not a better alternative for many developing countries.'

An alternative policy framework for economic developing in the South in the 1990s

The main parameters
Although the appropriate long-term economic policy for any individual developing country will depend on its particular circumstances, a realistic policy framework for the developing countries in the 1990s must, in my view, be based on the following main parameters:

(1) Despite the setback to the Southern economies in the 1980s, there is a continuing social imperative for fast long-term economic and industrial growth in the developing countries. The best estimates indicate that, on average, industry in these countries needs to expand at a long-term rate of about 8% per annum if there is to be any reasonable chance of (a) providing employment to the South's burgeoning labour forces (increasing at an annual rate of about 3.5% per annum in countries like Mexico and Brazil) and (b) meeting the minimum 'basic needs of the people' for food, shelter, health and education

over, say, a 20-year time-span.[12] Before the economic crisis of
the last decade, during the period 1960–80 the developing
countries as a whole were undergoing a veritable industrial
revolution and indeed achieving industrial growth rates of more
or less the required order. It is socially necessary for this
interrupted industrial revolution, particularly in Africa and
Latin America, to be resumed.[13]

(2) However, this fast growth of the South's economy and industry
during 1960–80 occurred in unusually propitious world economic circumstances. Up to 1973, the world economy enjoyed its
'golden years' (1950–73) of historically unprecedented growth
of output, consumption, productivity and employment.[14] During this period, the volume of world trade in manufacturing
expanded at a rate of about 10% per annum. Between 1973 and
1980, although the developed countries' economic growth was
nearly halved compared with their 1950–73 trend rate, the
developing countries were able, by and large, to maintain their
economic and industrial momentum mainly by their huge
borrowings during the 1970s. This situation ended with the
second oil price increase and the so-called Volcker shock (the
adoption of highly contractionary monetarist policies in the
USA at the end of the 1970s and the early 1980s; Singh, 1990a).

There are strong reasons to suggest that, over the forseeable
future (say the next decade), the economies of the industrial
countries and hence the world economy as a whole (as the OECD
countries account for nearly 80% of the non-Communist world's
GDP) will at best be able to expand only at their post-1973 long-
term rate rather than that achieved during the Golden Age.[15] The
slow growth of the world economy will have two significant
implications for industrial policy in the developing countries. First,
world trade and world demand for manufactures will expand at a
slower rate than they did in the pre-1973 period. Secondly, the
developing countries are unlikely to be able to recoup the terms of
trade losses they have suffered over the last decade; even in the
longer term, relative commodity prices will continue to be weak.

(3) As a consequence of these far-reaching changes in world
economic conditions, a very large number of countries in Latin
America and Africa – the two developing continents most
affected by the economic crisis – are today faced not only with a

short-term liquidity or balance of payments problem but also with the necessity of long-term structural adjustment. Many countries are in fundamental structural disequilibrium in the sense that their economies are unable to generate sufficient exports to pay for the required imports at a rate of economic and industrial growth that will keep their per capita income constant, let alone one which will permit a steady rise in living standards. The correction of this disequilibrium requires major changes in the structure of national production, both agricultural and industrial.

A strategic perspective on economic policy in the 1990s
Even in the industrially most underdeveloped Third World economies such as those of Sub-Saharan Africa, in the medium to long term industry will have to play a crucial role in the correction of the disequilibrium noted above. Two kinds of policy will need to be simultaneously pursued: (a) reducing the propensity to import without impairing domestic productive capabilities; (b) enhancing the capacity to import through promotion of exports. As a consequence of the balance of payments crisis, imports were severely curtailed in the 1980s particularly in the heavily indebted developing countries (Khan and Knight, 1988). However, this import compression led to greatly reduced domestic production. What is required for the correction of the disequilibrium is a phased reduction over time in the *import elasticity* of industrial production; this would represent a major structural change in the development and functioning of these economies. Given the size of the structural disequilibrium in many of the developing countries, this efficient import substitution is at least as necessary as export promotion for future economic and industrial development in these countries.

More significantly, it has to be appreciated that in the medium to long term, if the developing countries are to reach their socially necessary rates of growth in a slow-growing world economy, they will have to rely much more on domestic rather than world demand, on their own internal technological dynamism and on economic and technical co-operation amongst themselves. This does not mean that exports should be neglected; quite the contrary, in foreign exchange constrained economies they should be vigorously pursued through appropriate market (currency changes) or non-market (direct state assistance to particular firms or industries) methods depending on the circumstances of a particular country. Moreover, an extension of migrants' remittances can also make a significant contribution to a country's foreign exchange earnings. Nevertheless, as argued in Singh (1984), the essential point is that, with slow world economic growth, if the developing countries are to resume their golden years' growth path – their industrial revolution – the main dynamic will have to come increasingly from internal factors rather than from the external economy.

To illustrate with a specific example, consider industrial development in Mexico. During the 1960s (between 1960 and 1968), Mexican manufacturing industry expanded at an impressive rate of nearly 9% per annum, with a rate of growth of productivity of over 3% per annum. A critical element in this successful industrial development was the low value of the import elasticity of manufacturing production – it was about 0.8 (see Brailovsky, 1981). However, towards the end of the oil boom years (1980–81), the value of this elasticity rose to 4 (i.e. whilst manufacturing production increased at a rate of about 6% per annum, the volume of imports rose by nearly 25%). This large increase in import elasticity not only contributed to the subsequent balance of payments problems, but there is evidence that it also harmed rather than assisted domestic manufacturing production. After the onset of the debt crisis in 1982, the volume of Mexican imports fell sharply, but this led to a reduction in the rate of growth of manufacturing production from its long-term rate of 6–7% per annum to nearly zero over the period 1982–88. Notwithstanding Mexico's oil resources and its success with non-oil exports in the 1980s, if Mexican manufacturing industry is to re-attain its high long-term growth trajectory, the value of the import elasticity will have to come down to the level of the 1960s.[16] Singh (1986c) has argued that this would require *inter alia* a new technology policy and a purposive development over time of Mexico's capital goods industry. In capital goods production, Mexico lags behind other semi-industrial countries such as India, South Korea, Brazil or China. There is no reason, either on the demand or on the supply side, why Mexico, through efficient import substitution, should not be able to develop this crucial sector further (see Singh, 1986c).

Turning to the strategic question of how 'open' or how closely integrated a developing country's economy should be with the world economy, the answer clearly cannot simply be in terms of free trade and liberalisation. Even modern neoclassical theory rejects this view: in a world of imperfect competition, learning by doing and static and dynamic economies of scale (i.e. in the real world), the optimum level of trade for all countries is not free trade.[17] As argued in Chakravarty and Singh (1988) 'openness' is a multi-dimensional concept; apart from trade, a country can be 'open' or not so open with respect to financial and capital markets, in relation to technology, science, culture, education, inward and outward migration. Moreover, a country can choose to be open in some directions, say trade, but not so open in others, such as foreign direct investment or financial markets. Chakravarty and Singh's analysis suggests that there is no unique optimum form or degree of openness which holds true for all countries at all times. A number of factors affect the desirable nature of openness: the world configuration, the timing, the sequence, the past history of the economy, its stage of development. There may be serious irreversible losses if the wrong kind of openness is attempted or the timing and sequence are incorrect. The significance of the world configuration in this context cannot be exaggerated.

Policy lessons from past economic development

Apart from the above general perspective on medium- and long-term economic development in the 1990s, the developing countries must also learn from the successes and failures of their own economic history over the last three decades as well as that of countries like Japan (which is discussed by Gentaro Matsumato in the next chapter). Briefly, the following are some of the lessons which appear to be particularly relevant for the future.

(1) Although it was noted earlier that privatisation is neither a necessary nor a sufficient condition for improved performance, the efficiency of the state-owned industrial and commercial enterprises in many developing countries needs nevertheless to be greatly enhanced if these countries are to achieve fast economic growth. Experience suggests that the economic performance of public enterprises can be appreciably improved through measures such as greater managerial autonomy, setting of clear economic targets, transparency of accountancy and, where possible, introduction of private sector competition (Aylen, 1987; Chang and Singh,

forthcoming). Many developing countries have already successfully adopted such policies in the 1980s (e.g. India) without resorting to extensive privatisation.

(2)   The thwarted industrialisation of Sub-Saharan African countries during the last decade has important lessons for the future.[18] These countries of course started, after their independence in the 1950s and early 1960s, at a much lower initial level of industrial and skill development compared with the Asian and Latin American countries. The African governments were certainly right in their aim during the past two decades to attempt to change the structure of these economies by building up industry. However, the industries they established, although they may have been appropriate for the Golden Age, have turned out to be unsuitable for the new world economic conditions. The African economies diversified by moving from the production of mineral or agricultural commodities to the production of some manufactures. This reduced the imports of consumer goods, but overall dependence on manufactured imports increased. This was for two reasons: (a) the dependence on intermediate industrial imports did not decrease in most countries, and, more importantly, (b) capital goods imports increased as a consequence of both the industrialisation process itself and infrastructural development. As long as the world economy was expanding fast, foreign aid and other capital inflows were forthcoming and, equally importantly, the agricultural sector was functioning adequately, this pace of industrial and economic development was sustainable. However, once all these conditions changed simultaneously in the middle to late 1970s, the crisis was inevitable.

There were serious shortcomings in the model of economic development followed in Sub-Saharan Africa during the Golden Age, which were pointed out by observers at the time and which have become even more glaring in retrospect. In relation to industrial development, the most important of these were the lack of inter-sectoral linkages and in particular appropriate linkages with agriculture. As Guhlati and Sekhar (1981) note, African agriculture uses hardly any tools and implements locally manufactured by modern African industry. The main reason for this is that, by and large, African agriculture employs traditional technology, which does not use modern tools, or there are heavily mechanised pockets which use imported tractors and other heavy agricultural machinery. A more gradual and phased mechanisation of agriculture as a whole will not only help improve agricultural productivity but also aid sustainable industrial development. The local production of simpler modern agricultural tools and implements will promote small-scale industrial development, which in turn will increase industrial skills and employment.

Foreign aid and private foreign capital have played a leading role in establishing industry in Sub-Saharan African countries during the last two decades. Unfortunately, however, the African governments have tended to accept any industrial projects which the donors were willing to provide, regardless of the linkages with other industries and their suitability for the current state of the country's industrial development. In choosing industrial investment projects, African countries must in future pay close and serious attention to the inter-industry and the agriculture–industry linkages and to the viability of such projects in an uncertain world economic environment.

(3) Turning to the experiences of the 'large' semi-industrial countries, there is reason to believe that, at the present world conjuncture, external liberalisation for many of these countries is not just far from being the best policy, but may in fact harm their economic development. Nevertheless there may be gains from internal liberalisation, e.g. promotion of vigorous internal competition. Large countries have the advantage that they can substitute 'domestic competition' for 'external competition' without incurring the large penalties which external competition may impose on a foreign exchange constrained economy. In a recent paper on India's new economic strategy, Singh and Ghosh (1988) have argued that the external liberalisation policy which the Indian government has embarked on in recent years with the encouragement of the World Bank carries with it a serious danger of leading to an unsustainable debt burden, economic failure and low growth of output and employment. Instead of further import liberalisation and a greater integration with the world economy, Singh and Ghosh propose an alternative policy of more internal competition, greater internal technological development and a reduction in the propensity to import capital goods.

(4) There are some important lessons for small countries too from the experience of the last quarter century. Small countries must

necessarily rely on trade and specialisation in order to achieve economic development. There have therefore been a number of schemes for the establishment of common markets of contiguous countries to promote these aims. However, these integration schemes have not been conspicuously successful to date. The main reason is the large difference in the level of development of the various countries; in a common market with internal free trade, the more developed regions or countries have a tendency to develop even further without commensurate development in the less developed member countries (Kaldor, 1970). Nevertheless, industrialisation in smaller developing countries does require much more trade between developing countries; this is more likely to aid the development of all participating countries if it is planned, rather than free trade. Thus with the widely varying conditions of economic and industrial development in the small countries, for integration schemes to be successful what is needed is not so much the creation of a common market but the co-ordination of the trading, industrial and indeed macroeconomic policies of the participating countries. As the history of the development of the European Economic Community – from its initial beginnings in the early 1950s of six countries participating in the production only of steel and coal to its present state of wide-ranging economic integration among 12 countries – shows, such economic co-operation can occur only with political will and over time. In view of the very large possible gains from economic and technical co-operation, the small developing countries, despite all the difficulties they have experienced in the past, should therefore persist with their endeavours in this direction.

Conclusion

This paper has pointed to serious flaws in the industrial policy proposals of the international financial institutions – privatisation, deregulation, liberalisation, and closer integration with the world economy. The World Bank, the IMF and many mainstream economists often appeal to the industrial success of the East Asian NICs to support their policy programme. This paper suggests that a proper reading of the Japanese and East Asian experience lends scant support to the extensive liberalisation policies currently being recommended by the Bretton Woods institutions.

An alternative perspective on industrial policy for the developing countries is set out for the 1990s. This is predicated on the following postulates: (i) there is a compelling social imperative for Third World industry to expand at a long-run rate of 8% or so per annum – the kind of rate actually achieved during 1960–80; (ii) the world economy during the next decade will grow at its slow post-1973 trend rate rather than the rate which obtained during the Golden Years of 1950–73. This perspective *inter alia* recommends a strategic degree of involvement with the international economy, depending on the circumstances of an individual country and the world configuration that it faces; it also proposes an interventionist industrial policy to correct the structural disequilibrium which characterises many developing economies. In addition, it draws important lessons for the future from the actual experiences of industrialisation in the Third World countries during the last three decades.

However, with the blessing and more importantly the financial support of the Bretton Woods institutions, and in the new political climate engendered by the demise of communism and central planning in Europe, it is the former industrial policy programme which is being, or is likely to be, implemented in the next few years in several developing economies, particularly in Latin America (e.g. Mexico). The arguments of this paper suggest a pessimistic outlook for the success of such neo-liberal industrial policy experiments.

Notes

1   For an analysis of the reasons for this crisis, see Singh (1986a, 1990a and 1992); Dornbusch (1985); World Bank (1991) among others. For a discussion of the intercontinental differences and specifically for the reasons why the Asian countries by and large escaped the economic crisis of the 1980s and the Latin American countries did not, see Maddison (1985), Sachs (1985), Fishlow (1991), Hughes and Singh (1991), Singh (1986b).

2   In principle, the IMF is supposed to deal with short-term adjustment problems and the World Bank with long-term questions of economic development. In practice, because of cross-conditionality, the IMF's own structural adjustment loans and greater co-operation between the two institutions, the distinction has become very blurred. See further, Helleiner (1988).

3   See among others Singh (1986a), Avramovic (1988), Taylor (1988), Cornia *et al.* (1987).

4   For an expression of similar views by the current managing director of the IMF, see the IMF *Survey*, 10 December 1990.

5   See World Bank (1983, 1987 and 1988). See also the Berg Report on Sub-Saharan Africa (World Bank, 1981).

6 On this point, see Cosh, Hughes and Singh (1990), Hatsopoulos, Krugman and Summers (1988), Singh (1990b).

7 See for example Bishop and Kay (1989), Vickers and Yarrow (1988), and Yarrow (1989).

8 See further Sachs (1987), Lin (1985).

9 On these issues see Fishlow (1991) and Hughes and Singh (1991).

10 See Chapter 2 of World Bank (1987) on this point.

11 See Cline (1982) and Singh (1984). For a critique of this view, see Ranis (1985). See however the rejoinder by Cline (1985).

12 See ILO (1976), Singh (1979, 1990a).

13 See further Singh (1984).

14 See Maddison (1982)

15 For a fuller discussion, see Glyn *et al.* (1990). See also Singh (1990a).

16 See further Singh (1986c).

17 See for example Krugman (1987).

18 The analysis of the following paragraphs is based on Singh (1987).

References

Amsden, A. H. (1989), *Asia's Next Giant*, New York: Oxford University Press.

Aylen, J. (1987), 'Privatisation in developing countries', *Lloyds Bank Review*, January.

Avramovic, D. (1988), 'Conditionality: facts, theory and policy-contribution to the reconstruction of the international financial system', Helsinki: World Institute of Development Economic Research (WIDER).

Balassa, B. *et al.* (1986), *Towards Renewed Economic Growth in Latin America*, Washington, DC: Institute for International Economics/Mexico City: Colegio de México.

Bishop, M. and J. Kay (1989), 'Privatisation in the United Kingdom: lessons from experience', *World Development*, 17 (5).

Brailovsky, V. (1981), 'Industrialisation and oil in Mexico: A long-term perspective', in T. Baker and V. Brailovsky (eds), *Oil or Industry?* London: Academic Press.

Chakravarty, S. and Singh, A. (1988), 'The desirable forms of economic openness in the South', mimeo, Helsinki: WIDER.

Chang, H.-J. and Singh, A (forthcoming), 'Public enterprises in developing countries and economic efficiency', processed, Faculty of Economics, Cambridge University, September 1991.

Cline, W. R. (1982), 'Can the East Asian model of development be generalized?' *World Development*, No. 10, February.

Cline, W. R. (1985), 'Reply', *World Development*, 13 (4), April, 547–8.

Cornia, G., Jolly, R. and Stewart, F. (eds) (1987), *Adjustment with a Human Face*, Oxford: Clarendon.

Cosh, A., Hughes, A. and Singh, A. (1990), 'Takeovers and short-termism in the UK', Industrial Policy Paper No. 3, London: Institute of Public Policy Research.

De La Rosiere, J. (1986), 'The debt situation', *Labour and Society*, September.

Dornbusch, R. (1985), 'Policy and performance links between LDC datas and industrial nations', *Brookings Papers on Economic Activity*, No. 2.

Fishlow, A. (1991), 'Some reflections on comparative Latin American economic performance and policy', in T. Banuri (ed), *Economic Liberalisation: No Panacea*, Oxford: Clarendon Press.

Glyn, A., Hughes, A., Lipietz, A. and Singh, A. (1990), 'The rise and fall of the Golden Age', in S. Marglin and J. Schore (eds), *The Golden Age of Capitalism: Lessons for the 1990s*, Oxford: Oxford University Press.

Guhlati, R. and Sekhar, K. (1981), 'Industrial strategy for late starters: the experience of Kenya, Tanzania and Zambia', *World Bank Staff Working Paper*, No. 457, Washington DC.

Hatsopoulos, G. N., Krugman, P. R., Summers, L. H. (1988), 'U.S. competitiveness: beyond the trade deficit', July 15.

Helleiner, G. K. (1988), 'Growth orientated adjustment lending: a critical assessment of IMF/World Bank approaches', *South Commission, Geneva, Discussion Paper*.

Hughes, A. and Singh, A. (1991), 'The world economic slow-down and the Asian and Latin American economies: a comparative analysis of economic structure, policy and performance', in T. Banuri (ed.), *Economic Liberalisation: No Panacea*, Oxford: Clarendon Press.

ILO (1976), *Employment, Growth and Basis Needs: A One World Problem*, Geneva: ILO.

Jones, L. and Mason, E. (1982), 'Role of economic factors in determining the size and structure of the public-enterprise sector in less-developed countries with mixed economies', in L. Jones (ed.), *Public Enterprises in Less-developed Countries*, Cambridge: Cambridge University Press.

Kaldor (1970), 'The case for regional policies', *Scottish Journal of Political Economy*, XVII (3), November.

Khan, M. S. and Knight, M. D. (1988), 'Import compression and export performance in developing countries', *Review of Economics and Statistics*, May.

Kirkpatrick, C. H. (1986), 'The World Bank's views on state owned enterprises in less developed countries: a critical comment', *International Review of Economics and Business*, June.

Krugman, P. (1987), 'Is free trade passé?' *Journal of Economic Perspectives*, 1 (2), Fall.

Lin, C. (1985), 'Latin America and East Asia: a comparative development perspective', unpublished, Washington DC: International Monetary Fund.

Maddison, A. (1982), *Phases of Capitalist Development*, Oxford: Oxford University Press.

Maddison, A. (1985), *Two Crises: Latin America and Asia 1929–38 and 1973–83*, Paris: OECD.

Ranis, G. (1985), 'Can the East Asia model of development be generalised? A comment', *World Development*, 13 (4), April, 543–4.

Sachs, J. D. (1985), 'External debt and macroeconomic performance in Latin America and East Asia', *Brookings Papers in Economic Activity*, No. 2.

Sachs, J. D. (1987), 'Trade and exchange rate policies in growth oriented adjustment programme', in World Bank, *Growth Oriented Adjustment Programme*, Washington DC.

Short, R. (1984), 'The role of public enterprises: an international statistical comparison', in R. Floyd, C. Gary and R. Short (eds), *Public Enterprises in Mixed Economies: Some Macroeconomic Aspects*, Washington DC: International Monetary Fund.

Singer, H. W. (1988), 'Industrialization and world trade: ten years after the Brandt Report', Paper prepared for the International Symposium 'The Crisis of the Global System: The World Ten Years after the Brandt Report – Crisis Management for the 90s'.

Singh, A. (1979), 'The basic needs approach to development versus the new international economic order', *World Development*, Vol. 7, No. 6, June.

Singh, A. (1984), 'The interrupted industrial revolution of the third world; prospects and policies for resumption', *Industry and Development*, June.

Singh, A. (1986a), 'The great continental divide: Asian and Latin American countries in the world economic crisis', *Labour and Society*, September.

Singh, A. (1986b), 'The world economic crisis, stabilisation and structural adjustment', *Labour and Society*, II (3).

Singh, A. (1986c), 'Crisis and recovery in the Mexican economy: the role of the capital goods sector', in M. Fransman (ed.), *Machinery and Economic Development*, London: Macmillan.

Singh, A. (1987), 'Exogenous shocks and de-industrialisation in Africa: prospects and strategies for sustained industrial development', in RISNOC, *Africa's Economic Crisis*, New Delhi.

Singh, A. (1988), 'Employment and output in a semi-industrial economy: modelling alternative economic policy options in Mexico', in M. Hopkins (ed.), *Employment Forecasting*, London: Pinter Publishers.

Singh, A. (1990a), 'The state of industry in the Third World in the 1980s: analytical and policy issues', Working Paper No. 137, The Hellen Kellogg Institute for International Studies, University of Notre Dame, Indiana.

Singh, A. (1990b), 'The stock market in a socialist economy', in P. Nolan and F. Deng (eds), *The Chinese Economy and its Future*, Cambridge: Polity Press.

Singh, A. (1992), 'The actual crisis of economic development in the 1980s: an alternative policy perspective for the future', in A. Dutt and K. Jameson (eds), *New Directions in Development Economics*, Aldershot: Edward Elgar.

Singh, A. and Ghosh, J. (1988), 'Import liberalization and the new industrial strategy: an analysis of their impact on output and employment in the Indian economy', *Economic and Political Weekly*, Special Number, November.

Taylor, L. (1988), *Varieties of Stabilization Experience: Towards Sensible Macroeconomics in the Third World*, Oxford: Clarendon/New York: Oxford University Press.

Vickers, J. and Yarrow, G. (1988), *Privatisation: An Economic Analysis*, Cambridge, MA: The MIT Press.

World Bank (1981), *Accelerated Development in Sub-Saharan Africa: an agenda for action* (The Berg Report), Washington DC.

World Bank (1983), *World Development Report*, Washington DC.

World Bank (1987), *World Development Report*, Washington DC.

World Bank (1988), *World Development Report*, Washington DC.

World Bank (1991), *World Development Report*, Washington DC.

Yarrow, G. (1989), 'Does ownership matter?' in C. Valjanovski (ed.), *Privatisation and Competition*, London: IEA.

PART IV

JAPANESE, NORTH AMERICAN AND WEST EUROPEAN EXPERIENCES

The work of the Ministry of International Trade and Industry

Introduction

Since World War II Japan has achieved a miraculous performance in economic growth. Many economists have tried to explain Japan's postwar economic success. Their explanations range across a wide variety of factors such as the Japanese style of business management, a high investment ratio, an abundant labour force, the fiscal policy, the tax system, MITI's industrial policy, and the Japanese social structure and culture. In contrast with other countries (both advanced countries and developing countries), many people believe that in Japan there is close co-operation and/or harmony between government and industry. And it has been pointed out very often that, on the basis of that co-operative relationship, MITI was able to play the main role in postwar industrial policy and led the Japanese economy to its relative success.

MITI has certainly led postwar Japan's industrial policy. But is it true to say that, in a strict sense, MITI has controlled Japan's industrial organisation and that such a good performance would have been impossible without MITI's industrial policies? Are the industrial policies applied by MITI too unique to be introduced in other countries? Are they fair from the viewpoint of national welfare?

In this short paper, I will try to explain the role of the industrial policies applied by MITI in Japan's postwar economic success and to evaluate MITI's policies. In the next section, I will present a historical survey of the postwar Japanese industrial policy led by MITI. Then I will describe the nature of MITI's policies as selective and discriminatory, not competitive. The effectiveness of its restrictive policy is discussed in the case of a few industries. Lastly, I will analyse one aspect of the role of MITI's restrictive policies – the amalgamation and merger of many companies, because of a concern with excessive competition.

A survey of Japanese industrial policy

What is industrial policy? There is no rigid definition of industrial policy in Japan. Therefore, Professor K. Kaizuka's statements are very often ironically quoted, such as 'Industrial policy is the policy which MITI carries out' (1973). Japan's industrial policy is wide-ranging in nature and has wide-ranging targets: a macroeconomic goal, the protection and bringing up or nurturing of infant industries, the prevention of excessive competition, the conversion of industrial organisation, regional policy, etc. In order to achieve these targets, MITI has used various measures: discriminatory treatment of permission to import, restrictive laws, financial subsidies, guidelines, presenting a perspective on future industrial organisation. And its 'administrative guidance' (*gyosei shido*) has always been included. This ambiguity of definition and the variety of means is a characteristic of MITI's industrial policy. In the following I briefly survey MITI's industrial policy-making.

Recovery period (1945–mid 1950s)
As a defeated nation, in 1945 Japan's mining and manufacturing industries were at one-seventh of their 1941 level. The occupying Allied forces introduced three revolutionary policies: dissolution of the *zaibatsu* and decentralisation of business, reformation of the agricultural land ownership system, and the establishment of the rights of workers. These provided the framework within which Japan's economy had to develop.

In this period, greatest importance was given to the reconstruction and self-reliance of Japan's economy. An overall 'strengthening of international competitiveness' was declared and this slogan was maintained until the early 1970s. MITI's industrial policies reflected the idea of a controlled or planned economy. Production was stimulated by the famous 'priority production system', which meant using steel in order to increase the production of coal, in order to increase the production of steel. The fundamental (key) industries – steel, electricity, coal, shipping, and shipbuilding –

were favourably treated in several respects, especially finance and the import of materials. Aiming to achieve the expansion of production, the Reconstruction Finance Corporation was established and a price-control compensation system was introduced.

About 1950, the government planned the modernisation of industries. This was aimed at achieving the strengthening of international competitiveness by means of government support: the tax system, discriminatory finance by the national fund, restrictive treatment of foreign exchange, discriminatory allocation of foreign currency for importing materials and equipment, consolidation of fundamental equipment for industries, presentation of detailed guidelines for the modernisation of and expectations of each industry, and substantial relaxations of the Antimonopoly legislation. The revision and modification of the Antimonopoly Law to permit inter-corporate stockholding and the formation of cartels in cases of depression and rationalisation (the co-ordination of production and investment of plant), induced MITI's *gyosei shido* and administrative intervention.

Over 3.5 million repatriates were temporarily absorbed by the primary industry sector, agriculture, which accounted for over 40% of total employment. Labour-intensive light industries rapidly increased production in order to support the huge population of about 80 million. I therefore think that the problem of deep unemployment was not a great concern in the long run. The outbreak of the Korean War in 1950 accelerated the recovery of the Japanese economy and the succeeding boom encouraged enterprises to increase investment in new plant and equipment. In its White Paper of 1951, the Economic Planning Agency briefly remarked: 'Japan's economy could no longer be said to be "postwar".'

Period of rapid economic growth (mid 1950s–1960s)
It is frequently said that in this period the method of MITI's industrial policy was established. In the process of recovery, the slogan of MITI's industrial policy, 'strengthening of international competitiveness', meant not only import substitution but also export promotion. Targeting of industries was based on *the income elasticity criterion* and *the comparative technical progress criterion* (the dynamic comparative cost doctrine). MITI mainly promoted heavy and chemical industrialisation, that is to say, targeted the

capital-intensive industries. The introduction of new technologies was favourably treated.[1]

A typical case is the petrochemical industry, which reflected MITI's idea of industrial policy oriented to direct intervention in industrial structure. MITI intended to nurture the petrochemical industry and issued 'The Proposition for Nurturing the Petrochemical Industry' in 1955. This plan had three objectives: (1) securing materials for synthetic fabrics and synthetic resins, (2) promoting import substitution through increasing domestic production of ethylene products, (3) strengthening international competitiveness by means of cost reduction of the main chemical materials.

In Japan, the petrochemical industry had to depend for almost all technologies upon other advanced countries, so the difficulty of foreign currency finance was anticipated. Large-scale investment in plant and equipment was needed. Despite uncertainty over the future marketability of artificial resins, MITI's positive attitude induced an enormous amount of investment by the private sector with little concern about future risk. In its first plan (1955–1958), MITI permitted the establishment of four production centres: Mitsui Petrochemical, Sumitomo Chemical, Nippon Petrochemical, and Mitsubishi Oil and Chemical. In order to increase petrochemical-related production, MITI permitted the expansion of these four companies' capacity and five new entrants in its second plan (1959–1964). The Tax Exemption System for Important Products was revised in 1957 to allow favourable treatment of new industrial products such as petrochemical products. This discriminatory application of the tax system greatly improved the financial position of companies in the petrochemical industry. MITI decided the foreign currency quota of companies in the oil-refining industry in accordance with their quantity of supply of naphtha. This quota system forced more competitive behaviour on the oil-refining industry and led to lower material costs for the petrochemical industry.

MITI's plan of building up the petrochemical industry was changed to seeking more scale economies. Permission was given to construct new plant of dramatically increased size. This change of capacity for new plant also aimed to prevent new entry and to protect the existing firms' profitability. However, after tough negotiations, MITI had to permit three entrants and allow an increase in capacity for the five existing companies. In the early stages of MITI's plan, the import dependence ratio of petro-chemical products was over 90%. By 1965, exports exceeded imports and in 1970 that ratio had fallen to 1%.[2]

On the other hand, MITI planned to protect other modern industries, including the processing industry, on the basis of the criterion on page 147. This applied particularly to the motor vehicle industry, which has a wider input–output relationship in industrial structure. In 1951, MITI established a plan based on consensus with the motor vehicle companies. The plan comprised:

(1) protection of domestic makers from car imports and invest-ment by foreigners (tariff barriers, quantity quotas and a discriminatory commodity tax);
(2) favourable treatment for introducing technology from ad-vanced countries;
(3) low-interest loans and favourable finance (particularly, fin-anced by Nippon Developing Bank).

MITI treated almost all modern industries as 'infant industries'. However, this protective treatment of extensive industries was not always supported by all members of Japan's government. It is well known that the president of Nippon Ginko (the central bank of Japan) was against the domestic production of motor vehicles from the viewpoint of comparative advantage theory. MITI also had fears for the competitiveness of the automobile industry in the world market, so it planned to integrate the corporations into two or three groups. But that *gyosei shido* failed. In contrast, the new entrant, Honda, has been successful.

In general, MITI saw many of the capital-intensive big en-terprises as key industries. However, although protection was differential it covered almost all industries. MITI often struggled against a phased liberalisation of imports and capital investment. Japan had become a member of IMF in 1952 and GATT in 1955. The trade liberalisation rate reached over 90% in 1963. Japan acquired IMF Article 8 status in 1964. In the 1960s, the Japanese economy had to reconvert its industrial organisation in the light of the open-economy and/or trade and capital investment liberalis-ation. MITI recognised that the international competitiveness of industries was not enough and strongly feared takeover by foreigners. MITI considered that excessive competition prevented Japanese firms from enjoying scale economies. So did the businessmen. However, MITI did not object to the competition; rather it proposed 'orderly competition', which means 'effective competition' or competition in a cartel-like industrial organisation.

This phased liberalisation led to a number of large-scale mergers in the attempt to strengthen competitive power in the world market (for instance, Mitsubishi Heavy Industry, Fuji Steel and Yawata Steel, which became the newly named Nippon Steel, Mitsui Chemical, Kobe Steel, etc). Of course, MITI supported and promoted these mergers. Although the Fair Trade Commission and the majority of academic economists objected to the largest-scale merger of Fuji and Yawata, it was finally permitted in 1970. MITI's industrial policy has been based not on static price theory but on the prospects of a dynamic change in technology and comparative advantage over many years.

The heavy and chemical industries rapidly expanded their production and exports. Fixed investment in key industries led Japan's economy. In many industries, technical innovation and know-how increased beyond the 'borrowed technology' which was first introduced from the advanced countries, especially from the United States. New enterprises were born and small and medium-sized enterprises developed in the processing industries. Personal incomes generally increased. A huge domestic market made export promotion easier, because the complementary relationship between domestic demand and foreign demand induced suppliers of products considerably to reduce unit costs of production through mass production. (Shinohara, 1982, also insisted on this complementary relationship.) The fact that the Japanese economy had never experienced a deep recession or a negative growth rate before 1974 proves the importance of this complementary relationship. The development of capital-intensive industries did not bring about an unemployment problem because of the gradual development in processing industries, which were labour intensive. MITI was not much concerned to nurture the new types of consumer durable industries and innovative machines: sewing machines, cameras, fasteners, motor bicycles, transistor radios, TVs, watches, audio equipment, magnetic tape, tape-recorders, electronic calculators, NC machine tools, ceramics, robots, telecommunications equipment, etc. These industries became leading sectors of the Japanese economy in the next stage.

Transition to an economy with a stable rate of growth (from the early 1970s on)
Since the late 1960s Japan has consistently maintained a favourable international balance of payments and its international position has changed. Many industries have caught up with the level of advanced nations. Problems of environmental pollution, 'Nixon's shock', revaluation and the completely free floating of the yen, and the first oil crisis forced the thinking behind MITI's industrial policy to accept the necessity for changes of considerable magnitude. It became necessary to abandon the goal of strengthening international competitiveness. MITI could not continue with protective and restrictive industrial policies.

MITI shifted its fundamental policy attitudes from 'strengthening economic power' to 'good utilisation of economic power'. A new slogan was heard: 'the knowledge-intensive industrial structure', instead of 'the modernised capital-intensive industrial structure'. In some industries, particularly companies in the computer industry, MITI promoted co-operative research and development (R&D) through innovative methods of production. MITI's new vision attached importance to industrial structure policies, which emphasised such industries as:

(1) Research and development-intensive industries (computer, aircraft, industrial robot, atomic power-related industries, large-scale integrated circuits, fine chemicals, ocean development, etc.);
(2) High processing industries (office communication equipment, numerically counted machine tools, pollution prevention machinery, industrial housing production, high-quality printing, automated warehousing, educational equipment, etc.);
(3) Fashion industries (high-quality clothing and furniture, electronic musical instruments, etc.);
(4) Knowledge industries (information management services, information supplying services, education-related industries such as video, software, systems engineering, consulting, etc.).

('The Basic Direction of Trade and Industry in the 1970s', Industrial Structure Council, 1971; quoted from Shinohara, 1982, p. 32.)

This new policy emphasises the diversification of industrial policies in order to attain a high level of social welfare under conditions of a low but stable rate of growth. However, it is not clear whether MITI intended to intervene directly in these industries or not. Is this policy no more than a 'guideline' for the future? I do not think that MITI plans to build up these industries by means of protective policy or giving them priority, except in the case of a few industries.

On the contrary, MITI has had to protect the comparatively disadvantaged industries in respect of labour and energy costs (miscellaneous goods, yarns and textiles, shipbuilding, non-ferrous metals, etc). Many heavy and chemical industries depended on MITI's role as an arbitrator to regulate investment and production which could sustain the prices of its products in the world-wide recession.[3] However, MITI's policy frequently conflicted with the interests of business circles. Big business does not expect MITI to act as an authority. It expects MITI's role to be as an arbitrator between rivals in order to minimize their loss of profits when co-operation in investment and production is necessary.

Nature and background of MITI's industrial policy

MITI's industrial policy is fundamentally protective, even though the targeted industries have attained enough power to compete in the world market. The early goal of MITI's policy was the 'strengthening of international competitiveness', which corresponded with a national consensus to establish an international position, not by means of the prewar philosophy of colonialism linked with militarism, but by means of modernisation of the economy and lifestyle.

In the early stages of industrial policy, MITI's policy reflected the idea of a controlled or planned economy. The 'priority production system' was a representative example. MITI treated industries in a discriminatory manner when it allocated scarce funds for organising industries. At the same time, when big business wished to establish their equipment in the heavy and chemical industries MITI did not directly intervene to prevent them. After all, the principle of equal opportunity was applied to the big enterprises. In general, big business groups were able to competitively establish new firms in new industries and expand their capacity.

MITI's targeting of industries was based on *the income elasticity criterion* and *the comparative technical progress criterion*, not on neoclassical price theory. Although MITI's main concern was with heavy and chemical industrialisation and/or nurturing capital-intensive big business, protective industrial policies covered a wide range of industries. MITI's industrial policies consisted of various implementation measures. Professor Shinohara (1982, p. 27) has summarised the implementation measures used by MITI as the following:

special tax measures;
low-interest loans by quasi-governmental financial institutions;
import restrictions by means of duties, non-tariff barriers, etc.;
co-ordination of investment in plant and equipment;
promotion of economies of scale and improvement of production efficiency by merger and other combined production;
deferment of trade and capital liberalisation measures;
other administrative guidance.

Are these policies and implementation measures unique? It seems to me that these are the usual types of strategic implementation for building up industries. In Japan, these measures were implemented in a detailed and consistent manner. MITI's organisation has many bureaus, which include many sections that correspond to associations of companies in the same industry. These bureaus or sections are usually concerned with excessive competition or orderly competition in their respective corresponding industries. This one-to-one correspondence between MITI's organs and industries makes it possible to perform the role of negotiator or arbitrator even if there is strong opposition to MITI's policy. As well as Japan's usual way of decision-making, MITI's links with companies are useful for informal get-togethers between companies in order to take account of relevant factors through the exchange and transfer of information before formal decision-making.

MITI has been much concerned with effective competition (competition within an orderly industrial organisation) rather than excessive competition, in spite of its meaning being arbitrary. MITI always has worried about 'over-capacity', so companies could expect to use MITI as an arbitrator or co-ordinator if difficulties arose. In large-scale plant industries, in particular,

MITI's attitude toward industrial organisation reduced the risks involved in big investment. In the 1950s, some companies in the steel, chemical, and oil-refining industries strongly opposed MITI's restrictive policies. As a result, expansion of plants was permitted in accordance with the principle of equal opportunity. After two decades, these industries asked MITI to apply protective policies against new entry, such as NICs, and to play the role of arbitrator in co-ordinating investment and co-operating in reducing their productive capacity, and in scrapping their plants.

Another of MITI's roles is as a leader in co-ordinating research and development. In the 1960s MITI promoted the establishment of the Japan Electronic Computer Company (JECC), which aimed to provide financial support to domestic computer makers. In addition, MITI promoted the FONTAC project to develop the large computer. In this project, participants (domestic companies of course) specialised in their own superior elements. MITI strategically targeted the computer industry as a counterpart to IBM and promoted co-operative research and development throughout the 1970s. This nurturing policy was closely linked with other protective policy and subsidies. If I remember rightly, until the early 1980s, the Ministry of Education subsidised a university's purchase (rather than rental) of a large computer, which was an implicit strategy or implementation measure to protect the domestic companies against IBM. Although other big projects for research have been promoted by MITI, the evaluation of its effectiveness is not always positive. However, we must note that, in spite of their co-operation in research and development, domestic computer makers are in a state of free competition.

In the early postwar period, generally speaking, it seems to be correct to say that MITI's goals and criteria for industrial organisation were supported by popular opinion. Enterprises' flourishing investment in plant and equipment was financed not only through MITI's favourable treatment but also by Japan's high savings ratio. Japan's economy had huge domestic demand and world markets were open to traders. Except in the case of the United States, productivity in all advanced countries had been damaged by World War II.

In the long run, I do not think that targeting industries and the criterion of favourable treatment were wrong. MITI's policy was 'undoubtedly helped by the long-term perspectives of the typical

Japanese industrial firm, untrammelled by the threat of an active market for corporate control and supported by the long-term commitment of Japanese financial capital' (Cowling, 1990, p. 17). MITI's method of negotiating and arbitrating between companies is based on the Japanese tradition of the collective nature of the decision-making process. Without the close relationship or harmony between MITI and business, it would hardly be successful in the co-operative self-regulation of exports of motor vehicles to the United States. Moreover, business has supported this characteristic of MITI's industrial policy and their relationships.[4]

However, really innovative enterprises have been growing beyond the perspective of MITI's industrial organisation. Many small and medium-sized labour-intensive processing industries, as well as heavy and capital-intensive big business, have been expanding as a result of rapid technical progress. A qualitative change in the labour input, which has been significant in Japan but not in the United States, can lead to a significant cost advantage. In addition, for the manufacturing sector, 'Japan's system of conflict resolution is more efficient than the U.S. system in terms of productivity and cost' (Lam *et al.*, 1990, p. 431).

Industries frequently prospered only to decline, forcing companies to diversify in order to sustain employment. New competitors rapidly expanded and companies clearly changed position. I see flexibility in industrial organisation and a competitiveness between companies as the main characteristics of the postwar Japanese economy.[5] These characteristics cannot be attributed to MITI's industrial policy.

One aspect of MITI's industrial policy

MITI has had a tendency to underestimate the competitive power of Japanese industries in the world market. Even in the industries to which MITI applied a restrictive policy, productivity steadily grew and both domestic and international demand gradually increased beyond MITI's expectations. Entrepreneurs freed from the prewar order were able to extend their ability into economic competition.

For younger entrepreneurs full of animal spirits, what did MITI's restrictive attitude mean? Restrictive policy is no more than the exclusion of potential entrants, that is to say, entry-preventing behaviour, with concern about excessive competition. Both MITI and large-scale plant enterprises thought that industries needed moderate excess profits in order to attain further scale economies. But from the new entrant's point of view, the attractiveness of a particular industry is profitability both now and in the future. Further profitability depends upon technical progress.

In the static framework, the maximum entry-preventing price, p_0, is approximately shown by Modigliani's formula,[6]

$$p_0 = p_c \left(1 + \frac{\bar{x}}{e\,X_0}\right) \tag{9.1}$$

where e, X_0, and $\bar{x}$ are defined as the price elasticity of demand at the competitive price level, p_c, the level of demand at p_c, and the minimum efficient scale of production, respectively. From the above equation we can understand that the entry-preventing price, p_0, is largely dependent upon the relative scale of this market, $X_0/\bar{x}$. Unless the market price is higher than p_c, the entrant could not get any profit.

In a growing industry, as a matter of course, this relative scale changes over time and it will produce a change in p_0. For the new generation of able men with a spirit of bold enterprise (new entrant), challenging behaviour to acquire a share of excess profits is to be preferred to avoiding risk by being obedient to MITI's guidance. Denoting the rate of growth of market size after entry which is expected by the potential competitor (the new entrant) as g, the expected minimum scale of production for the entrant, $\bar{x}'$, should be rewritten as:

$$\bar{x}' = \Delta Q + g X_0. \tag{9.2}$$

The first term on the right-hand side denotes the increase in demand caused by the price decrease, while the second term denotes the increase caused by the growth of the market. If MITI's policy of industrial organisation is restrictive, the actual price will increase above p_c. And if the existing firm intends to set the entry-preventing price at the maximum level, then the effective entry-preventing price must be reduced to

$$p_0' = p_c \left(1 + \frac{\bar{x} - g X_0}{e X_0}\right). \tag{9.3}$$

It is reasonable to assume that the existing firm will expand production in accordance with its expected rate of growth, g_0. This will reduce the room for the entrant's demand. Then $\bar{x}'$ and the effective entry-preventing price are modified as follows:

$$\bar{x}' = \Delta Q + (g - g_0)X_0, \tag{9.4}$$

$$p_0' = p_c [1 + \frac{\bar{x} - (g - g_0)X_0}{e\,X_0}] \tag{9.5}$$

Because MITI tends to underestimate the potential size of the market, it prefers $g > g_0$. Therefore, it will be difficult for the existing firms and MITI to prevent potential competitors from making an entry into the industry. In this case, against the existing firms' will, MITI's restrictive policy stimulates new entry by keeping the price above the effective level of prevention. With their technology, the new generation of able men will succeed in obtaining a share of the market. For example, in the automobile industry, MITI intended to integrate the companies into two or three groups by means of *gyosei shido*, but could not prevent a new entrant, Honda. In 1962, MITI established the Law of Petroleum Industry, which aimed to protect Japanese capital and to prevent excess competition. Although MITI was authorised to intervene in the planned investment in equipment and level of production of the business, MITI failed to prevent Idemitsu's expansion of its plant. MITI had been requesting the steel industry, which is famous as the cartel-oriented industry, to self-regulate their investment in equipment. Even in that co-operative industry, MITI's restrictive intention was often strongly opposed by companies.

Concluding remarks

Many people believe that in Japan there is a close relationship and/or a delicate balance between government and industry (business). It has frequently been said that, because of this relationship, MITI was able to play the main role in postwar industrial policy and to guide the modernisation of the industrial structure; that is to say, MITI's industrial policy has largely contributed to Japan's economic success.

The goal of MITI's industrial policy was an overall strengthening of international competitiveness. This meant not only import substitution but also export promotion. Targeting of industries was based on *the income elasticity criterion* and *the comparative cost doctrine*, and was aimed at heavy and chemical industries and other capital-intensive industries. MITI promoted the introduction of the new technologies in these industries. Because MITI has always worried about over-capacity and been much concerned with effective competition, MITI has promoted the amalgamation and integration of companies in order to avoid excessive competition and to achieve economies of scale. In this MITI played the role of arbitrator and/or co-ordinator. However, despite MITI's attitude toward industrial organisation, business has often opposed such restrictive policies.

MITI's industrial policies consisted of a variety of implementation measures based on macroeconomic policy and the structural characteristics of Japan. Those measures were implemented in a detailed and consistent manner through *gyosei shido*. However, despite MITI's view, in almost all industries Japanese entrepreneurs have challenged and been successful in international competition. This entrepreneurship makes Japan's industrial organisation flexible and competitive.

Given Japan's rising relative position in international markets, MITI had to abandon the goal of strengthening international competitiveness and was unable to continue with its protective and restrictive industrial policies. MITI proclaimed a new slogan: 'the knowledge-intensive industrial structure.' However, I think it is doubtful whether MITI will be able to lead Japan's economy in the future to the extent that it did in the early stages of the postwar period.

Appendix: Principal events

1947:   Antimonopoly Law (Law Concerning the Prohibition of Private Monopolies and Maintenance of Fair Trade Practices)
1949:   Dodge Line
          Foreign Exchange and Foreign Trade Control Law (FEFTCL)
          Modification of Antimonopoly Law

1950:	Foreign Investment Law (FIL)
	Rule of Import Trade Control
	Nippon Export Bank (Nippon Export–Import Bank, 1951)
1951:	Nippon Developing Bank
1952:	Law of Company Rationalization Promotion
	Joined IMF
1953:	Relaxation of Antimonopoly Law
1955:	Joined GATT
	Proposition of Building up National Car
1956:	Machinery Industry Promotion Provisional Measures
1957:	Electronics Industry Promotion Provisional Measures
1963:	Designated Industries Promotion Provisional Measures (proposed to parliament but not seconded)
1964:	Acquisition of IMF Article 8 status
1971:	Special Electronics Industry and Special Machinery Industry Provisional Measures
	The report 'The Basic Direction of Trade and Industry in the 1970s'
1978:	The Special Machinery Information Industries Promotion Provisional Measures
	Stabilization Provisional Measures for Designated Depressed Industries
1980:	The report 'Trade and Industrial Policies for the 1980s'
1983:	Designated Industrial Organization Improvement Provisional Measures

Notes

I am grateful for Professor Cowling's invitation to report this short paper in the 1991 Warwick/Birmingham Workshop on Industrial Strategy and useful comments. I also wish to thank M. Shinohara (1982) for a great deal of information about MITI's industrial policy. However, I do not agree with his positive evaluation of MITI's role.

1   In the early stages, the symbolic industry was the heavy and chemical industry, which meant mass production in a capital-intensive organisation. In particular, steel was frequently called 'a rice of industries', because steel is the most important and useful material, having the widest variety of uses in modern industries.

In general, MITI endeavoured to reach a consensus with the private sector before proposing any law or measure to parliament. However, in 1963 MITI proposed the 'Designated Industries Promotion Provisional Measure' to parliament and it was not seconded because this proposition had no support from private sector business. 'The goal of the promotion measures was industrial reorganization based on neither free trade nor a controlled economy but a third method of 'cooperation between public and private sectors' comprised of industry, financial interests, and government' (Shinohara, 1982, p. 29). The designated industries were automobiles, steel and petrochemicals. The law aimed to strengthen international competitiveness by promoting co-operative behaviour among companies, concentration and the amalgamation of companies.

Private sector business was against this law because of its restrictive and authoritarian character. Because business disliked MITI's strong initiative, the Free and Democratic Party, Jimin-to, did not positively support it. Afterwards, however, the system of co-operation between the public and private sectors became the basic method when MITI wanted to lead or co-ordinate industrial reorganisation. We must note that, except in the petrochemical industry, this system is not supported by any law. (Companies in the petrochemical industry were under the control of the Law of Foreign Funds until 1972.) Co-operative adjustments of investment in plant and equipment were carried out in the steel, oil-refining, petrochemical, synthetic fibres, and paper and pulp industries in an informal manner through *gyosei shido*.

2   On nurturing the petrochemical industry, see Tsuruta (1982) and Komiya *et al*. (1984). See also Ito *et al*. (1988) for a theoretical analysis of nurturing policy.

Imports, exports and production of petrochemical products, 1957–1973 (million yen)

Year	Imports	Exports	Production
1957	16,278	—	1,789
1960	27,505	582	63,123
1964	30,023	6,192	251,486
1965	18,108	25,922	339,576
1968	25,272	41,859	705,331
1970	15,110	97,529	1,178,504
1973	28,837	101,010	1,596,756

Source: Tsuruta (1982), p. 181.

3   MITI proposed the 'Stabilisation Provisional Measure for Designated Depressed Industries' in 1978. This covers the electric furnace steel, aluminium refining, synthetic fibres, shipbuilding, chemical fertilisers, cotton and chemical spinning, and corrugated cardboard industries. After the second oil crisis in 1983, MITI proposed 'Designated Industrial Organisation Improvement Provisional Measures', which aimed to reconstruct the industries and promote a smooth exit of capital from the disadvantaged industries. These industries had become disadvantaged in terms of the developing countries and recession. These developments required MITI to establish a new type of industrial policy.

4   MITI's usual methods of communicating with business make it possible that, in practice, informal approval of all those involved is sought before a plan is formally proposed. Except in the early postwar period, MITI's industrial policy rarely involved direct intervention in industrial organisation. Although comparatively disadvantaged industries need MITI's protective policies, MITI's policy is fundamentally persuasive and is mainly supported by *gyosei shido*. Nippon Steel Corporation (1982) is very useful for understanding Japanese methods of decision-making. See also note 1.

5   In Japan's rapid economic growth period, the asset shares of the largest 200 companies gradually decreased (excluding the finance sectors), which did not happen in the UK. In Figure 9.1, I report the trend of net investments in three

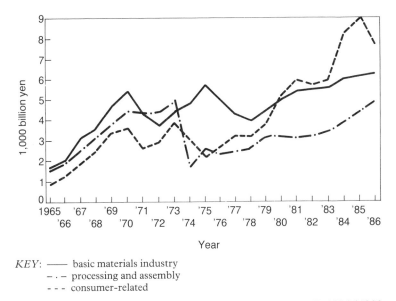

KEY: —— basic materials industry
— · — processing and assembly
- - - consumer-related

Figure 9.1 *Net investment in three manufacturing sectors, 1965–1986 (1980 prices)*

classified manufacturing sectors (not including the service sectors): basic material industries, processing and assembly industries, and consumer-related industries.

6 For the formulation of the entry-preventing price, see Waterson (1984), Chapter 4. Figure 9.2 will help in understanding the equations. Denoting the quantity of output of the existing firm as Q_0, the entry-limiting output is $X_0 - \bar{x} = Q_0$, i.e. the marginal quantity of demand which is left to the entrant is $\bar{x}$. By reducing its price to the level of p_c, the existing firm may increase its production by $\Delta Q = X_0 - Q_0$. When the entrant expects the market size to grow, the marginal quantity of demand and/or the minimum efficient scale of production will be $(X_c - Q_0) + gX_0$, because of the shifting of the demand curve from D to D'. AC' is the entrant's estimated average cost curve.

If the existing firm intends to frustrate the potential competitor's entry, it must restrict the entry-limiting output to less than Q' at pre-entry. It is reasonable that the entry-limiting output should be Q' at pre-entry. Considering $X_c - Q' = \bar{x}$ and the relation $X_c - X_0 = gX_0$, we get the equation (9.3).

References

Cowling, K. (1990), 'The strategic approach to economic and industrial policy', in K. Cowling and R. Sugden (eds), *A New Economic Policy for Britain*, Manchester: Manchester University Press.

Ito, M., Kiyono, K., Okuno, M. and Suzumura, K. (eds) (1988), *Sangyo Seisaku no Keizai Bunseki [An Economic Analysis of Industrial Policy]*, Tokyo: University of Tokyo Press.

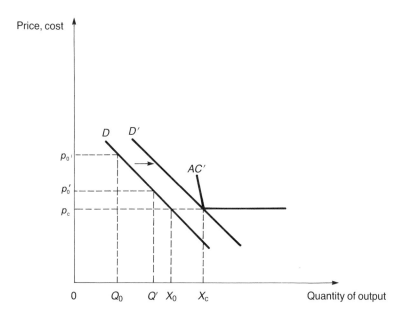

Figure 9.2   *Shifting demand curve and entry-preventing price*
(see note 6)

Kaizuka, K. (1973) *Keizaiseisaku no Kadai [Subjects of Economic Policy]*, Tokyo: University of Tokyo Press.

Komiya, Ryutaro, Okuno, M. and Suzumura, K. (eds) (1984), *Nihon no Sangyo Seisaku [Japan's Industrial Policy]*, Tokyo: University of Tokyo Press.

Lam, Alice C., Norsworthy, J. R. and Zabala, C. A. (1990), 'Labor disputes and productivity in Japan and the United States', in C. R. Hulten (ed.), *Productivity Growth in Japan and the United States*, Chicago: University of Chicago Press.

Nippon Steel Corporation (1982), *Nippon: The Land and its People*, Tokyo: Gakuseisya.

Shinohara, Miyohei (1982), *Industrial Growth, Trade, and Dynamic Patterns in the Japanese Economy*, Tokyo: University of Tokyo Press.

Tsuruta, Toshimasa (1982), *Sengo Nihon no Sangyo Seisaku [Industrial Policy in Postwar Japan]*, Tokyo: Nihon Keizai Shinbunsya.

Waterson, Michael (1984), *Economic Theory of the Industry*, Cambridge: Cambridge University Press.

10

Experience in Canada, the USA, Britain, Finland, Germany and Italy

Canada: industrial policy and economic integration

K. R. Stollery

Introduction

Canada is a small country that has found it necessary to involve the government in the economy to a considerable degree.[1] However, the United States as Canada's major trading partner has an economy about ten times the Canadian size, and economic and geopolitical links with the USA have profoundly conditioned Canadian economic policies.

The greatest recent challenge to Canadian industrial policies has been the US–Canada Free Trade Agreement, which was signed on 2 January 1988. The full effects of this agreement have not been fully felt, but as the results emerge they may be relevant to other regional economic groupings as well.

The following outlines the major Canadian industrial policies, beginning with the nineteenth-century 'National Policy' designed to promote economic growth.

The National Policy

Canada in its infancy did not have a well enough developed capital market to leave the infrastructure of nation-building to private interests, so there was significant government involvement from Confederation in 1867. The guiding industrial policy of the time was called the National Policy. This consisted mainly of subsidies to promote the building of an intercontinental railway transportation system (3000 miles across) and tariffs to promote manufacturing in central Canada (the Ontario and Quebec provinces), leaving the other regions as exporters of agricultural, mineral and forest products.[2] There were also later subsidies to steelmakers, metal refiners and paper mills to promote resource processing in Canada.

The subsidies involved were very large for the time, and subsequent research has suggested that they were unnecessarily large. To build the intercontinental railway, for example, the Canadian Pacific Railway company (CPR) was given $25 million and 25 million acres of prime land in western Canada, as well as the granting of a temporary monopoly of rail travel and exemptions from taxation (Bliss, 1982, p. 14); 25 million acres is nearly 40,000 square miles, out of perhaps 200,000 square miles of arable land in western Canada that has access to transportation. Thus, to subsidise a transportation link, nearly one-fifth of the land to be served was given to the railway company! That the subsidy was excessive is suggested by the fact that the railway was massively overbuilt, significantly before it was needed.

In fact, the railway was built so quickly for political rather than economic reasons. The transcontinental rail link was promised in the 1870s to British Columbia (Canada's most western province and then a separate British colony) in order to induce it to join Canada rather than the USA.[3]

The protective tariffs, as the other part of the National Policy, had the desired effect of promoting Canadian manufacturing but at the cost of creating other problems. Dales (1966) suggested that, while increasing the size of the manufacturing sector, the combination of high tariffs and unrestrained immigration did not increase the real incomes of pre-immigration Canadians. The tariffs have also been a major source of disunity in a country plagued with inter-regional rivalries, for they have been rightly perceived as indirectly harming the resource-exporting regions that were prevented from purchasing cheap imported manufactures.

Modern industrial policies

Modern Canadian industrial policies evolved slowly in response to a number of perceived needs, including the promotion of high-technology industries, the protection of Canadian sovereignty and culture and the reduction of regional inequalities. The promotion of high technology was attempted mainly through the agency of Crown corporations, most begun either during or shortly after World War II. Examples are the Atomic Energy Commission fostering a nuclear energy industry, and the promotion of aerospace technology and advanced petrochemical synthetics. Procurement policies by both the government airline and the armed forces were designed to support Canadian high technology.

The attempt to protect Canadian sovereignty arose when it was noticed in the early 1970s that more than three-quarters of resource industries and half of manufacturing were US owned, and that the subsidiaries of US companies were responding more to US than to Canadian law. During the energy crisis of the 1970s, for example, a US oil company was alleged to have diverted petrol from Canadian to US customers in response to US government pressure to alleviate the queues at domestic pumps. On the other side of the issue, Canadian consumers of potash benefited from the response of the subsidiary of a US company operating in Canada to the anti-monopoly pressure exerted by US authorities.

The Canadian response to the sovereignty issue was to control foreign investment in the early 1970s (creating the Foreign Investment Review Agency, FIRA), and to introduce a number of policies designed to promote Canadian ownership of energy supplies under the rubric of the National Energy Policy. This policy also imposed export taxes to keep Canadian oil prices below world levels and protect Canadian manufacturing.

The attempt was made to address regional inequalities by a number of means, including direct transfers to the provincial governments of the poorer regions to allow them to provide the same services as enjoyed by other Canadians (the Equalization Programme), tax concessions for companies locating in these regions (through a federal agency called the Department of Regional Economic Expansion, DREE) and special unemployment insurance provisions making it easier for people in high-unemployment regions to obtain unemployment benefits.

Lastly, a Canadian culture industry was fostered (with much wastage and the promotion of mediocre talent) through a national television channel and the promotion of Canadian firms.

The US–Canada Free Trade Agreement
A number of these policies may be under threat from the recently signed Free Trade Agreement with the USA. The motive for the

agreement was largely defensive on Canada's part – to forestall a growing rise of protectionism in Canada's major trading partner – but it may well have unfortunate consequences for Canada's industrial policies. The major provisions of the pact are:

- All tariffs to be removed between Canada and the USA on manufactured goods and many services, as well as the elimination of most non-tariff barriers. The average degree of price protection before the accord was only 6% in Canada and 5% in the USA, so this provision is not as dramatic as it sounds.[4]
- Freer investment across the border, raising the threshold for review under FIRA from $5 million to $150 million.
- A continental energy policy – forbidding the export taxes of the 1970s that kept Canadian oil prices low and prohibiting any reduction of exports to the USA in times of shortage that are more than proportional to the reduction in supplies to Canadians. Thus even though Canada has proportionally greater energy supply than the USA, the new agreement means that Canadian supplies must be fully shared, removing the right of Canadians to sell to whom they wish. This is obviously a complete reversal of former policy, and a significant infringement of Canadian sovereignty.
- A binational panel set up to settle trade disputes – something that Canada desperately wanted to forestall unilateral action by the USA against Canadian goods.

The weakening of FIRA significantly affects Canada's ability to control foreign investment and direct it in desired channels. Canada's regional industrial policies may also be under threat from the Free Trade Agreement. Because the two countries could not agree on the definition of a subsidy for the purpose of countervailing duties, it was left to the new binational panel to establish on a case-by-case basis, and this panel must base its decisions solely on the laws of the country whose firm is bringing the complaint (Green, 1990, p. 525). Unfortunately for Canada, the USA takes a very broad view of a subsidy and before the agreement imposed countervailing tariffs against what it considered unfair advantage given to Canadian industry. The celebrated cases were: softwood lumber – in which the USA claimed that the Canadian government (which owns the land the forest companies use) charged too low a rent – and Atlantic groundfish – where it was alleged that special unemployment assistance given to this poor region meant that the fishery could pay lower wages and thus had an unfair advantage over US fisheries.[5] This legislation will continue to apply in determining the decisions of the binational panel, and these decisions will determine the existence of many of Canada's industrial policies in the future.

Conclusions

Canadian industrial policies were devised on an *ad hoc* basis, and reflect a willingness to interfere with the market when perceived needs are not being met, as in the redistribution of income between rich and poor regions, for example. That some of these programmes are now under threat from the Free Trade Agreement illustrates the constraints as well as opportunities from economic integration.

Notes

1 The classic reference on the role of the state in Canadian economic life is Aitken (1967).

2 In the nineteenth century the term 'National Policy' referred just to the policy of tariff protection. The definition has only later been expanded to encompass the range of transport and other subsidies. For an extensive discussion of the National Policy see Bliss (1982).

3 For details of the Canadian political context in the 1870s see McNaught (1969), Chapter 10.

4 See Department of Finance (1988), Table 2, p. 20.

5 The softwood lumber case was analysed by Anderson and Cairns (1988), who concluded that the economic basis of the US claim was faulty.

References

Aitken, H. G. (1967), 'Defensive expansion: the state and economic growth in Canada', in W. T. Easterbrook and M. H. Watkins (eds), *Approaches to Canadian Economic History*, Toronto: McLelland and Stewart.

Anderson, F. J. and Cairns, R. D. (1988), 'The Softwood Lumber Agreement and resource politics', *Canadian Public Policy*, June, 186–96.

Bliss, M. (1982), *The Evolution of Industrial Policies in Canada: An Historical Survey*, Discussion Paper No. 218, Ottawa: Economic Council of Canada.

Dales, J. H. (1966), *The Protective Tariff in Canada's Development*, Toronto: University of Toronto Press.

Department of Finance, Canada (1988), *The Canada–U.S. Free Trade Agreement: An Economic Assessment*, Ottawa: Department of Finance.

Green, C. (1990), 'Trade and industrial policies', Chapter 18 of *Canadian Industrial Organization and Policy*, Toronto: McGraw-Hill Ryerson.

McNaught, K. (1969), *The Pelican History of Canada*, Harmondsworth, Middx: Penguin.

The USA: regulatory reform in the transportation industry

James Peoples

Introduction

Federal legislation, established primarily in the 1930s, directed the US government to set prices and restrict entry for a select group of industries. A desire to provide an affordable service for all customers was a major reason for implementing this industrial policy. Indeed, past research shows that cross-subsidisation was commonly practised as a way to maintain low prices for specific high-cost services.[1] By the early 1970s a growing number of studies seemed to suggest that less government intervention would actually allow firms generally to charge even lower prices. This notion hinged partly on the assumption that cost-saving advancements in technology since the 1930s allowed for increased competition in markets that were previously government-sanctioned oligopolies. Using these studies as a springboard to enact new legislation, the US government adopted radical changes in the regulation of product markets. Firms in the cable, petroleum, natural gas, telecommunications, transportation and banking industries faced reduced regulation of rates and entry in the 1980s.

In general, sufficient time has elapsed to comment on the effectiveness of this deregulatory industrial strategy. In what follows I will limit my attention to the airline and trucking industries of the transportation sector. Choosing these two industries with such inherently different market structures should provide useful information on the appropriateness of government decontrol.

Market characteristics under regulation

Before deregulation, potential competitors for high-density routes were prohibited from airline routes. During this time, 11 carriers served these markets, and low-density routes were usually served by only one of these carriers. In an attempt to eliminate non-competitive pricing that could evolve from limiting entry, the government set prices according to the distance between destination points. Thus carriers charged similar fares on low- and high-density routes of the same distance. Since carriers were prohibited from engaging in price competition, they instead focused on distinguishing their product with service quality. For example, it was common for carriers to add extra flights even though this practice resulted in the costly reduction of the number of passengers per flight.

The market structure of the regulated trucking industry differed substantially from the airline industry, with the eight largest trucking companies combined having only an 11% market share in 1976.[2] Still long-term competitive pricing did not ensue. Entry regulation, though, prohibited potential competitors from applying for route certificates in certain parts of the industry unless they provided service to new locations. Furthermore, these new permits were allowed only after incumbent carriers were solicited, and given the chance to provide the service themselves. The result was much higher concentration on individual trucking routes.

To avoid the possibility of price collusion among carriers in concentrated markets, rate regulation was applied to the part of the industry facing the least amount of competition from other modes of transportation: those hauling less than a truckload of general freight (LTL carriers). Their rates for shipments were determined using mark-up pricing methods. On the one hand, this pricing policy allowed LTL companies to subsidise low-density routes at the expense of customers along high-density routes. On the other hand, the mark-ups were such that this pricing practice provided economic rent for the LTL segment of the industry (Moore, 1986). Unlike carriers providing LTL service, carriers shipping full truckloads of special freight (TL carriers) competed with rail carriers to receive shipping contracts, and as a result faced little rate regulation.[3]

In sum, in an attempt to provide inexpensive universal service, industrial regulation in the USA seemingly promoted inefficient operations and costly services. The reaction of the US government was to invoke a new policy that allowed carriers greater ease of entry and discretion in setting prices and in choosing routes.

The record on deregulation
Since 1981, route authority has been awarded freely and airline carriers allowed to set prices with complete discretion under the terms of the 1978 Airline Deregulation Act. The removal of entry

restrictions resulted in an initial surge of new passenger carriers from 28 in 1976 to 61 in 1983.[4] Increased competition put downward pressure on price hikes, especially for high-density routes (Kaplan, 1986). However, the influx of new competitors was not long lasting as the introduction of the hub-and-spoke network reduced the number of planes needed to serve major city pairs. This type of network allowed airlines to fill a large proportion of their seating capacity by routing originating flights to a central airport (the hub). In turn, airlines with hubs took advantage of economies of aircraft size and current US merger policy to increase their market share. Indeed, by 1985 the two-firm concentration ratio for domestic carriers averaged over 70% at hub airports, compared with 52.24% in 1978, before deregulation.[5]

In conjunction with the use of the hub-and-spoke network, air fares for short-haul services outpaced fare increases for routes served by the hub-and-spoke network. Proponents of the contestability hypothesis suggest that the threat of potential entry partly contributed to the maintenance of low fares despite high market shares (Bailey and Baumol, 1984). None the less, high concentration at major city pairs could lead to future price fixing if potential entrants face substantial barriers to entry.[6] Past research reveals that the prevailing method of allocating gate space and take-off and landing slots has given incumbent airlines significant control over entry into their markets by other airlines. Risk-averse behaviour by airport operators led to long-term lease agreements, especially with solvent hub airlines. This in turn limited the access of potential competitors. The common practice of providing landing and take-off slots to hub airlines further enhanced barriers to entry into these markets. When combined with the control of major carriers over the reservation booking system, the height of entry barriers could be non-trivial.

In contrast to the declining numbers of competitors in the airline industry after 1983, the total number of regulated carriers increased from 16,000 in 1975 to over 30,000 in 1986 following regulatory reform in the trucking industry.[7] The new entrants were mostly small TL carriers. Rate analysis of trucking deregulation shows that the influx of these new entrants limited the ability of firms to pass through costs in the most competitive sector of this industry (Perry, 1986).

Presumably, fixed costs were sufficiently low to allow such a significant increase of new entrants. These costs, though, were not the same across type of carrier. In particular, the cost of constructing terminals inhibited entry into the profitable LTL market. Established LTL firms could set up their terminals as a hub-and-spoke network to further deter entry into their markets. Hence, techniques to enhance efficiency in this industry may conceivably lead to less competition, but such is not the case.

Concluding comments
In the airline industry the conventional method of allocating leases and slots gave incumbents, in particular major hub airlines, significant control over entry into their markets. Although few analysts have advocated returning to the past system of regulation, some have questioned whether some types of regulatory action might be needed. It has been suggested that, to lessen the market dominance of hub carriers, regulators should prohibit long-term leasing, as well as discourage airlines that fail to use their gate space (Bauer, 1987). Additionally, charging higher take-off and landing fees at the busiest times could allocate airport resources more evenly and thereby lower the entry barriers that have developed under the present system. The success of these recommendations depends partly on the willingness of airport managers to dissolve their current lockstep relationship with incumbent airlines and on the ability of potential entrants to pay competitive rates for peak-load departure and arrival times. Even if barriers to entry were low, the common occurrence of incumbents acquiring new entrants dampens the prospects of lowered market concentration along hub-and-spoke routes.

The difficulty encountered in sustaining competition in the market place suggests that the transition to complete decontrol was inadequate. Only for the case of an industry such as trucking, which has relatively low fixed costs, has this policy encouraged long-standing competitiveness. And even in this industry conditions for maintaining low barriers to entry may now be in jeopardy. In the case of airlines, a competitive market structure can be maintained only by active intervention to lower existing barriers, and a strong merger policy to allow new entrants to prosper and remain independent.

Notes

1 Before regulatory reform, low prices for local phone calls were offset by revenue generated in the less expensive long-distance sector. Similarly, low fares for low- density routes in rail, air and trucking were compensated by the profit received from providing service along high-density routes.

2 *Source*: the American Trucking Association.

3 It is the nature of the shipment size that results in the competition against rail service, since large hauls allow rail carriers to benefit from economies of train size.

4 *Source*: the Airline Transportation Association.

5 This group of airports does not include major hub airports such as DC National, New York, Kennedy, New York, Laguadia, and Newark International. Thus, this measure possibly understates the true increase in market concentration at the hub airports (Bauer, 1987).

6 Airline reservation agencies are currently under investigation for alleged price fixing.

7 *Source*: the Interstate Commerce Commission.

References

Bailey, Elizabeth E. and Baumol, William J. (1984), 'Deregulation and the theory of contestable markets', *Yale Journal on Regulation*, 1, 111–37.

Bauer, Paul W. (1987), 'Competition, concentration, and fares in the U.S. airline industry', *Economic Commentary*, The Federal Reserve Bank of Cleveland, 15 September.

Kaplan, Daniel P. (1986), 'The changing airline industry', in Leonard Weiss and Michael W. Klass (eds), *Regulatory Reform*, Boston: Little Brown.

Moore, Thomas G. (1986), 'Rail and trucking deregulation', in Leonard Weiss and Michael W. Klass (eds), *Regulatory Reform*, Boston: Little Brown.

Perry, Charles R. (1986), *Deregulation and the Decline of the Unionized Trucking Industry*, Philadelphia: Wharton School's Industrial Research Unit.

Britain

Malcolm Sawyer

In this paper we provide a schematic outline of industrial policy in Britain in the postwar period. Many would treat industrial policy as virtually synonymous with competition policy. Our view is that industrial policy should be regarded much more widely, but we begin our discussion with competition policy (defined to include policies on mergers, monopolies and restriction practices), and move on to consider policies which can be seen as more developmental in nature.

Competition policy in Britain can be traced through a series of Acts of Parliament, starting in 1948, which can be seen as gradually strengthening and extending the operation of competition policy. A policy of investigation of monopolies (defined initially as a firm having a one-third market share, since revised to a one-quarter share) by a quasi-independent commission (now called the Monopolies and Mergers Commission, hereafter the MMC) was initiated in 1948. The emphasis was on the potential for monopolies to have adverse economic consequences and on conduct and performance rather than structure. The range of industries which can be investigated by the MMC has been gradually widened (e.g. in 1965 to cover services and the professions). However, monopoly investigations have been a rather low-key affair, in terms of both numbers investigated (of the order of three a year) and the rather minor effects of the findings of the MMC. Restrictive practices were initially subject to investigation by the forerunner of the MMC but have been under the auspices of the Restrictive Practices Court since 1956. The legislation (and more particularly its interpretation) has involved a strong presumption against restrictive agreements and cartels and has been implemented through the judicial system (unlike the monopolies and mergers legislation). The scope of the legislation has also been gradually extended, most recently in 1976 to include services. It is probably the case that the extent of cartel-type agreements amongst firms has been considerably diminished by this legislation from a very high level in the 1940s, though there is occasional evidence of some continuing agreements.

The examination of proposed mergers by the MMC was introduced in 1965, where a merger was to be judged in terms of the public interest (rather similar to the judgement of monopoly situations) and the criteria for possible referral of a merger were the creation or enhancement of a monopoly position or the size of firms involved (measured in terms of assets, with the present cut-off level being £30 million). During the period since 1965 (which has included two massive waves of merger activity in the late 1960s and the second half of the 1980s), only a small proportion (of the order of 3%) of mergers which met the criteria for referral have been referred to the MMC. The investigations of the MMC have led to around 1% of mergers being stopped by government action whilst a further 1% were abandoned during the period of investigation. Besides the small impact of the merger policy, another aspect to note is the question of what constitutes the public interest. Whilst this has not been fully defined in the legislation, the public interest was initially considered in terms of factors such as unemployment (both level and regional distribution), and research and development, but has now become identified with competition. Apart from difficulties in defining competition (discussed elsewhere in this volume), this has the effect of virtually ruling out any consideration of diversified mergers.

Within competition policy there has been a gradual extension of its coverage and a shift towards a more explicit concern with the promotion of competition. In so far as economic analysis has had an influence on this policy, it has been a mixture of the 'market failure' paradigm and aspects of Austrian economics. Whilst it is difficult to be sure whether economic analysis has had much influence, it would appear that there was some influence from the 'market failure' approach initially in terms of the focus on structure (market share, cartels), whilst the Austrian approach has been more influential in the 1980s with an emphasis on conditions of entry into an industry and government's role in raising barriers to entry. This can be seen to some degree in the operation of monopoly policy but also in decisions on the deregulation of bus and long-distance coach services. Whilst much attention is given in textbooks to discussion of competition policy, there must be severe doubts as to whether it has had much impact on industrial performance, for the policy has been operated on a rather small scale.

There have been a variety of measures to restructure industry. The nationalisation programme of the Labour governments not only transferred ownership into the public sector but also changed industrial structure (generally creating a monopoly situation). The privatisation programme since 1979 has transferred many of these industries back to the private sector but with the monopoly position largely maintained, though generally subject to some regulation, particularly over price increases. The privatisation programme has viewed ownership as a more important determinant of performance than competition. There has also been some restructuring of 'sunset' industries (such as textiles, aircraft production), and much of this occurred during the 1950s and 1960s. Whilst there were numerous motives and pressures involved in these policies, they could be seen as involving the notion that changing structure leads to changes in performance.

Competition policy involves an essentially regulatory role for the state in industrial affairs. It also involves an essentially arms-length relationship between government and enterprises. In some contrast, a developmental role for the state involves the active promotion of industrial development, with the state adopting an entrepreneurial role, either in its own industrial operations and/or in its promotion of private business. The idea of a developmental role for the state has never been widely accepted in Britain, and has clearly had no influence over policies of the Conservative government which came to power in 1979. Although not expressed in these terms, a number of policies pursued during the 1960s and 1970s (mainly though not exclusively by Labour governments) can be viewed as involving a more developmental role for the state. An early example of this was the establishment of the National Economic Development Office (NEDO) on a tripartite basis to identify obstacles to faster economic growth. The short-lived National Plan of the mid-1960s sought to use indicative planning, the fostering of favourable expectations and the identification and then removal of bottlenecks to generate faster growth. The role of the Industrial Reorganisation Corporation was to stimulate rationalism and modernisation, particularly through the promotion of mergers. The National Enterprise Board of the 1970s operated both as a hospital for sick companies (such as British Leyland) and also as the promoter of and investor in small high-technology companies. The industrial strategy, introduced in 1975, built on the institutional framework of NEDO and sought to analyse the difficulties facing particular sectors (in manufacturing) and to search for ways to overcome these difficulties (with the aid of government finance). Some sectors of the economy were viewed as particularly important for future success, and the idea behind the strategy was to identify and then aid those sectors. Throughout these attempts at tripartite policies, however, there was an emphasis on securing agreement and few instruments to ensure their implementation.

British industrial policy has taken many twists and turns in response to changes in government, economic and political ideas, etc. in the search for a remedy for continuing relative economic decline. However, whilst there has been some flirtation with a developmental role for the state, the main thrust of British industrial policy has been for the state to adopt a rather regulatory role with an emphasis on competition policy.

Note

This paper draws heavily upon my previous writings, notably 'Industrial policies of the Labour government of the 1960s and 1970s', in K. Cowling and H. Tomann (eds), *Industrial Policy after 1992*, London: Anglo-German Foundation, 1990; 'Industrial policy', in M. Artis and D. Cobham (eds), *Labour's Economic Policies, 1974–79*, Manchester: Manchester University Press, 1991; and to a lesser extent *Economics of Industries and Firms*, London: Croom-Helm, 1985, Chapter 16, and 'Industry', in M. Artis (ed.), *A Manual of Applied Economics*, London: Weidenfeld & Nicolson, 1989.

Finland

Johan Willner

Background: industrial structure in Finland

The Finnish economy is highly concentrated. The three largest firms in each industry had on average a market share of more than 50% in 1982. To mention two comparative examples, the US four-firm concentration ratio was on average 47.8% in 1977, while the UK five-firm concentration ratio was 50.6% in 1975. Not surprisingly, there is a substantial potential for welfare losses in a number of industries, at least if firms behave according to traditional oligopoly theory (Willner and Ståhl, 1991).

However, it is unfair to describe the Finnish economy only as dominated by private oligopolies. There are a number of industries with low concentration and high demand elasticity. The producer cooperative owns a significant part of the food industry and the consumer co-operative is active in retail trade, as well as owning hotels and restaurants. More important from a policy standpoint is that the state is a big owner in many industries, with a share of the domestic value added amounting to about 20%. Therefore the public sector has an at least potentially important tool for industrial policy-making.

Finnish industrial policy before 1990

Intervention to promote growth

The state has in fact played a very active part in Finland. This activity includes selective promotion of industries and financial support in the form of tax exemptions and also direct support. The policy also included state ownership of important firms. A shift towards a more market-oriented policy started in 1985–90.

Finland's oldest state companies date from 1918. The state bought and established a number of firms, predominantly in pulp and paper, fertilising and mining industries. The aim was to encourage industrialisation and development where private risk capital seemed insufficient. It was at that time felt important that production and natural resources remained under national control. During the depression a number of new acquisitions were made and public enterprises were reorganised as state-owned limited companies to give easier access to capital markets and weaken their dependence on the state budget. After the war, a number of state companies were established partly because of the needs of reconstruction but also because of reparations to the Soviet Union. In 1950–1970 an important motive was to promote employment and regional balance. After 1970, the state has initiated only joint ventures with the private sector.

State activity has been motivated more by the lack of private risk capital rather than ideologically. Therefore, the state firms have usually been instructed to behave like a private firm. This is made clear in a government decision from 1983, but in most cases firms had to conform to 'sound business principles' even before that. Exceptions have been of the kind that private firms have been supported with low energy prices and cheap railway freight. As a consequence, state companies are usually as profitable as comparable private firms; energy production is however much more profitable than on average (*Valtionyhtiöt markkinataloudessa*, 1989).

Competition policy[1]

Finland became independent in 1917. Its development towards a market economy started in the second half of the nineteenth century. No need to restrict monopolies was perceived until after World War II, but there was some legislation against unfair competition. The first Competition Law is from 1957. It outlawed bidding cartels but otherwise collusion was permitted. However, the authorities were obliged to monitor and register restrictive trade practices. No major revisions were made until 1988. Most prices have at times been subject to regulation, but that has been part of macroeconomic stabilisation policy.

The high industrial concentration in Finland has never been perceived as a problem, and mergers have even been encouraged as part of a strategy creating strong export companies. Typically, the only privatisations that have taken place have made the largest firms in their industries even stronger. Also, large profits have been seen as an incentive for innovation, not as a symptom of allocative inefficiency.

A summary of the experiences

Industrial policy in Finland has not traditionally been concerned with allocative efficiency. It has been subordinated to the purpose of promoting economic growth and success in export markets. Given these limited ambitions, the policy has been in part successful. The country's growth performance has been impressive. However, the policy has been associated with growth to an extent that has conflicted with other important targets. Unemployment might have been high without the emigration to Sweden. Domestic monopolies have been strong, and there has been no active anti-trust policy. Creating competition and restricting monopoly power have not, until quite recently (see below), been on the agenda. Not surprisingly, recent research shows that Finland has relatively high productivity but low real wages and low unit labour costs. The country is known for its high prices, but that is partly the result of profitability being about 10% higher than in all other highly industrialised European countries except for Italy (Pohjola, 1991).

Recent developments

Refinements to the Competition Law[2]
At the end of the 1980s, we can perceive a new emphasis on microeconomic efficiency. It is related to the so-called controlled restructuring in Finland, initiated by the government (dominated by conservatives and social democrats) in 1987.[3] The tax reform is a case in point, and the same can be said about the revision of the Competition Law that took place in 1988. However, in contrast with the EC legislation, Finnish legislation was based on outlawing the abuse of a dominant position, not on prohibiting the position as such. Barriers to entry were to be removed and agreements implying horizontal limitations of competition were declared invalid.

However, the Competition Law since 1988 is at present subject to revision. A recent committee report (*Kilpailulainsäädännön uudistaminen*, Helsinki, 1991) suggests some changes that would make the Finnish legislation closer to the principles that are followed in the rest of Europe. The suggestion does not depart from the abuse principle. Sanctions for restrictive practices are suggested to take the form of administrative–judicial fines. However, the possibilities for regulating prices have been reduced. There will be no sanctions against mergers, and the suggestions are based on emphasising dynamic rather than static efficiency. Mergers and high profits are even seen as promoting dynamic efficiency.[4]

Another recent tendency is the focus on the public sector not only as an owner of monopolistic companies but also as a regulator. The Office of Free Competition finds unnecessary regulation of the private sector more worrying than restrictive trade agreements (Reimavuo, 1991). Most regulation can be found in the transport sector and in agriculture. The credit market has recently been deregulated.

The Office of Free Competition (established in 1988) can report some successes in abolishing collusive agreements, as reported by its director (Purasjoki, 1990). The need for a microeconomic policy is recognised. However, it represents no major departure from the tradition supporting rather than restricting private sector concentration. To promote dynamic rather than static efficiency is a new way of expressing the traditional orientation towards growth rather than fair prices and justice.

Privatisations and flexibility in the public sector
At the time of writing, no decisions about major privatisations have been made. However, the current scepticism towards public sector activities has been present in Finland in two ways.

First, there already exists a Ministry of Trade and Industry working party report suggesting privatisation of most of the state companies in Finland (*Visio yksityistämisestä Suomessa 1990-luvulla*, 1991). The motives are, as in most countries, the belief that state companies are inefficient – despite the experiences of profitable state companies in Finland – and the dangers of a too dominant public sector. Privatisation is not about promoting competition. The report even suggests that it is easier to accomplish mergers creating sufficiently large companies if there is no distinction between a state-owned and a private sector of the economy. The report thus dismisses the mixed oligopoly idea because it wants to decrease rather than increase domestic competition.

Secondly, even if state railways, telecommunications and post are not subject to privatisation, they have been reorganised as limited companies. They are not allowed to cross-subsidise and unprofitable activities have to cease. There is an obvious danger that measures that minimise the companies' costs will in fact increase the costs carried by the rest of society. Closely related to this development is the change of status of civil servants, who can now be made redundant.

Conclusions

Where policy has affected the industrial structure in Finland it has been aimed at growth, not allocative efficiency and justice. The large proportion of state companies in the economy can be explained by that motive. The outcome has been a fairly rapid growth rate, but also comparatively low real wages and high profitability.

The present changes in the competition policy are, at least to some extent, based on visions about how industries should work and they have resulted in the removal of some restrictive trade agreements. Nevertheless, they do not restrict the influence of large companies; rather they increase it by reducing the importance of the state as an owner or a regulator. The privatisations which have been suggested would increase the market power of big private firms, not reduce it. The state has never used its firms for creating competition, but nevertheless privatisations would leave the public sector without a powerful tool for intervention.

Until the present crisis, the Finnish experiences were often described as a success story. At the moment, the export companies have difficulties and the economic policy is deflationary. However, there is some evidence that high profits rather than high real wages explain why Finnish products are too expensive. Therefore I cannot escape the conclusion that a higher standard of living might have been possible without distorting competitive power in the international markets.

Notes

I am indebted to Jan Otto Andersson and Markus Jäntti for helpful discussions. The shortcomings are my own.

1   This section uses material from Rissanen (1989), Wilhelmsson (1989) and the committee report on revising the Competition Law, *Kilpailulainsäädännön uudistaminen* (Ministry of Trade and Industry, Helsinki, 1991).

2   This section is based on the committee report with suggestions for revising the Competition Law, *Kilpailulainsäädännön uudistaminen* (Ministry of Trade and Industry, Helsinki, 1991) and Hallberg (1991).

3   Further details about this change of emphasis are described in English by Andersson (1989).

4   The influence of Austrian economic thought is quite explicit, as follows from Virtanen's (1991) contribution to the Yearbook issued by the Office of Free Competition.

References

Unfortunately, most references are in Finnish. However, there is an English summary of those articles that are published in the Yearbook of the Office of Free Competition.

Andersson, J. O., (1989), 'Controlled restructuring in Finland', *Scandinavian Political Studies*, 12 (4), 373–89.

Hallberg, P. (1991), 'Kilpailulainsäädännön uudistaminen', *Kilpailuvirasto, Vuosikirja 1991* [Yearbook of the Office of Free Competition], 22–6.

Pohjola, Matti (1991), 'Tulopoliittinen neuvottelujärjestelmä ja Suomi', in P. Forsman, *et al.*, *Korkean Hintatason Suomi*, Helsinki: Paulon Säätiö.

Purasjoki, M. (1990), 'Vad felas konkurrensen i Finland', *Ekonomiska Samfundets Tidskrift*, 43 (4), 273–82.

Reimavuo, S. (1991), 'Deregulaation teoria ja käytäntö', *Kilpailuvirasto, Vuosikirja 1991* [Yearbook of the Office of Free Competition], 27–31.

Rissanen, K. (1989), 'Kilpailusta ja sääntelystä', *Oikeus*, 7 (4–5), 352–61.

Valtionyhtiöt markkinataloudessa (1989), Helsinki: Liiketaloustieteuine tutkimuslaitos.

Virtanen, M. (1991), 'Kilpailupolitiikka ja itävaltalainen talousteoria', *Kilpailuvirasto, Vuosikirja 1991* [Yearbook of the Office of Free Competition]

Visio yksityistämisestä Suomessa (1991), Helsinki: Kauppa-ja Teollisuusministeriö (Ministry of Trade and Industry), 12.2.

Wilhelmsson, T. (1989), '1980-luvun oikeuspolitiikkaa: kilpailuaatteen uusi nousu', *Oikeus*, 7 (4–5), 348–51.

Willner, J. and Ståhl, L. (1991), 'Where are the welfare losses of imperfect competition large? European Journal of Political Economy (forthcoming).

Germany

Horst Tomann

The 1990 OECD Report on Industrial Policy indicates a general shift of industrial strategies towards measures improving corporate competitiveness. That, I think, defines exactly Germany's industrial strategy during the 1980s and reveals the underlying philosophy of fostering the investment process through the increased profitability of firms. The strategy consisted of four areas:

(1) *Tax reform*

Decreasing the tax burden on corporate profit was a major issue in the conservatives' government programme. The government implemented a tax reform in several stages – some of them yet to come – which have reduced marginal rates of income tax and provided a more favourable tax treatment for small and medium-sized enterprises (SMEs), which are subject to personal income tax. At the same time, the tax system was simplified with the effect of avoiding misallocation of investment. The basic idea was to replace specific subsidies by general tax concessions and to abolish incentives which induced rent-seeking behaviour. For example, the tax system formerly induced 'overinvestment' in real estate.

(2) *Measures related to research and development*

Financial support of R&D has been a traditional area of industrial strategy. Germany even has a Federal Ministry of Science and Technology. Emphasis, however, shifted from support of specific projects to general measures in favour of 'innovative activities'. In this field, intangible investment increasingly plays the dominant role: provision of infrastructure for technology transfer, subsidisation of R&D personnel, financial aid for external expertise, support of inter-firm co-operation.

(3) *Measures in favour of SMEs*

Fostering SMEs has become a strategic area of industrial policy for several reasons. On the one hand, SMEs are in an unfavourable position as far as risk-taking is concerned. Hence, they cannot fully avoid discrimination in the capital market. On the other hand, the crucial role of SMEs in providing a diversified industrial structure has been recognised. In particular, technology policy in favour of SMEs proved to be a reliable measure of growth policy. The new techno-industrial paradigm requires the combination of established technologies rather than invention of new ones as a precondition of technological evolution. Here, SMEs play an active role. The German experience supports the OECD thesis that profitability does not increase with firm size. Furthermore, jobs in SMEs are probably more long term.

(4) *Measures towards increased labour market flexibility*
German labour market deregulation has had a significant effect on profitability in two respects. First, in 1984, IG Metall started negotiations on shortening the working week to 35 hours. The employers' association would only accept a contract which at the same time introduced a scheme separating machine operating from individual working time at the firm level. That increased capital utilisation rates and, hence, profitability for many firms. Secondly, an Employment Promotion Act in 1985 enabled firms to offer labour contracts of limited duration. That should improve the chances of re-employment for the long-term unemployed, in particular for unskilled labour. This regulation will be in force until 1995 and had rather good results during the first phase.

How does such a strategy fit into the German concept of 'Ordnungs-politik'?
Traditionally, according to this concept, industrial policy has to play a subsidiary role in enhancing structural change and reducing the social cost of change. In particular, targeting, i.e. opening up new directions of sectoral change, has not been an issue for industrial policy. There are three exceptions, justifying state intervention at industrial level:

(1)   provision of basic sectors of national interest;
(2)   restructuring of declining industries;
(3)   fostering innovative activity.

To understand the German policy concept, two qualifications should be made. On the one hand, the German policy system is a two-tier system with a rather liberal 'Ordnungspolitik' at the federal level and much industry promotion at state level. Let me give two examples. First, the famous Baden–Württemberg model of technology transfer, in particular to SMEs, shows a strong relationship between state and industry (not to mention the political fate of Lothar Späth). Secondly, North-Rhine Westphalia has successfully managed the process of restructuring the declining Ruhr area. The crucial role in this revitalisation process was assigned to the educational system, which has been considerably extended during the last two decades. As educational policy is in state competence, here again the active role of industrial policy shows.

On the other hand, in a more general sense industrial policy has played a subsidiary role. As regards industrial strategy, the main strategic device in Germany has been a tight monetary policy. Although German policy was not very successful in attracting strategic sectors (what we call 'strategic trade policy' in an environment of monopolistic competition), it was successful in providing a competitive environment for German industry. Only recently did we learn that German monetary policy does not have its origins in a special German fear of inflation, or a national preference for stability, but was conceived from the very beginning as a means of improving competitiveness in world markets.

In a regime of fixed exchange rates, this strategy evidently works: relative price stability immediately devalues the own currency in real terms – this explains the huge current account surplus accumulated by Germany within the EMS. As long as the EMS is stable and the fixing of exchange rates is credible, the current account surplus will be balanced by net capital exports. So, by its tight monetary policy Germany became a lender country.

In a regime of flexible exchange rates, a policy of price level stability works as well. Although the currency tends to revaluate, some undervaluation may remain in real terms. The crucial point, however, is that in a flexible exchange rate system the country with price level stability does not need net capital imports and thus can afford relatively low real interest rate levels. As the OECD Report on Industrial Policy shows, real long-term interest rates during the 1980s were lowest in Germany and Japan.

Moreover, a tight monetary policy opens the way for a strategy of open markets: there is no need for a protectionist trade policy, as the monetary policy already provides favourable conditions for industry to withstand the pressures of international competition.

New challenges: does German unity require an active industrial strategy?
Germany unity would seem to require a return to the robust, old-fashioned measures of an industrial development strategy (see also Chapter 15). It is true that at first federal government tried to achieve unification at least cost by establishing monetary, economic and social union in mid-1990. However, the provision of a stable and convertible currency; a German Unity Fund (DM 112 billion) to finance investment in infrastructure for the next few years; and transfer payments to establish a social security system in East Germany proved to be insufficient. But it was not until early 1991 that the heads of the state governments in Sachsen and Brandenburg, Biedenkopf and Stolpe exerted political pressure. The state and local governments would certainly have become insolvent without additional help. This prospect induced re-negotiation of the unity treaty between the federal and state governments.

Today, industrial policy for East Germany means a role in development. Four areas are to be distinguished:

(1) Promotion of private investment by soft loans and subsidies of up to 40% of the amount invested. Moreover, special arrangements provide real estate to private investors.
(2) Public investment in infrastructure, especially for transport and telecommunications: it is said that a modern telecom network will be operational throughout East Germany by 1997.
(3) Trade finance guarantees and financial assistance to support trade with Eastern Europe, especially the Soviet Union.
(4) Measures to support retraining and re-education of the workforce.

To finance this programme the conservative government returned to deficit spending and some tax increases. The budget deficit will amount to 8% of GNP over the next few years, which is high by international standards. Lastly, in February 1991, the West-Länder accepted the East in to the 'Finanzausgleich', a scheme of tax revenue redistribution. In particular, VAT revenues are to be redistributed on equal terms per capita.

Although much money has been spent, the process of structural change is only slowly getting under way. There were some major shortcomings of the reform blocking the transition process:

(1) The currency reform did not include a realistic reassessment of enterprise debt. Rather, the firms' liabilities were converted, by and large, at the same rate as were private savings accounts, i.e. at a rate of 2:1. Only in late 1990 did the government consider a debt release on individual terms.

(2) The privatisation programme, which simply aimed to sell firms through a government agency called 'Treuhandanstalt', did not work properly because of an inadequate institutional framework and narrow markets for enterprises. Furthermore, the government missed the opportunity of using this programme for distributional objectives as well.

(3) To postpone the rise of visible unemployment the government financed large-scale 'unemployment on the job'. This led to an adverse pattern of payments, with unemployed people receiving more money than people undergoing retraining and re-education. In some cases people even refused to take on new jobs, instead staying with their former employer.

Meanwhile, optimistic voices grow louder: by the end of 1991 East German economic progress will be under way, if not in employment then in production.

Italy

Patrizio Bianchi

The origin of the Italian industrial system

The Italian industrial system emerged a century later than the English Industrial Revolution. Political fragmentation limited the modernisation of local industries; a core of modern manufacturing was established in the northern states under the Austrian Empire. Unification of the Italian states under the King of Piedmont-Savoy (1861) was the opportunity for creating a domestic market, wide enough to permit the reorganisation of industry.

Nevertheless, the scarcity of national capital promoted the entry of foreign financial groups, and the spread of German-style commercial banks. These banks collected small amounts of individual savings, which they invested in industrial firms, which in turn acquired share control of the banks themselves. This mechanism allowed commercial banks with relatively little capital to control a large share of industry, especially steel, shipbuilding, energy, telecommunications, arms production, producer goods, which were largely bought by the state. At the very beginning of the 1930s, the international financial slump made it impossible to regulate this fragile mechanism: the three largest banks collapsed, causing the general insolvency of the banking system.

The basic characteristics of the Italian industrial system

At the beginning of 1933 the Instituto per la Ricostruzione Industriale (IRI) was founded by the government in order to rescue the banking system; IRI absorbed assets (firm shares controlled by banks) and liabilities (banks' debts and losses). The new public body tried to privatise firms and banks, but it was immediately clear that the financial and human resources did not exist to acquire those companies. Thus, IRI, the public shareholding company controlling the industrial base of the country, was established as a temporary expedient to overcome the financial crisis, but it became a structural element of the Italian economy.

The Banking Reform Act was issued on 1 March 1936; it forbade deposit banks to invest, directly or through long-term lending to manufacturing companies; special banks, owned by the largest banks, were established in order to provide investment credit. Thus, the second structural element of the Italian economy – the public ownership of the banking system and a rigid division between deposit banks and investment banks – was established as a temporary solution to the financial slump.

Both these elements are still in operation.

At the end of World War II, the Constituent Assembly of the new republic debated whether to maintain or dissolve the public shareholdings. The largest private companies, such as Fiat, and the new Christian Democratic Party were in favour of maintaining public companies working in the manufacturing sectors. The most dynamic of Italian industries argued that private firms had to produce finished goods on a scale appropriate to the international market; therefore, the state had to provide basic and intermediate goods such as steel and cast iron and a communications network, by investing directly in these highly capital-intensive sectors.

The role of state-owned companies

Thus, IRI reorganised its firms and expanded its activities in basic production and in the telecommunications network, such as in motorway building and management. In the early 1950s the 'IRI formula' was applied to the energy sector; ENI was set up to manage companies in oil refining and distribution, chemical industries, fibre and fertiliser production.

In 1960 IRI, ENI and the other minor public shareholding companies were used as an industrial policy instrument, to invest in the less-advantaged areas of the country, especially in the Mezzogiorno. In the 1970s, public bodies were required to acquire all collapsing firms in order to avoid individual crises becoming a general slump of the industrial system.

In the 1950s, developing countries considered the Italian public ownership model an attractive example of positive state involvement; it was a powerful instrument managed by the government to force the industrialisation of the country. In the 1970s the model became a clear example of the risks of extensive public involvement in economic life. Almost all the basic sectors were in crisis, and the big plants established in the South faced a dramatic slump.

Thus, at the beginning of the 1980s the state-owned companies almost went bankrupt. The government appointed new chairmen, not from the political mileu; public companies were reorganised and returned to positive results; some companies in the textile, auto and steel sectors were privatised. By the end of 1988, internal funds obtained by profits and privatisation drastically reduced public support of state-owned companies. But, it is a matter of fact that the political parties reacted against this claim to autonomy by public managers, and new chairmen, with links with political parties, were appointed in 1989. The privatisation process stopped, inefficient investment in the Southern regions started again, and quite clearly the 1991 budget was again in deficit.

State aid to industrial firms

State aid to industry has been a constant element of Italian industrial policy. The European Commission has criticised the Italian government for the quantity and quality of these subsidies. Since the end of the war, the Italian government has provided subsidies in order to promote the development of less-favoured areas and to favour the innovate efforts of small and medium-sized firms. Table 10.1 lists the main laws concerning public aid: it shows that most of the laws provide subsidies for the acquisition of new machinery.

The basic concepts were, first, that small firms and companies working in the marginal areas were financially disadvantaged in getting loans from the banking system; and, secondly, that the only innovation considered was acquisition of new machinery. The aid has been given to individual firms in the form of a discount on the normal rate applied by the banking system. Thus, subsidies paid to individual companies to acquire new machinery are nothing less than compensation for higher interest rates imposed by a very rigid banking system, which is able to discriminate on price according to the size and location of companies.

After the 1970s industrial slump, a massive intervention was undertaken to favour the reorganisation of large enterprises (law 675/1977), and to promote R&D activities (law 46/1982). Both laws went into effect many months after their approval, because of opposition by the European Commission. Community authorities considered the two laws to be infringements of Article 92 of the Treaty of Rome and re-examined the intervention programmes in order to accept only those specific aids which were in accordance with Community rules (see Table 10.2).

Table 10.1   *Italy's main industrial policy laws*

Year	Act	Content
1952	L 949	Development of small and medium firms
1957	L 634	Industrialisation of Southern regions
1960	L 1061	Credit to commercial companies
1961	L 1470	Industrial reconversion of small and medium firms
1965	L 1329	Acquisition of new machines by small and medium firms
1967	L 131	Buyer credit
1968	L 1089	Applied research
1971	L 184	Creation of the public body to rescue bankrupt firms (GEPI)
	L 1101	Restructurating of textile firms
1972	L 464	Restructurating of small and medium firms
1975	L 517	Modernisation of commercial companies
1976	L 183	Creation of the Fund for small and medium firms
	DPR 902	Restructuring of Northern small and medium firms
1977	L 675	Industrial restructuring; revision of all the laws on industrial intervention
1979	L 95	Official legal regime for managing large bankrupt firms
1981	L 240	Export pools for small and medium firms
1982	L 46	National Fund for technological innovation
	L 63	Restructurating of consumer electronics
	L 308	Energy saving and development of new energy sources
	DL 697	Modernisation of commercial companies
1983	L 696	Acquisition of new machines by small and medium firms
1986	L 64	Extraordinary intervention in the South
1987	L 399	Acquisition of machinery by small and medium firms

Table 10.2   *Disputes between Italy and the EC over the application of laws 675/1977 and 46/1982*

Sector	Outcome
Fashion	
textiles – clothing	1
footwear – leather	1
Electronics	
computers and microelectronics	2
appliances	3
Steel	5
Chemicals	
man-made fibres	1
secondary	3
Mechanical engineering	3
Paper	
mass	1
special	3
Food and drink	3
Cars	4
Car parts	3
Aerospace	5
Environment	5

Key:

1 – national subsidies forbidden
2 – national subsidies allowed
3 – national subsidies allowed, notification to EC required
4 – national subsidies allowed only in situations specified by EC
5 – national subsidies allowed only within Community Programmes

This high level of aid testifies to a rigid, central bureaucracy, which provides subsidies to compensate for operating disadvantages simply because it is not able to impose a real process of institutional change. Ultimate evidence of this rigidity is the public support of investment in the Mezzogiorno. Central government has for decades given public subsidies to relocate industrial plants to the Southern regions of the country. Money was given from central government to individual companies through the banking system to acquire machinery, without any attempt to create the network of relations that is the real core of industrialisation. The result has been a large proportion of firm failure.

On the other hand, central government intervention has weakened regional government, and the new structural approach proposed by the EC has not been implemented. The Integrated Mediterranean Programmes, which require an active role from local authorities, are not working, so the Commission recently redirected grants from Southern Italy to France.

The banking system and financial market
After half a century, the Italian banking system is still governed by the 1936 law. The banking system is largely directly owned by the state (almost 90% of deposits), the ordinary banks are not allowed to act as commercial banks, and the international operations of Italian banks are still very limited.

On the other hand, it has to be noted that the Italian stock market is not large enough adequately to control the efficiency of individual companies: 207 companies are quoted on the Milan stock exchange, and of these 91 belong to 9 conglomerates, accounting for 80% of total capital quoted. These conglomerates are either state controlled or closely controlled by family concerns, so that takeovers are very difficult.

Less than 5% of mergers and acquisitions involved companies listed on the Milan stock exchange. The recent wave of mergers and acquisitions has largely been realised through direct agreement between companies, without any protection for minority owners and without public information on what is happening. The Antitrust Commission was established only on 1 January 1991. Nevertheless, the completion of the Single Market will promote a change in this rigid situation by inducing increased competition within the banking and financial system. The potential (and, in the near future, actual) competition from the European banks is rapidly inducing a process of modernisation among Italian banks, and a strong effort by parliament to initiate financial regulations in order promote the creation of new financial institutions.

Concluding remarks
Italian industrial policy has been used as a buffer against international crises and to compensate for structural features of the

domestic industrial and financial system. The completion of the Single Market, the reinforcement of Articles 92–94 (concerning state aid) and of Article 90 (regarding public companies), and the reform of structural policies (Article 130) are forcing the Italian government to face the crucial aspects of industrial strategy managed by the government. A positive result has been a reform of university rules (23/11/90), making it possible for universities to co-operate with local authorities and private companies to develop applied research and undertake testing for industry.

Part V

THE EUROPEAN
COMMUNITY

Industrial strategy and structural policies

Different perspectives on European integration

The present stage of European integration, promoted by the Single European Act signed in 1985 and having effect from 1 July 1987, may be seen from two different perspectives.

The first view emphasises that the completion of the Single Market offers a great opportunity for improving firm efficiency. The potential gains to be derived from the removal of the residual barriers to trade inside the Common Market concern possible reductions in unit costs of production through company reorganisation in a more competitive context (Commission, 1988a, Cecchini, 1988).

In this sense, the economic theory concerning the completion of the Single Market, the so-called 'Economics of 1992' (Commission, 1985) does not appear to differ from the already consolidated economy of the Common Market, where consumer advantages stem simply from intensive use of economies of scale. In practice, this approach provides clear support for mergers, offering powerful sustenance to the present process of economic concentration.

The second view stresses that the Single Market approach is a different pathway to European integration based on a very complex process of institutional harmonisation, aimed at linking the efficiency, equity and stability targets. The 1985 White Paper (Commission, 1985) and the Padoa Schioppa Report, (1987) stated that the process of European integration is definitely based on the promotion of market forces. However, it requires the implementation of a set of public regulations and structural policies to prevent the search for efficiency from favouring monopolization and market distortion, and squeezing the equity rights established for all the members of the Community.

It is a matter of fact that the present stage of European integration is based on a substantial U-turn in the policy-making approach of the Community. The Single European Act represents the transition from a centralised model of public intervention (the Commission acting as a central bureaucracy directly managing policies and commanding national administrations) to an approach based on the co-operation of various national and local authorities, all with the power to formulate norms and implement policies which must conform with those enforced by other authorities. This model of diffused political power has a central authority whose basic function is to promote the harmonisation of local powers (the principle of reciprocal recognition) and to intervene in situations where the scale of operations is beyond the scope of a single local authority (the principle of subsidiarity). The 'central' authority (that is to say, the Commission) also has to prevent 'local' public policies (of national and regional governments) from distorting competition among companies by subsidising inefficient producers. This marks a shift from a 'French' approach to a 'German' approach to policy-making.

The acceptance of the principle of institutional harmonisation starts a process of competition among public authorities to establish regulations and standards for industry and to define public policies for favouring the competitiveness of local producers. This principle of institutional competition clearly indicates an evolutionary model of policy-making, which leaves the most active national and local authorities to drive the process of economic and political integration.

This U-turn in the policy-making approach was supported by the adoption of the majority rule for the basic decisions taken by the Community authority. The first stage of European integration was crucially based on the central role of the member states, which had to decide *de facto* on a unanimous basis. The unanimity rule, required for all important decisions of the Council of Ministers, gave a strong power of 'veto' to the less efficient governments.

This approach became a substantial constraint on Community operations during the years of the economic crisis, when each national government tested its legitimacy by guaranteeing the conditions for survival of their national production structures. From the late 1960s to the mid-1980s the process of European integration slowed down, despite the fact that during this period the Community expanded from the original six to ten members, because each government used its veto power to protect its weaker competitors.

The acceptance of the principle of reciprocal recognition, which was strengthened by the majority rule, reinforced the need to ensure a balanced expansion of the Community, not through the reinforcement of the veto, but by providing the means to accelerate the development of the less-favoured areas.

To prevent the unified market from becoming ruled by dominant companies restricting new entry and trade practices (Jacquemin, Buigues and Ilzkovitz, 1989), and to prevent national and local governments from supporting domestic champions, hence altering market competition, the completion of the European Single Market requires full application of competition policies. The Commission recently passed regulations on concentration (Regulations EEC n.4064/89, 21 December 1989, *EC Official Bulletin* L.395, 30 December 1989) and reinforce strict control over those national actions which could infringe Articles 92 – 94 of the Treaty of Rome (Commission, 1989c).

Both actions are a necessary complement to the removal of residual non-tariff barriers and to the promotion of reciprocal recognition of local standards (Cecchini, 1988). Nevertheless, the efficiency approach, based on the recognition of the leading role of the most efficient competitors (both companies and governments), has been coupled with a thorough reform of Community structural policies, in order to promote small and medium-sized firms, especially in the less-developed areas.

The 1985 White Paper (Commission, 1985) clearly established that competition has to be sustained not by simply creating a wider internal market and applying a stringent competition policy, but by encouraging the entry of new companies, and by giving the weaker competitors the opportunity to grow. The efficiency goal has made it necessary to pursue the complementary aims of stability and equality in all the regions of the Community, as was clearly stated by the Padoa Schioppa Report (1987).

This perspective necessarily takes into account the relation existing between policies to promote market forces and policies to develop the less-favoured areas. The risk is that stronger competition could lead to inequality and instability throughout the

Community. Therefore, the full application of the new approach to policy-making requires a reinforcement of the structural policy of the Community. Because the European Community is essentially based on the promotion of free trade, public regulation and structural policies are acceptable only if they create the conditions for more effective competition. This means giving favourable opportunities to weaker competitors to increase their efficiency, and therefore promoting more balanced, equal and stable growth.

The reform of structural funds

The Commission of the European Communities defines 'structural policies' as those actions oriented to sustaining the development of the less-favoured areas and sectors of the Community, in order 'to promote throughout the Community a harmonious development of economic activities, a continuous and balanced expansion . . . closer relations between the States belonging to it', as required by the opening statement of the Treaty of Rome. These structural actions are: the so-called structural funds (the Regional Development Fund – ERDF, the Social Fund – ESR, and the Agricultural Guidance and Guarantee Fund – EAGGF, only for promoting farm reorganisation – the so-called 'orientation'); European Investment Bank (EIB) interventions; the Integrated Mediterranean Programmes (IMPs); the Development Integrated Operations; the programmes supporting the industrial modernisation of Portugal and intervention in natural disaster areas; specific programmes in training, promotion, and for information connected with these funds (Commission, 1989b, sections 4 and 10).[1]

In its early stages, the Community was oriented to a sectoral approach to policy-making. Territorial disparities were considered to be a matter for national government intervention.[2] The creation of the European Regional Development Fund in 1975 was based on the notion that regional policy was a national matter, and, therefore, fund allocation was based on fixed quotas agreed among the national governments. A new stage of reform began in 1984, when the fixed national quota system was abandoned and a mixed system was established, based on a minimum quota plus an amount to be negotiated with the Commission.

Substantial reform was enacted only with Single European Act approval. The Single European Act amended the Treaty of Rome by introducing the new Article 130 A – E. This reinforces the equality and stability goals of the Community and defines the policy instruments to achieve these aims (130 A and B); the ERDF is defined within the Treaty of Rome as an instrument devoted to correcting territorial imbalances (C); the structural funds (ERDF, ESR and EAGGF) are reformed so that they can be used, together with EIB resources and other EC policies, to develop the less-favoured areas (D and E) (Commission, 1989a).

The reform of the structural funds, which went into effect on 1 January 1989, must be regarded as one of the main changes in the policy-making approach of the Community. The new allocation model is based on national plans submitted to the Commission for approval. Since these plans have to involve the regional governments, the main result of this reform is an explicit recognition of the role of the regional governments.

The IMPs pioneered the new approach of integration of policy interventions by the three levels of policy-making (European, national, regional). The structural fund reform fully conforms to this territorial concentration of integrated policy interventions, managed by different political actors. The new strategy for European integration enacted by the Commission is to overcome the previous dominant role of national governments, by bringing the regions into play as primary actors in the policy-making process.

Thus, in the first phase, the allocation of the structural funds was decided by the national states; in the second phase, allocation was decided as a bilateral game, played by the Commission and national governments, within a rigid framework of national balances; in the third phase, the Community is moving toward a multilateral game, based on a very complex intergovernmental arrangement involving the Commission, national governments and regional governments (Leonardi, 1990).

Although Community funds have rapidly increased over the last few years, the most important element of the new phase is that the Community state aids have 'directed' national interventions: the structural funds have to be allocated jointly by the Community, national and regional authorities on the basis established by the Community itself.

Local partnership is the key element of the structural fund reform (Commission, 1989a, pp. 14–15). Not only is this principle crucial for ERDF intervention in the less-favoured areas, but it becomes the basic approach for any operations of the Community that concern small, and medium-sized enterprises (Commission, 1988b), and by and large for any action having a territorial impact.

Structural action expenses have rapidly increased in the last few years: 'structural actions' represented 23.6% of the 1990 EC Budget, compared with 14.4% in 1983, 16.6% in 1986 and 20.4% in 1989.[3] The Commission decided that the structural funds must be doubled between 1988 (4.1 billion ECU) and 1993 (9.2 billion ECU); interventions for Objective 1 (the promotion of development in the less-favoured areas of the Community) account for 63% of the expenses (Commission, 1990c, pp. 14 and 15).

Although expenses for the EAGCF-guarantee operations have decreased over time and those for innovation promotion programmes have increased, agricultural protection costs still absorbed 54% of the EC Budget in 1990 (compared with 70% in 1985), while innovation promotion was only about 4% of the Budget (compared with 2.5% in 1985).

Competition policy and control of state aid

The reinforcement of structural policies is a crucial aspect of the Single Market approach to industrial policy. The Bangemann Report, issued on 26 November 1990, clearly states that the new industrial policy approach is based on the balanced development of the Single Market (see also Commission, 1990b). This balanced development requires the full application of four sets of policies:

(1) the removal of the residual non-tariff barriers and the harmonisation of market standards throughout the Community, in order to create the institutional conditions for the effective establishment of a single market for goods, services, labour and capital;

(2) an effective competition policy to avoid restrictive practices, monopolisation, excessive concentration and unfair public aids to national companies re-creating internal barriers to new competition in this Single Market;

(3) public support for innovation, especially for very innovative sectors, and for the development of small companies through the promotion of a network of innovators;

(4) structural policies to create a positive environment in which to develop new industrial and service activities in the less-favoured areas.

Market competition is seen as the engine of a dynamic economy, but it requires an effective competition policy to prevent monopolisation by the existing competitors and structural policies to promote the entry of new competitors. Nevertheless, full application of this approach to industrial policy has considerable political impact on national state power, because it limits national states' ability to manage industrial strategy directly.

Member states have resisted this approach. A very interesting case is provided by Italian industrial policy towards small and medium-sized firms. The Commission criticised the Italian government for the volume and nature of subsidies given to national firms. According to data provided by the Commission, (1989c, 1990d), state aid to Italian firms is twice that given by the French, German and British governments (see Table 11.1). Moreover, in France, Germany and the United Kingdom, most of the subsidies are granted because of Community rules (agriculture, fishery, transport, steel and coal), whereas in Italy these represent only one-third.

Table 11.1 *Subsides distributed by national governments*

	Total subsidies		To manufacturing industry		To manuf. industry minus steel and ship building	
	% of GDP	ECU per employee	% of value added	ECU per employee	% of value added	ECU per employee
Italy (EC est.)	5.66	1,357	16.72	6,226	15.8	5,951
Italy (Bank of Italy est.)	4.26	1,022	10.97	4,086	10.1	3,084
France	2.68	792	4.93	1,649	3.6	1,223
Germany	2.53	761	3.03	982	2.9	940
UK	1.79	396	3.81	971	2.9	757

Note: Subsidies to manufacturing industry do not include contributions to agriculture, fishery, transport or coal where subsidies are given because of Community rules.
Source: Commission (1989c).

Italian industrial policy laws are disputed by the Commission acting under the provisions of Articles 92 – 93 of the Treaty (see, for instance, Table 10.2). The Commission considers that the Italian policy approach is still based on direct transfers to individual firms aimed at compensating for inefficiency not removing the causes of inefficiency.

Italian industrial policy to small firms has traditionally been aimed at reducing the high interest rates for machinery acquisitions; it is simply an intervention to support the inefficient Italian financial system, which is still based on a very rigid state-controlled banking system (see also Chapter 10). This approach considers the individual firms in isolation, having the ultimate aim of acquiring machinery at a reasonable price so as to be individually more competitive.

This policy is even more indefensible when account is taken of the success of the Italian districts, founded on the flexible specialisation model. This pathway to industrialisation is largely focused on the integration of a variety of actors, interacting at local level. A stable social community is the core of the industrial system, and the promotion of endogenous forces stems from a strengthening of social and productive integration. A variety of experiences throughout Europe, from Emilia Romagna to Baden-Württemberg, from Catalonia to Jutland, shows clearly that acceleration of growth in the 1980s was not just a matter of individual productive efficiency, but was essentially a matter of promoting the establishment of a network of innovators, and providing information, training, research facilities, and entry opportunities to final markets.

This model has positively influenced the reform of European structural policy. Nevertheless, the Italian government refused to apply these principles in full and reinforced a policy approach based on direct transfers from the central government to individual companies. This approach was applied in the Southern regions. The Mezzogiorno has been considered a special intervention area since the postwar period: a central agency was created in 1952 (Cassa per il Mezzogiorno) in order to manage all the interventions directly, because local administrations were not considered capable of driving the industrialisation process. After the closure of the Cassa in 1986, the intervention was still managed through a restricted number of central agencies, despite the fact that a constitutional reform established regional governments in 1976.

The basic assumptions behind this special intervention were: (i) the Mezzogiorno is a homogeneous area, with common problems; (ii) the local authorities have neither the technical capacity nor the political legitimation to intervene in these problems, thus a central intervention, going beyond local authorities, is required. Public policy was designed to force a process of development through the relocalisation of large plants. Public shareholding companies were ordered to invest in the Southern regions in order to create new jobs; they invested in capital-intensive sectors, which were seen as the core of the rapid industrialisation process (refining, chemicals, steel, auto). The 1970s economic crisis had a very negative impact on most of these new plants, inducing a further decline of these depressed areas.[4]

The result of this policy is clearly indicated by the evidence that unemployment in the South grew in the second part of the 1980s, while the Northern regions were near to full employment. Italy is thus the only country in Europe to have increased internal regional disparities in terms of unemployment (less than 5% in Emilia–Romagna and Lombardia, more than 20% in several areas of the Mezzogiorno; Commission 1991.)

It is also a matter of fact that the present condition of the Mezzogiorno is quite different from in the past. Some regions have shown significant growth. Eastern regions such as Abruzzi, Molise and Puglia present a clear development, at least in terms of income per capita (unemployment is increasing because of the entry of women and young people into the labour market). The other regions have experienced a clear decline in terms of both employment and income per capita; they are also facing a dramatic collapse in the social fabric of life, with an explosion of criminal activity.

The Adriatic Sea regions succeeded because an endogenous process of growth, based on small and medium-sized companies, started in the late 1970s. This process flourished in Abruzzo e Molise largely because central intervention ignored these mountainous regions and no large plants were installed by public companies.[5]

The entire Mezzogiorno is regarded as a less-favoured area, and therefore it is part of the Objective 1 zone. However, the Commission has disputed most of the interventions made by the Italian government, because they are based on subsidies, they are not targeted at specific areas and sectors, and they are neither coordinated with the Commission nor integrated on a local basis with the regional authorities' actions. Recently, the Commission transferred 250 million ECU from Italy to France because the Italian regions have not used the Community aids for IMPs. Checking the IMPs, it is also evident that Molise, Abruzzi and Puglia, like the Northern regions, have well-managed IMPs and therefore they have received Community subsidies. The least-favoured areas were not able to organise a local network of productive partnership, and therefore they missed the opportunity because prolonged dependency on the central government reduced their capacity to promote endogenous development.

It is also a matter of fact that the Spanish regions, which gained autonomy in the recent past, performed very well in the 1980s, relative to the very bad results of Italian regions, especially those receiving massive central interventions (Commission 1991).

The risks and opportunities of the new policy-making approach

The new approach adopted by the Commission reverses the old practice of the national governments of providing subsidies to individual firms to compensate for structural imbalances. The aim is to enforce a progressive structural adjustment by reinforcing the local network of productive and service relations in order to stimulate endogenous market forces. This policy approach is consistent with the general attitude of the Community towards market forces. It is introducing competition among European regions, based on the local environmental and institutional conditions for industrial development. The present goal of the reformed structural funds is to help the less-favoured areas to take a part in this game.

Nevertheless, regional roles vary from country to country. The regionalisation process in Europe has been the result of different political processes. The very concept of 'region' and the extent of regional powers differ from country to country (e.g. West Germany is constitutionally a federal state while the UK and France are still very centralised). Thus, a crucial aim of the new approach is to enforce a difficult process of harmonisation between the very different administrative organisations of member states by promoting an effective strengthening of the regional administration level, and by supporting an internal restructuring of the regional administration to be involved in the multilateral policy game.

It has also to be stressed that regional governments are not equally active. In all the European countries, the most active regional governments are those that administer the most favoured areas (such as Catalonia, Lombardy and Emilia–Romagna, Baden–Württemberg, Rhone Alps). They claim autonomy from the national level by looking for transnational alliances with other strong regions, and for an explicit direct relation with the Commission (Cooke, 1990).

In contrast, the economic ills of the less-favoured areas are usually accompanied by a weak local administration, which is traditionally dependent on the central authority and used to dealing with local problems by claiming support from the national government rather than directly implementing new development projects. The new approach risks failure because the most active actors, which are able to participate effectively in the game, are already the strongest areas of the Community, and the national governments can reinforce their position by claiming the less-favoured areas.

Several studies stress that regional disparities have increased in the recent past and could be greater in the future (DATAR, 1989; Pirelli, 1990; Commission 1991). The core of Europe is still restricted to the central regions of West Germany and the Paris and London areas; this area accounts for 20% of total European territory and for 40% of annual income. There is a rapidly growing area (the southern regions of France, the northern regions of Italy, Catalonia and Valencia), but Europe is still characterised by a large periphery with slow growth and poor infrastructure. The need for structural action seems to be greater than was expected when the Single Act was signed and the structural funds reformed (Commission 1991).

The new structural policy approach, coupled with the reinforcement of Article 92 of the Treaty of Rome, makes it clear that these disparities often affect local authorities' autonomous capacity to formulate structural policies. Therefore. a crucial issue for the future of Europe concerns the efficiency and autonomy of local authorities and, moreover, the promotion of democracy throughout Europe. This needs to take into account the diversity that exists in social, economic and cultural terms among European regions, but also should allow and force them to take part in the same process in order to provide equal opportunities for all citizens (Hingel, 1990).

This process of institutional reorganisation is more complex than it was at the end of the 1980s. The German reunification, the Eastern European countries' political and economic reorganisation, the dramatic events in the Soviet Union, the persisting weakness of the Southern regions, the immigration pressures from less-developed countries, the threat of a new global recession are all introducing a variety of institutional problems that could seriously constrain the present stage of European integration. The main risk is that the European Community will not be able to face and tackle these problems, and therefore that an oversimplified approach to European integration emerges.

Notes

1 The EAGGF is based on two separate sub-funds the EAGGF-orientation fund is defined as a structural fund, while the EAGGF-guarantee is not (Commission, 1989b, section 13).

2 Although sectoral policies in coal, steel, agriculture, transport and shipbuilding contained provisions to correct the regional problems arising out of the structural adjustment of these sectors, the only general instrument of an explicitly regional policy provided by the Treaty – Article 3(j) – was the European Investment Bank, which was limited to providing loans to member states for developing basic infrastructures. During the first 20 years of operation, from 1958 to 1977, the EIB allocated 65% of its loans to regional development projects in the less-favoured areas of the Community. In 1978 the EIB created the New Community Instrument to help small and medium-sized companies to finance productive investments. Also the European Social Fund, provided by Article 3(i) of the Treaty of Rome to promote the re-employment of workers involved in industrial crisis, had a clearly territorial impact, but was designed to support sectoral policies.

3 Because the EC Budget organisation has changed many times, I have reclassified the entries of the 1983–1988 budgets according to the 1989–90 scheme, in order to compare expenses over time (Commission, 1989b and previous Annual Reports).

4 Most of these plants were called 'cathedrals-in-the-desert', not because they were built in a desert, but because the rapid construction of a new plant in the modern sector, largely subsidised by the central government, destroyed the traditional sector by attracting the best manpower, inflating real estate prices and distorting traditional social and economic values.

5 A modern Fiat plant was established in south Molise; it had a positive impact because Fiat also relocated some of its subcontractors, looking to reorganize a local network of medium-sized firms. On the other hand, the currently most depressed areas of Puglia are those that in the past received the most active public intervention in the steel, shipbuilding and chemical industries (Taranto, Brindisi).

References

Cecchini, P. (1988), *The European Challenge 1992*, Aldershot, Hants: Wildwood House.

Commission of the European Communities (1985), *White Paper on Completing the Internal Market*, Brussels.

Commission of the European Communities (1987), 'The Single Act: a New Frontier for Europe', *Bulletin of the EC*, Supplement.

Commission of the European Communities (1988a), 'The Economics of 1992', *European Economy* No.35, March.

Commission of the European Communities (1988b), *Operations of the European Community concerning small and medium sized enterprises*, Task Force SME, Brussels.

Commission of the European Communities (1989a), *Vademecum sulla riforma dei fondi strutturali comunitari*, Documento, Brussels.

Commission of the European Communities (1989b), *XXII Relazione generale sull'attività delle Communità Europee*, Brussels.

Commission of the European Communities (1989c), *Primo censimento degli aiuti di stato nella Comunità Europea*, Brussels.

Commission of the European Communities (1990a), *Quinto rapporto della commissione al consiglio e al parlemento europeo relativo al completamento del mercato interno*, Brussels, 28 March.

Commission of the European Communities (1990b), *Industrial Policy in an Open and Competitive Environment, Guidelines for a Community Approach, Working Paper*, Brussels, 14 September.

Commission of the European Communities (1990c), *Relazione annuale sull'attuazione della Riforma dei fondi strutturali*, Brussels, 15 November.

Commission of the European Communities (1990d), *Second Survey on State Aids in the European Community in the Manufacturing and Certain Other Sectors*, Brussels.

Commission of the European Communities (1991), *Le regioni degli anni novanta. Quarta relazione periodica sulla situazione socioeconomica e sullo sviluppo delle regioni della Comunità*, Brussels.

Cooke, P. (1990), Globalization of Economic organization and the emergence of regional interstate partnership', mimeo Department of City & Regional Planning, University of Wales College of Cardiff, Cardiff.

DATAR (1989), 'Les Villes européennes', *La Documentation Française*, May.

Jacquemin, A., Buigues, P. and Ilzkovitz, F. (1989), 'Horizontal mergers and competition policy in the European Community', *European Economy*, No.40.

Hingel, A. J. (1990), *Diversity, Equality and Community Cohesion*, FAST Working Paper PD1/01, Brussels.

Leonardi, R. (1990), '*The regional revolution in Europe: the Single European Act and the Regional Fund*', mimeo, European University Institute, Florence.

Mueller, D. (1986), *Public Choice*, Cambridge: Cambridge University Press.

Padoa Schioppa, T. (1987), *Efficiency, Stability and Equity. A Strategy for the Evolution of the Economic System of the E.C.*, Brussels.

Pirelli – Ufficio Studi Economici (1990), '*Le regioni europee in prospettiva*', mimeo Milan.

A critical assessment of the 1992 project agenda for industry policy

The Single European Act 1987, due to come into force on 31 December 1992, has provided a platform for the most ambitious attempt by far to date to establish a European industry policy. Since the Commission of the European Communities (CEC) has struggled for a very long time in this area to establish an agenda with real substance and force relative to national programmes, the opportunity is unsurprisingly being grabbed with both hands. The agenda is not what is popularly supposed, however, though the objectives actually sought have long antecedents in EC thinking. This paper sets out to clarify EC policy, and to comment thereon.

Industry policy is generally distinguished from macroeconomic policies (fiscal or monetary) chiefly by its discriminatory intervention in the allocation of resources between sectors or companies. It is usually justified as a means of correcting or improving on the operation of the market in the real world (e.g. where unrestrained activity produces concentrations of power inimical to 'free' competition, where externalities exist, or where strategic developments are not encouraged by market signals or require greater resources than are available to firms; see also Part I of this volume). There are well-rehearsed debates over the desirability of such intervention at all, and over the validity of this being orchestrated at a European (rather than national or local) level if it should be judged appropriate.

1992 and industry policy

Textbook accounts of EC industry policy focus on three chief elements:

(1) *Competition policy*. Empowered by several articles of the Treaty of Rome, this covers policy against cartels (under Article 85); against the abuse of monopoly power and, derivatively, for the control of mergers (under Article 86); and against unfair subsidisation by member state governments of their national champions (under Article 92).

(2) Support of *research and development* programmes in areas, such as electronics, where European companies have lagged behind, with spin-off debilitation for the general competitiveness and level of technological development in European industry. This has been led by the ESPRIT programme.

(3) *Restructuring of traditional industries*, particularly steel and textiles. This has sought to manage the social and economic consequences of decline, and to even out some of the regional impact thereof.

Although neo-liberals and interventionists in the EC have disagreed sharply on the appropriate extent of such activities, there has been some tacit consensus on the practical need for some policies in these areas, and that they should be European rather than just national, even through the torrid years for interventionism of the 1980s. Disagreements have to some extent concerned whether the role of a European (or national) state should be regulatory, husbanding the working of management and competition, or more actively developmental. Most of the policies outlined above have been regulatory or mildly supportive of business, and as such have not tested the limits of assent.

However, the completion of the Single Market adds a more extensive potential role for the CEC, laid out in a policy document seeking to define the remit of EC activity published on 26 November 1990 (CEC, 1990). The elements proposed in that document emphasise 'adjustment', with the EC's tasks revolving around the catalysis, acceleration, and provision of the prerequisites for this. It is the nature and direction of the adjustment that is perceived as central to the 1992 project, and the particular developmental slant which it embodies, that must be clarified.

The direction of the CEC's underlying approach to the problems of the European economy, and the means for tackling it, was in many respects already in place by the 1970s. The Memorandum on Industrial Policy of March 1970 (the Colonna report) presented five key themes for a European initiative. These included the already familiar removal of trade barriers and the harmonisation of rules and regulations, but added the improvement of management techniques, European solidarity against extra-EC competition, and the promotion of mergers within the EC (but across national boundaries) to meet that competition. A Eurocompany Statute was drafted that year as a first facilitative step to providing the legal basis for trans-European incorporation. However, it ran foul of the fierce debate on industrial democracy owing to its German-style worker participation proposals, and went into suspension for more than two decades.

A major inspiration of this had been a growing concern about the growth of foreign, almost entirely American, investment in Europe, most dramatically depicted in the forebodings of Servan-Schreiber's *Le Défi Americain* (1967). Servan-Schreiber had advocated the encouragement of European business collaboration to build a counterforce to this threat, and now his idea was to be adopted and, over the next 20 years, rationalised and developed into a policy for the promotion of Euro-champions. European companies were to be the main means of enhancing Europe's lagging performance, by uniting into giants capable of taking on American (and latterly Japanese) competitors at home and in the global market place.

This policy does glint through in the practice of the less controversial elements of EC industry policy outlined earlier. Actions against cartels, for instance, are restrained in the case of arrangements which facilitate the production and distribution of goods or aid technological progress; these can thus be represented as joint ventures. The Industrial Affairs Directorate even sponsored a cartel to share out the market in synthetic fibres between the main producers in 1978, which was sustained despite criticism from the Competition Directorate. Similar arrangements effectively accompanied the management of decline in the steel industry.

In the meantime, the ESPRIT programme was actually the result of pressure from the 12 largest European companies in the information technology industry, and has concentrated on attempting to promote co-operation and build exclusively European players in the high-tech fields. When two participating UK companies, ICL and STC, were taken over (by Fujitsu and Northern Telecom of Canada, respectively), the European Parliament Budget Committee expressed fears of 'foreign raiders' reaping the benefits of EC spending (*International Management*, February 1991).

Periodic attempts through the 1970s and 1980s to define a more active and explicit policy on industrial affairs, pushed most strenuously by the French outside Brussels, fell on the stony ground of the upsurge of the New Right. The Single European Act allowed this preoccupation with creating a European big business counter-challenge to the USA to find new life. Its prominence in the 1992 project is readily appreciated from a cursory examination of certain features of the analysis of the supposed benefits to flow therefrom in the CEC's *Costs of Non-Europe* studies. Economies of greater production scale, in particular, are the expected result, and in the *CONE* studies these are expected to yield benefits at least as great as those from the lowering of non-tariff barriers, and greater than (as well as implicitly contrary to) those expected from the erosion of monopoly power in single member states (Cecchini, 1988, p. 80).

There are numerous critical assumptions in this claim. They include the supposition that the restructuring of European capital will take the form of an intra-European process, and in three ways: *internal restructuring*, involving the rationalisation of product lines in a single company; *external restructuring*, via mergers and takeovers across European borders but within the EC; and *co-operation*, through the development of joint ventures between European companies to pool expertise and resources. Four-fifths of scale economies are expected to flow from this restructuring, the presumption again being that scale and restructuring are viable routes to the enhancement of efficiency. The preferred format is cooperation, since takeovers run the risk of obliterating what may still be important national symbols within member states. Lastly, it is assumed, apparently, that European companies are somehow more beneficial to European economies than foreign-owned companies, even when both are multinationals.

A critique of Euro-champions policy

Once identified, this 1992 agenda becomes vulnerable to a series of criticisms. First, the last assumption noted is far from easy to justify – particularly in the economic terms of analysis adopted by the CEC. In neither neoclassical nor radical economic theory is it easy to find any justification for supposing that a country or region's 'own' MNCs are more likely to enhance local economic welfare than are foreign-owned companies.

Of course, the basis of this contention is really political nationalism enhanced by the fear of the invader, bearing US imperialism, as epitomised in Servan-Schreiber's original onslaught. Yet such has been the growth in investment outflows from Europe, and the relative decline in those from the USA, that investment holdings by European firms in the USA are now at least as great as those the other way, even provoking a backlash resentment from the USA in recent years which ironically echoes that of *Le Défi Americain*.

On the other hand, many American companies have been established in Europe for decades, with an estimated total of 2 million employees in European subsidiaries of US corporations by the late 1980s. Moreover, 85% of US company sales in Europe were locally produced, implying too that employment was European (Gittelman, 1990). Whether this European employment base is even more likely to apply to European MNCs competing abroad is dubious (and, on past records, most unlikely for UK companies in particular). More relevant may be the branch-plant syndrome fear: that non-European companies will operate largely low-tech, low R&D, low-control 'screwdriver' operations in Europe, and keep the key strategic operations for their home base. This has some potential substance, undoubtedly, but would need to rely on a detailed assessment of the costs and benefits of foreign direct investment (FDI) by MNCs from overseas (and from Europe to other economies). It could be argued that the fear is more real for certain peripheral employment regions within the EC, and that Europe is such a crucial market that it tends to attract many key functions and not just assembly operations. In any case, the CEC analyses singularly fail to even recognise, let alone address, the issues and problems in this area, for all the central role of Euro-MNCs in their proclaimed benefits from 1992.

In some respects, the arguments raised above may exacerbate the fears in Brussels. The invaders are already among us! Not just the Americans, but the Japanese, their threat reflected in the resistance in some EC quarters to allowing production by Nissan in Washington or Toyota in Burnaston to count as EC output for purposes of import quota calculation. The second criticism which may be raised, then, concerns the EC's misunderstanding of the whole process in which they are seeking to intervene. In labelling some MNCs as 'theirs' and embracing others as 'ours', they are failing to understand what is happening is a global international-isation of capital, from whatever home base (Grahl and Teague, 1990). Promoting concentration and collaboration of Euro-capital, on this account, will only accelerate the whole process a little.

Thirdly, though, there are also doubts whether the process will take the shape that Brussels hopes it will. One problem may be that mergers will be not so much cross-border and intra-European, as the CEC exhorts, but a result of acquisitions by US and other 'outsiders' trying to get themselves inside the walls of a potential Fortress Europe and at the same time to exploit 'the new Klondike' (*Guardian*, 21 May 1990) of the completed market. The figures for the late 1980s do show some signs of such a rush (CTC, 1989), but more significantly they suggest that the preferred joint venture approach is liable to draw European companies closer not to other Europeans, but to the Americans or Japanese. Kay (1990, 1991) identifies such a pattern, and suggests that it is logical: companies wish to co-operate not with their closest competitors, but with firms that have other advantages and are less direct rivals. They prefer to take over their competitors. Such a viewpoint has been confirmed in a recent British Institute of Management survey of British business opinion, and is also buttressed by recent decisions by some European electronics companies to look for 'more dynamic alliances with the US and Japan' than they can find in Europe (*International Management*, July/August 1991).

In any case, fourthly, there are extremely good reasons for doubting the efficiency benefits of a policy based on scale. The argument that the greatest disadvantage of European companies is the size of their home market and their consequent limited production scale is relatively easily questioned. Geroski (1989) shows that three-quarters of European industries have a min-imum efficient scale of production that is less than 5% of the total Community market. Only aircraft, chemicals, electric motors and paper are seen as plausible sectoral sites for significant scale economies as a result of 1992. Moreover, Rugman (1986) demonstrates that the largest European companies fall short only of the largest ten US corporations in size – and those ten are no more efficient than other US corporations, suggesting that it is other management features which account for differentials in profitability.

Fifthly, the same argument applies *a fortiori* to a case for efficiency based on joint ventures and mergers. Studies of mergers in operation have been almost unanimous in their conclusion that the effect is not synergy but dissipation (Cowling, 1982; Whittington, 1980). One international study of almost 800 mergers in six countries concluded that no price, efficiency or sales benefits could be found; only empire-building made much sense of the activity at all (Mueller, 1980). The tasks involved in bringing together different organisations tended to create managerial havoc, though they may be less obdurate than those of managing joint ventures where no one organisation has the ability to make and enforce decisions. The problems of Renault–Volvo or GEC–Siemens in making their alliances pay illustrate this in recent times in the European context.

The sixth point extends the above with reference specifically to the encouragement of multinational operation as well as scale. Geroski criticises the CEC proposals on the grounds that 'they focus on what is technologically possible without considering organizational or managerial constraints' (1989, p. 39). Indeed, Cecchini himself notes that success in the pursuit of the intended restructuring requires 'new modes of company management and organization' (1988, p. 87), while the CEC case elaborated by Emerson *et al.* acknowledges that 'firms' ability to meet these challenges depends on their managerial capacity' (1988, p. 170). These uncertainties appear then to be set to one side, however, and the risk of failure is quietly erased from the deliberations.

Yet problems and dilemmas of the management of MNCs are now well documented (Ramsay, 1990). They include pervasive difficulties in reconciling the marketing demands and managerial incentives of local responsiveness with the production and co-ordination demands of centralised organisation. Constant shifts in organisational structure reflect these contradictory pressures, compounded by the predicaments created by the tenuousness of control over geographical and cultural space and the rivalry between different managerial functions.

The implications of the critique

The analysis presented here holds out gloomy prospects for the effect of 1992, especially in so far as it relies on an industry policy resting on the creation and performance of Euro-MNCs. The economic benefits, especially in terms of jobs and competitiveness, appear far less secure than the costs in employment terms predicted for the early stages of 'adjustment'. Nor has this paper touched on the sectoral and geographical unevenness of the likely impact of the problems identified in this paper and elsewhere. Finally, the promotion and sponsorship of concentrations of capital in Europe threaten the democratic intentions of the Social Charter, and also disable the CEC, the main protagonist of the reforms associated with this, from defending them in the face of arguments concerning the imperatives of restructuring.

These conclusions should not be allowed to get out of proportion. The likely negative or neutral effects identified above may dispel optimism concerning 1992, but their effects will be at the margins in the real world. Other global and European economic developments are likely greatly to outweigh them in the scales. Moreover, the opportunities for a newly unified European labour movement (aided further by the decline of Cold War splits in the EC union ranks, let alone between the EC unions and labour organisation in Eastern Europe), and the enhanced opportunities for lobbying and joint action, and for resourcing the collection and dissemination of intelligence for collective bargaining, all provide countervailing grounds for optimism. The European labour movement, both industrially and politically, none the less needs to be aware of the real agenda and likely impact of 1992 in order to tackle the challenges effectively.

References

Cecchini, P. (1988) *The European Challenge 1992: The Benefits of a Single Market*, Aldershot: Wildwood House.

Centre on Transnational Corporations (1989), 'The impact of 1992', unattributed article in *CTC Reporter*, No.27, Spring, 21–4.

Commission of European Communities (1990), *The Impact of the Internal Market by Industrial Sector: The Challenge for Member States*, Brussels: EC.

Cowling, K. (1982), *Monopoly Capitalism*, London: Macmillan.

Emerson, M., Aujean, M., Catinat, M., Goybet, P. and Jacquemin, A. (1988), *The Economies of 1992: The E.C. Commission's Assessment of the Economic Effects of Completing the Internal Market*, Oxford: Oxford University Press.

Geroski, P. A. (1989), 'The choice between diversity and scale', in Davis E. *et al.*, *1992: Myths & Realities*, London: Centre for Business Strategy, London Business School.

Gittelman, M. (1990), 'Transnational corporations in Europe 1992: implications for developing countries', *CTC Reporter*, No.29, Spring, 35–9, 41–2.

Grahl, J. and Teague, P. (1990), *1992 – The Big Market: The Future of the European Community*, London: Lawrence & Wishart.

Kay, N. (1990), 'Industrial collaborative activity and the completion of the Single Market', mimeo.

Kay, N. (1991), 'Mergers, acquisitions and the completion of the Single Market', mimeo.

Mueller, D. C. (1980), *The Determinants and Effects of Mergers: An International Comparison*, Cambridge, Mass: Oelgeschlager, Gunn & Hain.

Ramsay, H. E. (1990), *1992: The Year of the Multinational? Corporate Restructuring and Labour in the Single Market*, Warwick Papers in Industrial Relations No.35, Coventry: Industrial Relations Research Unit, University of Warwick.

Rugman, A. M. (1986), 'European multinationals: an international comparison of size and performance', in K. Macharinza and W. Staehle (eds), *European Approaches to International Management*, Berlin: De Gruyter.

Servan-Schreiber, J. -J. (1967), *Le Défi Américain*, Paris: Denoël.

Whittington, G. (1980), 'The profitability and size of United Kingdom companies, 1960–74', *Journal of Industrial Economics*, June.

A competitive strategy for Europe

Introduction

My aim in this paper is to propose that there is a need for a *new explicit criterion* on which European competition policy should be based, and also to suggest a competitive strategy for Europe in line with the proposed criterion. The criterion suggests that competition policies should satisfy four propositions. The need for such a criterion is derived from my discussion of the concept of competition in theory and practice, and my assertion that existing policies lack a criterion or are based on implicit ones. The criterion is then proposed and discussed. Policies for Europe in line with the proposed criterion are then examined, with qualifications and conclusions.

Competition in theory and practice

The concept of competition has a very prominent place in economic theory, a prominence which moreover tends to cut across ideological boundaries. Mainstream neoclassical, Austrian and Marxist theorists all regard competition as all-important, but differ as to what exactly competition is and does. In the mainstream neoclassical tradition, for example, *competition* is primarily a type of market structure.[1] This can be perfect or imperfect. When perfect, it can be shown that a market economy can allocate resources efficiently in the Pareto sense. Departures from perfect competition hinder this outcome, and lead to 'market failure', monopoly 'welfare losses' and, thus, a need for intervention (e.g. by the state) to 'correct' the situation.[2] This is supported by theoretical models of oligopoly, such as the limit-pricing model (see e.g. Modigliani, 1958), and, in particular, by the generalised oligopoly model of Cowling and Waterson (1976). It need not be the case if oligopolistic markets are perfectly contestable, i.e. characterised by free entry and costless exit, as such markets result in price-taking behaviour (see Baumol, 1982), thus re-establishing the perfectly competitive outcome.

The above is now standard in the literature. This makes it sufficient for me to conclude that, so far as the mainstream goes, departures from perfect competition necessitate (state) intervention to (re-)establish conditions of perfect competition or perfect contestability. The exact mechanics of this unfortunately are not discussed in the mainstream. This is not surprising given the patent unrealism of some assumptions, for example perfect knowledge in the case of perfect competition. Given the potential non-feasibility of the perfect competition ideal, the alternative of *workable competition* has been proposed (see Clark, 1940). Also see Reid (1987) for a critical assessment of the notion. Establishing conditions for perfect contestability appears an easier alternative. However, this underestimates the problems associated with the assumption of free entry and costless exit. Besides the many existing critiques of this assumption, surveyed e.g. in Pitelis (1991a), in an ironic anticipation of these ideas Schumpeter (1942) had observed that 'perfectly free entry into a field may make it impossible to enter it at all' (p. 105). This is simply because free entry defeats the very *raison d'être* for entry, 'excess profit'! Accordingly, it is fair I believe to conclude that beyond the suggestion that, if a 'mythical' state of perfect competition exists, this is good, so that in its absence intervention should aim at 're-inventing' it, the mainstream approach fails to answer how exactly this is to be achieved. From a policy perspective this leaves a lot to be desired.

Given the above lacuna in theory, competition policies in *practice* are primarily concerned with the control of (the abuse of) monopoly power, as qualified by additional *static* and *dynamic* considerations such as: the impact of size on technology (and vice versa) and/or efficiency (or vice versa) – what are known as the 'Schumpeterian' and 'differential efficiency' hypotheses, respectively, in the literature; the impact of size on *international competitiveness* and (thus) export surpluses (the 'Servan-Schreiber condition'); whether size is the result of efficiency in terms of transaction cost reductions (the 'market-hierarchies' scenario of Oliver Williamson); whether monopoly results in lower costs, thus offsetting any consumer surplus losses (the Williamson trade-off); whether monopoly is associated with higher X-efficiency (the Leibenstein argument); whether or not monopoly results in lower rates of invention (the Arrow–Demsetz debate).[3] Detailed discussions on the above and full references are in Pitelis (1991a). Here all I want to point to is the conclusion that the mainstream neoclassical approach's policy implications are also unclear about the degree of intervention: depending on static and dynamic theory, evidence, ideology and their interaction, neoclassical theory can favour a lot of intervention or very little intervention.

In part, the above is the result of neoclassical theory's influence by other perspectives. Chicago school perspectives, such as those of Harold Demsetz, are now part of the orthodoxy, while some post-Keynesian (Kaleckian) and Marxian views underlie the 'generalised oligopoly' model (see Pitelis, 1991a, for discussion). An important difference between the mainstream and alternative perspectives, however, like Austrian, Schumpeterian and Marxist ones, is that all these consider competition as a *process* and not as an 'equilibrium' market structure, (but see note 1).

Schumpeter (1942), for example, stresses the role of *potential* competition as a disciplining power in the long run, namely as a means of erosion of any short-term monopoly positions. In his view monopoly is transient, as are monopoly profits. Perfect competition of the textbook type is simply a myth. This Schumpeterian perspective (but in a short-run version which Schumpeter himself had warned against) is incorporated in the contestable markets view. Given Schumpeter's focus on potential competition, and his (related) view that (temporary) monopoly is the result of successful innovations, the Schumpeterian perspective is in line with little policy intervention. This is also true, and more so, in the Austrian tradition; where competition is viewed as a process of discovery of new information by alert entrepreneurs, whose success is rewarded by profits, which, however, are eventually eroded by the actions of other (actual or potential) successful entrepreneurs. By synchronising the previously unco-ordinated plans of buyers and sellers, entrepreneurship is beneficial for society at large, and state intervention can only be harmful by interfering with the competitive market process.

The Marxian perspective has various strands. One is of the neoclassical market structure type, represented by Baran and Sweezy (1966), who regard modern markets as oligopolistic and behaving as if they were monopolies, i.e. they maximise joint profits and try to prevent new entry. Other Marxists adopt a dynamic perspective on competition, sometimes with rather 'Austrian' overtones (see the survey in Jenkins, 1987, and my discussion in

Pitelis, 1991a). In part this is due to Marx himself, who had stressed two types of competition as the driving force of capital accumulation: first, competition between capital and labour (I call this conflict); and, second, competition between different capitals (firms), which is inter-capitalist competition (or rivalry). Concerning the latter, Marx had pointed to a dialectical relationship between 'monopoly' and 'competition' where the one produces the other, and where monopoly can be maintained only by continually entering the struggle of competition (see Jenkins, 1987, for more). This view (as nearly always with Marx) allows both types of interpretation. It can be claimed that competition (rivalry) is a dynamic dialectical perpetual process, or that through perpetual competitive struggle monopoly positions *are* maintained (the Baran –Sweezy view). For my purposes here, what is interesting is that the whole logic of the Marxian scheme leads to a contradiction as regards policy implications. Even if one accepts the Baran–Sweezy view, monopolisation is part and parcel of the maturing of capitalism, which is a precondition of 'socialism'. Given this, should the state (which in any case in the final analysis represents the interests of the monopolies) intervene to protect the 'consumers' (labour), or should the process be welcomed, given its long-run implications (potentially socialism?) There are proposed solutions to this dilemma, but for the purposes of this paper suffice it to note that, in the Marxian tradition, the issue of 'policy' is less straightforward than in other traditions.

The discussion so far allows me to conclude that economic theory of all perspectives gives prominence to the concept of competition, but often conflicting policy proposals. This allows policy-makers at a national level great scope for manoeuvre. In *practice*, national competition policies, in the UK, USA and Germany for example, are guided, I believe, by a presumed trade-off between the potential static welfare losses of monopoly of the neoclassical type (as modified by the current influence of views such as Chicago, contestability, etc. at any point in time) and the potential dynamic gains from big size for the country in question. In recent years the balance of these (following in particular the ideological assault of the 'New Right') has favoured little intervention *against* monopoly power.

A difference between the policies of countries, however, is whether, and to what extent, they pursue active, conscious policies to promote their country's business. Here Japan's Ministry of International Trade and Industry (MITI) is viewed as the exemplar of an active 'developmental' policy, as opposed to the more passive role of, for example, Britain and the USA. MITI's apparent success (see also Chapter 9) has led to widespread demands for a similar (suitably adjusted) role of the state in countries such as Britain (see, for example, Cowling, 1989). Accepting that a developmental approach can be of benefit to a country's business sector, it still leaves unclear a number of important issues concerning: intra-country distribution of income, the relationship between 'private' and 'national' interest, and the very definition of 'national' interest. Concerning, moreover, a 'multi'national entity, such as the European Community (EC), the concept of 'national' interest acquires added complexity. All these point to the need for an explicitly, well-analysed criterion on which competition policies should be based, in general and for the EC in particular.

A proposed criterion-basis for competition policy

The concept of developmental industrial or competition policy which benefits a country's business sector (and therefore enhances its ability to compete successfully in international markets) is based on the assumption that increased international competitiveness of a country's business sector benefits the country (the nation) as a whole, both in the short run and also in the long run. This need not be true, however, for three reasons. First, potential benefits from increased competitiveness may be distributed unevenly, accrue to only the business sector or even lead to intra-country redistribution favouring the business sector through increased monopolisation (reduced 'consumer surplus'). In brief, the issue of intra-country distribution of income has to be explicitly addressed. Second, in the face of internationalised production and the emergence of the transnational corporation (TNC), it is not obvious that potential benefits to a TNC will accrue to the home country of the TNC at all. In other words, the relationship between TNCs and national interest also needs to be addressed. Third, short-term benefits to the business sector through increased competitiveness need not be independent from long-term effects. The relationship between the two, in theory positive, negative or one of independence, has to be analysed, so that an informed decision can be made.

The above problems are complicated further if one considers the policies of a multi-country entity such as the EC. Besides the three issues raised above, one needs also to consider the intra-EC inter-country distribution of any potential benefits from increased EC competitiveness, in the short run and in the long run. Similar to the case of intra-country distribution, inter-country (intra-EC) distribution of benefits can be unequal, accrue only to some countries or even in the longer term harm some countries (regions), through, for example, undermining the competitiveness of their industrial (regional) base.

Issues such as these (and perhaps others too) need to be addressed for a competitive strategy for Europe to be derived – a strategy, that is, based on an explicit criterion which guides the specific policies. I attempt to address them below.

Assuming a constant intra-country distribution of income and a given set of terms of international trade, then any increase in the export surplus of one country implies a decrease in the export surplus of the rest of the world and an increase in the effective demand and (*ceteris paribus*) income of the country whose export surplus has increased. In this static world what one wins someone else loses, i.e. we have a zero-sum game. Given the assumption of a constant distribution, gains and losses are distributed evenly, which implies that winners are faced with Pareto improvements, and losers with Pareto-inefficient changes. Assuming that export surpluses can increase through an increased international competitiveness of a country's business sector, the above may imply that 'what is good for General Motors is good for the nation'.

This statement, however, ignores the potential link between increased competitiveness and the impact of acquiring it and maintaining it on income distribution within the winning country. To the extent, for example, that increased international competitiveness is achieved through increased firm size, concentration and prices, this will tend to redistribute income to the business sector. The stream of discounted *ex ante* and *ex post* losses in 'consumer surplus' will need to be weighed against the benefits from increased 'export surpluses' for a decision to be drawn as to whether even the country winner has achieved a Pareto improvement. Even disregarding the important issues of the original distribution of income (not accounted for by the Pareto criterion), the relationship between competitiveness and distribution is more complex than it seems to be believed. This leads me to

> **Proposition 1** National industrial competition policies should at the very least satisfy an *inter-temporal Pareto-type criterion*; that is, policies should be adopted *if* expected benefits from increased competitiveness (increased total income) outweigh expected losses (consumer surplus) resulting from the process of acquiring and maintaining competitiveness. The resulting 'surplus' distribution, moreover, should not enhance existing income disparities.[4]

So far we have assumed a positive relationship between the competitiveness of a country's business sector and this country's economic welfare (export surplus income). This need not necessarily be the case. A corporation can become privately more competitive and yet the benefits from this may not be realised in its home-base country. An example is a firm which undertakes foreign direct investment (FDI) activities. As its degree of competitiveness increases, so may its FDI activities. Profits from the latter, however, need not be repatriated. They can be used to finance further FDI activities and/or deposited in tax-havens, and/or 'dissipated' through 'transfer pricing'. In this sense a privately successful TNC can originate from (result in) a declining nation. The 'deindustrialization' of the UK is a case in point here (see Coates and Hillard, 1986). From this discussion follows my

> **Proposition 2** Subject to proposition 1 being satisfied, industrial competition policies should satisfy the *national interest criterion*; that is, they should be adopted *if* potential positive expected benefits from increased corporate competitiveness are expected to accrue to the nation.

The above discussion has taken place within the framework of an assumed zero-sum game. If this is true then any short-term benefits from a firm's (country's) increased competitiveness may result in reductions in the income of the rest of the world. This might eventually undermine the very source of success of the winning country.[5] There are two ways through which this outcome need not come about:

(1) If, within the zero-sum assumption, a country's firms favour other countries. This is possible in the case, for example, of

TNCs.[6] From our national policy perspective, however, it does not satisfy Proposition 2.

(2) If the game is not zero-sum, but positive-sum, in the sense of leading to increasing global income from economic activity. This is possible if we relax the assumption of a given income and allow for economic development-growth through international trade and the activities of TNCs. This can come about through the usual channels of exporting technology, skills, organisational and management know-how, etc. Accepting this, and given propositions 1 and 2, it follows:

Proposition 3   Subject to satisfying Propositions 1 and 2, national policies should satisfy an *international Pareto-type criterion*; that is, policies should be adopted when they have an expected overall positive impact on global economic welfare (here income).[7]

Assuming that the EC is an extended nation state, EC policies could be considered in the light of Propositions 1, 2 and 3. The EC, however, consists of many (currently 12) countries, each with different cultures, expectations, policies, etc. Participation in the club is on the basis of expected benefits, including economic. In their absence, problems may arise which threaten EC coherence and stability; see Pitelis (1991c) for further discussion of this point. In order to guard against this, EC policies should also satisfy the following:

Proposition 4   EC policies should satisfy Propositions 1, 2 and 3 *and* an *intra-EC Pareto-type criterion* concerning intra-EC inter-country distribution; that is, adopted policies should be expected to increase one country's welfare without reducing the welfare of another.

From the above I can summarise and conclude by proposing the following criterion basis for European industrial competition policies, defined here as 'Criterion X'.

'Criterion X'

Industrial and competition policies of the EC should satisfy Proposition 4 and, subject to that, Propositions 1, 2 and 3. To the extent moreover that separate (intra-EC national–regional) policies exist, these should be consistent with the overall policies.

A competition policy for Europe

Existing competition policy in the European Community appears to be derived from the orthodox perfect competition monopoly dichotomy of market structures. In particular, Article 3(f) of the Treaty of Rome appeals to a system which ensures non-distortion of market competition. The two main articles concerning such distortions are Article 85 on restrictive practices and Article 86 on dominant firms. Article 85 is concerned with collusive agreements, between two or more firms, usually assuming the form of price fixing (collusion). Firms intending to reach agreements potentially infringing Article 85 can inform the Commission, in which case exemptions may be granted in certain cases, in particular agreements which are not thought to limit competition and/or which improve the production and distribution of a good. In the absence of such information, no exemptions are granted and the Commission can (and has on a number of occasions)prosecute and fine the companies involved in such practices (see for example Barnes and Preston, 1988, for examples).

Article 86 is concerned with the abuse of a monopoly (dominant) position. Focus on abuse rather than monopoly *per se* is indicative of the Commission's regard for the potential efficiency gains of big size. Mergers are not specifically covered in the article. Their relevance lies in the fact that they can serve to establish a dominant position and/or to avoid Article 85, namely be an alternative means of price fixing to collusion. The European Court has thus ruled that mergers are covered by Article 85.

It is widely acknowledged that the Commission had little success with the application and enforcement of Article 85. A most glaring case was that of Hoffman-La Roche, the Swiss transnational. Its attempts to obtain and maintain dominance in the vitamins market defy the imagination of the best industrial organisation theorists (see the vivid exposition in Stanley Adams, 1985).

The failure of the Commission to take tough measures in cases such as these can only partly be attributed to 'bureaucratic' inefficiency. A more important reason, I think, is the Commission's concern with *international competitiveness*. It was observed especially during the 1960s and 1970s that Europe was lagging behind the USA, particularly in the field of technology (see Servan-Schreiber, 1968). Big size was thought to be the means through which

European firms could become more competitive, that is, reply to the 'American challenge' (see also the previous chapter in this volume). Governments (particularly the French) and industry alike were taken by this view, which might have influenced the Commission's attitude towards mergers and big size (see e.g. Swann, 1988). While the EC recognised the 'vices' of monopoly, in practice more emphasis was given to its virtues, with a resulting permissive, if not encouraging, stance towards mergers and big EC-based (transnational) corporations. This implicitly assumed that any short-run European consumer welfare losses will be offset by dynamic gains (P1). Also that this will further European 'national' interest (P2 and P4) and that it will not be at the expense of Europe's rivals (USA, Japan and the newly industrialized countries, NICs) and the Third World (P3) (or if it is, it does not matter).

As I have already suggested (and explain further below), none of these assumptions needs be true. Moreover, what is interesting is the case of the transnational corporation. At the time of the undisputed hegemony of American TNCs, the promotion by the EC of concerns competitive to the American giants might be viewed as promoting actual and/or potential competition, with potential beneficial effects on European consumers' welfare, but also that the rest of the world, through, for example, reduced prices. However, following the growth of European TNCs, the latter appear keener to 'co-operate' with their American, Japanese and other 'rivals'. Over 30% of all European industry is now controlled by 'foreign' TNCs (Ionian Bank, 1989), raising question marks about the very definition of 'European TNCs'. Viewed in this light, the Commission can ill afford to stick to its old attitudes.

Granting my proposed criterion and on the basis of previous analysis, a competition policy of Europe should contain three elements:

(1) a tough attitude towards actions and policies by TNCs 'foreign' and 'European',[8]
(2) relatedly, a conscious attempt to encourage actual and potential competition within Europe;
(3) an avoidance of the possibility of a 'fortress Europe', that is, a Europe protected from the sources of international competition.

These are obviously interrelated. They all point to containing the forces potentially leading to dominance, through e.g. collusion by global TNCs.

Starting with the first element above, Articles 85 and 86 represent only *negative* encouragement to *actual* competition. They do not take *positive* steps to encourage competition, actual or potential. They still have a useful role to play, but only if the Commission pursues a tough policy of identification of culprits and implementation. There are very good reasons why this should happen. First, very substantial empirical evidence has been accumulated concerning the inefficiency and unprofitability of mergers. This evidence is summarised in Cowling and Sawyer (1989). It provides a big blow to the efficiency of big size argument. A second reason is the observed footloose nature of foreign direct investment by transnational corporations and their patent disregard of 'nationalistic feelings', or indeed any feelings other than the lust for profits. This is not surprising. It is certainly in line with established economic theory (profit maximisation). It may, however, lead to (or facilitate) the process of *deindustrialisation*, which has manifested itself in a number of early industrialised countries, most obviously the United Kingdom (see the discussion in Coates and Hillard, 1986). The fact that the UK has had a worse economic performance in the recent past than other major industrialised countries, despite being the home country of a big number of important and (privately) successful TNCs, patently demonstrates the fallacy of the argument that there is a one-to-one correspondence between being a home TNC country and being *internationally competitive*. Being lenient to 'European' TNCs therefore need not imply increased international competitiveness for Europe.

The opposite is more likely, as the resultant increased mobility and power of TNCs will tend to lead to increased bargaining leverage towards the Commission and European labour unions (see Pitelis and Sugden, 1991, for discussions).

The above does not address the *research and development* (R&D) issue. There is little doubt that big TNCs are in a better position than smaller firms to undertake R&D efforts and in particular to *apply* inventions[9] (innovate) for reasons related to access to finance (either through retained profits and/or from financial institutions) and/or the fact that the very uncertainty of the outcomes of the R&D effort makes it more likely that a big diversified firm will end up finding a commercial use for an existing invention. Moreover, the intra-firm transfer of intermediate goods, such as technology, and its arguably associated reduction in market transaction costs, represents one of the main reasons proposed to explain the very existence (and efficiency) of TNCs (see, for example, Buckley and Casson, 1976). Yet, even here the case for the free reign of TNCs is precarious. Indeed, the very reasons allegedly leading to TNCs, namely market failure due to high market transaction costs in intermediate product markets, could (should) equally plausibly lead to state intervention intended to remove such market failures. Further, and related to the above, the possibility that TNCs are in a better position to undertake R&D does not imply a superior capability to states, the EC and/or networks of small firms.

Even if a case for advantages by TNCs could be made on the basis of increased international competitiveness, this is undermined by the increasing tendency of European-based TNCs to co-operate rather than compete with their Japanese, US and other 'rivals'. The car industry is a case in point. This raises the real possibility (a daunting one too) of global collusion of global TNCs. Allowing a free rein to European TNCs does nothing to prevent this.

It follows that the EC should take specific *negative* steps to counteract the increasing power of TNCs: first, by actually applying Articles 85 and 86; second, by taking specific steps to reduce the mobility of 'European' TNCs and the power this mobility entails; third, by taking specific measures to reduce the ability of TNCs to reach international agreements with other TNCs, i.e. potential global collusion.[10]

The above prescriptions do not originate from any desire for anti-TNC rhetoric or an anti-TNC romanticism. It is claimed not that TNCs are *per se* 'evil' or inherently inefficient; simply that, in their pursuit of profit, they are likely to attempt to contain competition, and thus eliminate its potential benefits. Therefore, the EC should guard against this, devising a legal framework and enforcement mechanism designed to prevent its occurrence.

That my proposals for a competition policy are in line with my proposed criterion should be obvious. The negative and positive steps to enhance competition are of benefit to European consumers (reduced prices), but also to the smaller firms, without having a negative impact on the welfare of other (non-European) countries. Moreover, the openness of Europe to outside competition further enhances the welfare of European consumers, while simultaneously having the same effect on peoples of non-European countries, *ceteris paribus*. Indeed, in the longer term it does not even undermine the profitability of European-based TNCs. The threat of competition might make them more alert to new opportunities for profitable expansion, while protectionism might result in 'sleepy giants' (see below).

The above policies are *negative* in the sense that they try to prevent further reductions in competition arising from TNC behaviour. The EC, however, also needs *positive* action to enhance competition. Such action should be directed either towards facilitating the emergence of new players, or towards advancing the relative position of existing (networks of) small and medium-sized firms. The logic behind such actions needs little elaboration. The challenge by existing concerns and/or the fear of the emergence of new ones (especially if such fear enjoys the declared support of the EC) could either give rise to actual competitors to existing firms or at least generate the threat of *potential* competition, thus creating conditions of contestability. Specific measures along these lines could include: the publicly financed provision of education and skills to the public in the areas and specialisations most needed by the small and medium-size sector, as well as in new fields where potential new players may arise; easy access to finance (another potential barrier to entry) for new players and/or existing ones where obvious potential does exist; support to the R&D efforts of small, medium and potential new firms, either through financial assistance or through the direct handling of publicly owned R&D initiatives to interested parties thought to be able to make good use of it.

Of particular interest here is the *subcontracting* phenomenon. Despite the lack of reliable information on the extent of this, there are strong indications that big TNCs are making ample use of this practice and this is now on the increase (see Cowling and Sugden, 1987, for a discussion and some data). The problem with subcontracting is that big TNCs are taking control of the operations of smaller players, the very source of potential rivalry and competition to them. Thus, they eliminate a potential source of competition, further increasing their grip on international production. Although subcontracting arrangements can often be beneficial to the smaller firms too, as they provide them with a degree of certainty concerning their expected future business, they tend to reduce competition.[11] This necessitates steps towards this trend. Cases of subcontracting, for example, could be investigated and disallowed where it was felt that the smaller firms could have an independently successful future, for example with some support. Alternatively, TNCs could be requested to report all their (intended) subcontracting arrangements before they are allowed to proceed with them.

The third dimension of European competition policy should be preventing the emergence of a 'fortress Europe', protected from international competition. It has been noted, for example, that one reason for the British decline was Britain's reliance on the existing cheap raw materials and labour of the Empire, and thus its lack of intention or need to compete internationally (see Hobsbawm, 1969). The same could happen in Europe if, for example, it tried to become insulated from the outside world through neo-protectionist policies. This could be damaging in two complementary ways. First, by insulating European TNCs from potential new entrants from outside the EC, in particular from newly industrialised countries (NICs) and the Third World, it would eliminate potential sources of competition not only for European TNCs, but also for the numerous American and Japanese TNCs already operating in Europe. Protection of such firms from outside competition would further enhance their relative strength in world markets and defeat the very reason of protectionism, since they are *not* European! Second, such policies could reduce the incentive of European-based TNCs to compete internationally in advanced technology sectors, given their ability to extract profits from the protected, enlarged European base.[12]

So far we have treated the EC as one homogeneous nation state. Once the reality of the 12 (at the moment) is allowed, a new major dimension enters the picture: *intra-EC competition*. Although the open European market will generate *static* gains for Europe as a whole,[13] and the increased competitiveness of European products may lead to further *dynamic* gains for the EC, the extent to which each European country is going to gain will depend on its relative competitiveness and/or its ability to claim assistance from the various EC funds. This brings the issue of the relative strength of each country to the centre of the analysis.

The route most commonly adopted by European member states in order to achieve increased relative competitiveness is state aid to domestic producers (see also Chapter 11). State aids are covered by Articles 92 and 93 of the Treaty of Rome. The general idea is that state aids are not allowed unless they are for a special purpose, and/or they are intended to remedy a serious problem in a national economy, and/or they are directed to areas of high unemployment or low incomes. In the last case they should not be 'excessive'. Apart from the obviously mild nature of Articles 92 and 93, most member states tend to bend the rules by giving the aid first and then asking the Commission for permission (see Barnes and Preston, 1988).

This tendency of member states renders their views about competitiveness of the utmost importance. Not surprisingly such views appear not to differ very much from the European Community's own in their emphasis on the competitiveness of 'their' firms. Much of the recent debate on industrial policy and industrial strategy appears to be in terms of 'picking winners' and/or 'creating winners' (see, for example, the UK Industrial Strategy Group, 1989; also Vernardakis, 1989, for a similar observation). An institutional device, much like Japan's Ministry of International Trade and Industry (MITI), is often viewed as the means by which such policies could be adopted in particular countries (see, for example, the interesting analysis and prescriptions for the UK in Cowling, 1989).

A problem with this emphasis on 'winners' is the underlying absence of a clear-cut welfare criterion as regards the rest of Europe, the rest of the world and indeed the welfare of the very country which focuses on 'winners'. If, for example, such 'winners' are existing established TNCs, as originally thought by the EC, their impact on world welfare is unlikely to be positive. Indeed, their impact on 'their, country's (and EC) welfare too need not necessarily be positive, for reasons already explained. This makes it necessary that careful consideration is given to the definition and nature of 'winners' both by member states and by the EC.

Starting with the member states, my discussion so far would point to a definition of 'winners' as firms (existing or potential) whose operations will represent a challenge to the existing (domestic or foreign) TNCs and thus will further competition and accordingly tend to increase domestic and global welfare. The processes through which this result comes about, I have already explained. As for the EC, it should support such actions by member states by allowing state aid directed to such firms and by itself assisting them.

My prescriptions above have interesting implications for the competition policy of 'the South' of Europe. The term 'South' refers to the group of countries, or regions (such as Portugal, Greece, Spain, Ireland, most of South Italy and a number of northern UK regions, in particular Northern Ireland) whose relative performance in terms of a number of economic indices, such as real GDP (expressed in purchasing power standards) and/or the importance of agriculture as a percentage of total economic activity, is judged to be 'substantially below' the European average.[14] Although mainly referring to the Mediterranean countries, it is obviously the case that the term 'South' is not purely geographical. The importance of my previous discussion for the competition policy of these states/regions is that they could and should qualify for exemption by the EC of their state aids towards their firms, on the basis of Article 93(3), which allows such (non-excessive) aids for areas of low incomes. Indeed, considering that the domestic firms or industrial sectors of these regions are often small or medium sized (thus the obvious targets for support as potential rivals to TNCs and as sources of competition within Europe), the EC itself should extend its support towards selected industries/firms in these states/regions.

In the absence of such policies, the possibility of a 'fortress Europe' may become a very real one. Big European-based (European, American and Japanese, but in fact Profitlandese) TNCs will find it very tempting to focus on reaping the fruits of the expanded European market, being protected themselves from international competition. The end product could be not only the economic dependence of the 'South' on such companies, with associated political repercussions (see Pitelis, 1991c, for a discussion), but also the potential deindustrialisation of Europe as a whole. European countries (in particular the Southern ones) should try to avoid these daunting prospects.

To summarise, European competition policies should satisfy a criterion basis for policy which accounts for intra-country, intra-EC, Pareto efficiency, European 'national' interest, intra-EC, inter-country, Pareto-type efficiency, and global (EC versus non-EC) Pareto-type efficiency. Control of 'monopoly' power, promotion of competition and openness to external competition are three dimensions of proposed EC policy which satisfy my proposed criterion. Crucial for their implementation is the identification of the actors who can assist the achievement of these objectives. Such actors were proposed to be (relatively) small and medium-sized firms. For smaller ('South') European countries, this can be interpreted to include support for the creation of some (relatively) big players as potential challengers to the existing giants (see also Pitelis, 1991c, for more of this on the Greek case).

Market versus government 'failures'

A premise on which my suggestions here are based is that of *state intervention in market economies*. Alternatively put, the need to use the market is implicitly allowed, as is the need to use the state. This presupposes the existence of 'market failure', 'private sector failure' and 'state failure', the last most commonly known as 'government failure'. A detailed discussion of these issues is in Pitelis (1991a). A summary version of the main issues follows.

The pervasiveness of 'market failure' is now acknowledged widely enough to have led to attempts to explain the emergence of 'hierarchies', in particular uninational firms and TNCs, in terms of 'market failure' (see, for example, Coase, 1937, Williamson, 1975, 1981, and the contributions in Pitelis and Sugden, 1991). There is also little doubt that 'hierarchies' themselves 'fail', for example by creating monopolies and thus restraining competition and/or by underproviding or failing to provide 'public goods' (see Dasgupta, 1986, and Pitelis, 1991b, for extensive discussions). The failure by both 'markets' and 'hierarchies' introduces the notion of 'private sector failure'.

Private sector failures are traditionally regarded as the *raison d'être* of state intervention in market economies. If such intervention could replace the market perfectly, the market would become superfluous. Accordingly, the lack of a call for replacement of the market by the state here can be justified only if states too fail. The concept of 'state or government failure' has indeed become very popular these days, gathering the support of a very diverse group of economists, ranging from the Chicago school theorists to Marxist ones (see the discussion in Green, 1987, and Pitelis, 1991b). The failure of centrally planned economies has added additional weight to the plausibility of the notion.

The presence of both market failure and state failure is a case for the use of both market and state in the allocation of resources[15] –

thus justifying my focus in this paper.[16] Indeed much of my analysis in this paper could (and should) be applied to state offices themselves, that is, they should become contestable (see also Lively, 1979); i.e. subjected to continuous actual and potential competition by, for example, rival parties.[17]

Related to the above issue is the question of the relationship between nation states (or international states such as the EC) and TNCs. This again is a particularly interesting issue that has been widely and hotly debated since the 1960s (see, for example, the collection in Radice, 1975). My underlying theory of state–TNCs relationships is one of 'rivalry and collusion'. This view is based on the presumption that the state has a 'relative autonomy' from the economic base-agents, that is, it rejects the simple 'instrumentalist' view of the state of the Marxist or Friedman variety (see Pitelis, 1991a, for more). Given this autonomy, the states (and their agents: politicians, bureaucrats, etc.) could take a hostile stance towards big TNCs if the latter's operations were against their interests, or collude with such TNCs if the opposite were the case.

In line with the above, the state's interests and the TNCs' interest go hand in hand to the extent that the TNCs' policies, through for example repatriated profits, increased international competitiveness and/or employment creation, are in line with the interests of the state (see below). The footloose nature of TNC operations, however, and the associated fear of deindustrialisation, as well as the related increased bargaining power of TNCs towards states, could be viewed as threats to the states' relative autonomy/interests. In that case counter-threats can be used, such as the withdrawal of political and/or military backing of TNC operations. Such treats can help TNCs think 'nationalistically', or, in our framework, think European.

My proposed policies in the preceding discussion are obviously in line with this 'rivalry/collusion' framework, in that constraints on the relative power of big TNCs enhance the relative power/ autonomy of the national states of the EC vis-á-vis such firms, thus satisfying the interests of states and their agents, invariably taken to be the reproduction of the status quo and/or the re-election of politicians and/or the reappointment of bureaucrats.

Concluding remarks

By way of concluding the paper, a summary of the main arguments is as follows. Economic theory provides a strong basis for competition policy, favouring actual and/or potential competition in the market place. Subject to the acceptance of a composite 'criterion X', a competition policy for the EC should contain an attempt to restrain the power of TNCs, the encouragement of actual and/or potential competition within Europe, and a continuous attempt to avoid the possibility of a 'fortress Europe'. Individual member states should adjust their policies accordingly. This could imply different policies in different countries, in particular Northern and Southern ones respectively. In contrast with the Northern countries, support for the creation of 'giants' by the Southern countries could at times be in line with the proposed maximand. Important prerequisites for the successful adoption of such policies are related to the ability, willingness or need of the states to adopt such policies, which in turn is related to their interests vis-á-vis TNCs and consumers/electors. My proposals are based on the notion of *state intervention in markets* in an environment characterised by rivalry and collusion between states and TNCs. The proposed policies are realistic to the extent that my underlying theoretical theses are a plausible description of reality. The existing evidence to which I have referred in this paper does, I believe, lend some support to my suggestions.

Notes

An earlier version of this paper was prepared for the 'Europe 12 Committee' meeting in Bonn, 1990. The paper was presented to the European Research Conference in Nottingham, April 1991, and the Warwick/Birmingham Workshop on Industrial Strategy, Birmingham, July 1991. I am grateful to the participants of these meetings for helpful comments. In particular I am grateful to Keith Cowling, David Mayes, Malcolm Sawyer and Roger Sugden for written comments and suggestions, all of which I have tried to incorporate in the present version. I am also grateful to Keith Cowling and Roger Sugden for their invitation to the particularly stimulating Warwick/Birmingham Workshop.

1 Besides its main focus on competition (and monopoly) as types of market structure, there is an *implicit* competitive process in the neoclassical tradition in the assumption of entry. Perfectly easy entry, for example in the case of perfectly competitive structures, implies, at least up to a point, that the *structure* is shaped by the process, i.e. a structure–process interaction.

2 For a discussion of instances and reasons of market (and government) failure, see Pitelis (1991b).

3 These conditions also underlie discussions on industrial policy. The boundaries between industrial and competition policies are often blurred. In theory, competition policy is seen as interventionist–regulatory, while industrial policy is seen in broader terms, i.e more proactive. In practice, the two are often hard to disentangle.

In part this reflects difficulties of definition, reflected (for the case of competition) in the discussions in the section. Similar difficulties are associated with the concept of industrial policies; the theoretical industrial organisation-derived form of this concept is often broadened beyond recognition in practice (see below).

4 Relaxation of this last sentence is possible under the guise of the so-called 'compensation criteria' in welfare economics. Problems with such criteria are well known, however, and I will not be entering this discussion here.

5 Reasons for this are economic (a reduction in the sources of further benefits) and political ('anti-imperialist' feelings and their potential consequences).

6 For an extensive discussion on 'dependency', 'dependent industrialisation', etc. see Pitelis (1991a).

7 Keeping within the economic bias of this article, welfare is viewed throughout as equivalent to growth income. This need not be the case given problems of measurement and interpretation of e.g. per capita incomes, the recent focus on economists such as Sen (1988) on criteria such as 'life expectancy' (which, incidentally, can often differ radically from rankings of welfare based on income), and more generally that economic-type criteria tend to ignore socio-politico-cultural and environmental issues.

8 It is worth mentioning here that recent tough measures towards 'foreign' TNCs (e.g. 'local contents rules'), although welcome, do not address the fundamental issues raised here, concerning in particular the threats from the mobility and power of *all* TNCs, not just 'foreign'.

9 No more can be credited to big firms than *ability* to innovate. Concerning inventions, it is standard knowledge that the vast majority originate from small firms or individual inventors (see Scherer, 1980). Whether ability to innovate, moreover, implies higher innovation rates is very debatable in theory and evidence (see the discussion in Pitelis, 1991a).

10 Three years since the writing of this paragraph in an earlier version of this paper, the recent announcement of international co-operation between the two car giants, Mitsubishi (Japan) and Daimler-Benz (Germany), indicates, I believe, that EC policy is misdirected.

11 The 'degree of certainty', moreover, is itself precarious. Japanese giants, for example, are well known not to extend their life-time employment contracts and other fringe benefits to the subcontractors, who are the first to suffer the consequences of adversity.

12 It is disturbing that there is some evidence to suggest that this is currently under way. In recent years European industries seems to have lost their edge in high-technology areas. Moreover, while European balance of payments surpluses with the USA and Japan are declining, the original surplus countries such as Germany still exhibit surpluses but these are now accounted for by the smaller countries (see Vernardakis, 1989).

13 Estimated by the Cecchini Report (Cecchini, 1988) to be around 6% of EC GDP. This should be seen as an upper bound, however (see Sawyer, 1989).

14 My economic (see note 7) and *ad hoc* definition of 'South' here is a per capita GNP in purchasing parity standards of less than 90% of the European average and/ or an above 15% proportion of agriculture to total employment. All the above-mentioned countries qualify as 'South' on this basis (see the Commission of the EC, *Annual Economic Report 1986–87* and the *Basic Statistics of the Community*, 23rd edition; figures relate to 1985).

15 This should not be taken to imply support for the wider distributional disparities brought about in most market economies through the unfettered operation of markets/firms. The coexistence of market and the state could at least equally well apply in the case of an original equitable distribution of income.

16 A specific proposal regarding the role of each for the case of Britain is Cowling (1989). He proposes the use of the state for strategic planning purposes and the use of the market for the day-to-day running/operational decisions in the system.

17 The exact ways through which this could be achieved are beyond the scope of this paper and my present abilities. The major problem of agency however is worth noting; that is, someone needs to persuade/force the state to adopt policies which make its monopoly power on legal violence contestable. This problem is widely discussed for the case of the control of firms' controllers. 'Who monitors the monitor' is now a classic question posed by Jensen and Meckling (1976). Its relevance for the case of the state is obvious here.

References

Adams, S. (1985), *La-Roche vs Adams*, London: Fontana.

Baran, P. and Sweezy, P. (1966), *Monopoly Capital*, Harmondsworth, Middx: Penguin.

Barnes, I. and Preston, J. (1988), *The European Community*, London: Longman.

Baumol, W. (1982), 'Contestable markets', *American Economic Review*, 72, 1–15.

Buckley, P. and Casson, M. (1976), *The Future of Multinational Enterprise*, London: Macmillan.

Cecchini, P. (1988), *The European Challenge 1992: The Benefits of a Single Market*, Aldershot: Wildwood House.

Clark, J. M. (1940), 'Towards a concept of workable competition', *American Economic Review*, 30, 241–56.

Coase, R. (1937), 'The nature of the firm', *Economica*, 4, 386–405.

Coates, D. and Hillard, J. (1986), *The Economic Decline of Britain*, Sussex: Wheatsheaf.

Cowling, K. (1989), 'The strategic approach', in Industrial Strategy Group (1989).

Cowling, K. and Sugden, R. (1987), *Transnational Monopoly Capitalism*, Sussex: Wheatsheaf.

Cowling, K. and Sawyer, M. (1989), 'Merger and monopoly policy', in Industrial Strategy Group (1989).

Cowling, K. and Waterson, M. (1976), 'Price cost margins and market structure', *Economica*, 43.

Dasgupta, P. (1986), 'Positive freedoms, markets and the welfare State', *Oxford Review of Economic Policy*, 2(2).

Green, D. G. (1987), *The New Right*, Sussex: Wheatsheaf.

Hobsbawm, E. (1969), *Industry and Empire*, London: Pelican.

Industrial Strategy Group (1989), *Beyond the Review: Perspectives on Labour's Economic and Industrial Strategy*, Edinburgh: Industrial Strategy Group.

Ionian Bank of Greece (1989), *1992: The Development of the Internal Market in Europe and the Case of Greece*, Athens (in Greek).

Jenkins, R. (1987), *Transnational Corporations and Uneven Development*, London and New York: Methuen.

Jensen, M. C. and Meckling, W. (1976), 'Theory of the firm: managerial behaviour, agency costs and ownership structure', *Journal of Financial Economics*, 3, 304–60.

Lively, C. (1978), 'Pluralism and consensus', in P. Birnbaum, *et al.* (eds), *Democracy Consensus and Social Contract*, London: Sage Publications.

Modigliani, F. (1958), 'New developments on the oligopoly front', *Journal of Political Economy*, 66.

Pitelis, C. N. (1991a), *Market and non-Market Hierarchies*, Oxford: Blackwell.

Pitelis, C. N. (1991b), 'Market failure and the existence of states', *International Review of Applied Economics* 5(3).

Pitelis, C. N. (1991c), '1992: Industrial policy issues for Greece and the EEC', *European Research*, 2(5).

Pitelis, C. N. and Sugden, R. (eds) (1991), *The Nature of the Transnational Firm*, London: Routledge.

Radice, H. (ed.) (1975), *International Firms and Modern Imperialism*, Harmondsworth, Middx: Penguin.

Reid, G. (1987), *Theories of Industrial Organisation*, Oxford: Blackwell.

Sawyer, M. (1989), 'Industry', in M. Artis (ed.), *Prest and Coppock's the UK Economy*, 12th edn, London: Weidenfeld & Nicolson.

Scherer, F. M. (1980), *Industrial Market Structure and Economic Performance*, 2nd edn, Chicago: Rand McNally.

Servan-Schreiber, J. (1968), *The American Challenge*, London: Hamish Hamilton.

Schumpeter, J. (1942), *Capitalism, Socialism and Democracy*; London: Unwin Hyman, 5th edn, 1987.

Sen, A. (1988), 'Freedom of choice', *European Economic Review*, 32.

Swann, D. (1988), *The Economics of the Common Market*, 6th edn, Harmondsworth, Middx: Penguin Books.

Vernardakis, N. (1989), 'Structural and Technological imperatives in the light of development prospects for the Greek economy', *International Economic Association 9th Congress Proceedings*, Athens.

Williamson, O. E. (1975), *Markets and Hierarchies*, New York: Free Press.

Williamson, O. E. (1981), 'The modern corporation', *Journal of Economic Literature*, 19(4).

Part VI

EASTERN EUROPE

Privatisation in small European Soviet-type economies

Options strategies and consequences for industrial structure

Introduction

This paper will deal with four aspects of the privatisation process in five economies which are now frequently referred to as 'reforming small Soviet-type economies'. The economies in question are those of Poland, the Czech and Slovak Federation (CSFR), Hungary, Yugoslavia, Romania, Bulgaria and Albania. Privatisation in the Soviet Union and some Asian countries will not be discussed even though many of the issues raised in the paper are highly relevant for these economies as well.

In the economics profession, privatisation in the context of the mentioned economies is used in two ways. The first deals with the changing property rights of existing state ownership while the second deals with the changing share of the private sector. This paper will deal only with the former aspect of privatisation.

Privatisation will be defined as an orderly change of property rights from present state (social in the case of Yugoslavia[1]) ownership (enterprises, land, housing, etc.) to private ownership. While this definition stresses the orderly nature of the process, it still considers privatisation as a very wide concept. Thus it encompasses various ways in which the process can be managed (by including both spontaneous and tightly controlled change), it does not define the new owner (thus including restitution as well as new owners, foreign or domestic), nor is it limited by the nature of the assets (including all existing enterprises regardless of size, as well as land and housing).

This definition is broader than the one usually assumed in the profession. All too often privatisation is implicitly reduced to only of the aspects included in the above definition, namely, to that of the state finding new private owners for existing large state-owned enterprises, i.e. to what is referred to as 'large privatisation from above'. Since the other forms of privatisation seem equally important, their discussion will be included in the paper.

The four aspects of privatisation discussed are:

(1) single-owner privatisation;
(2) policy options of 'large privatisation';
(3) the expectations from privatisation; and
(4) the role of the state in a prolonged 'interregnum' period.

Space does not permit a detailed analysis of the privatisation paths chosen by the five economies, nor is there yet sufficient knowledge or understanding of them, so the empirical data will be largely in anecdotal form and confined to the notes.

Single-owner privatisation

Under 'single-owner' privatisation this paper will include the privatisation and restitution[2] of small and medium-sized enterprises (usually referred to as 'small privatisation'[3]) and the privatisation and restitution of land and housing.

Even though they can involve more than one owner (worker buyouts or many heirs), such a grouping seems justified because of the many important economic features they share. The most important are that they: (i) provide seedbeds for entrepreneurship, (ii) reduce the scope for the second economy, (iii) irreversibly increase the reliance on market exchange, (iv) cause short-term effects and rapid changes in the economic and political landscape, (v) enable 'normal' growth paths for firms, (vi) make a major contribution to structural change in terms of the size distribution of firms and agricultural holdings, (vii) provide the much required impetus for growth, and finally (viii) are prone to 'bottom–up privatisation'. In this way small privatisation and restitution can make a major contribution to the 'delivery' expected from privatisation in general.

If this is so it is surprising that they share two more characteristics. First, they are outside the spotlight of the economics profession in spite of causing heated discussions in the parliaments of the countries. Initial discussions almost wholly ignored them, concentrating instead on the 'glamorous topic' of large privatisation from above, and even the latest surveys give them insufficient attention, (see Jackson, 1991, Portes, 1991, or Grosfeld and Hare, 1991). Secondly, policy-makers have treated them in the same way as the economists, i.e. as a set of simpler issues with secondary effects which merit less attention and can largely be left to themselves (see World Bank, 1991).

Restitution and privatisation of land and housing
The restitution of land is simplest since it is easy to determine the original owner and the present owner[4] (or user), while the nature of the resource itself has changed little, making valuation problems simpler. The more serious difficulties here arise in determining the way in which the land was nationalised. Indeed, the indirect pressures being 'voluntary donations' and sales at fictitious prices as well as the brutality of collectivisation are well known (see Brus, 1986).

Private agriculture (i.e. commercial farming with competitive markets) forms the basis of new agricultural policies in all of these economies. Consequently land privatisation is high on the agenda. In spite of these new policies the policy-makers have not completely escaped the old approach in that they favour agricultural co-operatives or renamed state farms[5] and limit private holdings.[6]

Restitution of housing is more complicated. This is not only because of the changed nature of the resource involved (owing to urban growth and bad maintenance), but also because of the distributional and, more importantly, re-distributional issues involved. Subsidised rents, inheritable tenancy, postwar housing allocation and later criteria for allocating new housing have made inequalities in housing the main source of inequality in Soviet-type economies (see Szelenyi, 1983). Understandably, then, the issues related to the restitution of housing are socially and politically extremely charged. Privatisation and restitution of housing has further come against the barrier of the very low savings of the population.

Restitution of enterprises
The restitution of firms is the most problematic. As in the case of land, nationalisation was often based on 'voluntary donations' or sales of undervalued firms made under threat (see Brus, 1986).

Furthermore, in many cases the nature of the resource has changed since nationalisation. Frequently these firms provided the basis (without using the name, usually) from which giant 'socialist enterprises' emerged. These problems are compounded by those of evaluating enterprise value in an environment with no capital markets, heavily distorted prices and undefined tax and monetary systems. The issue is further complicated since many of the owners have left the countries concerned.

To what extent the issues of enterprise restitution are complicated, important and disregarded can be seen in the way restitution-related issues have influenced privatisation. Most recent surveys, e.g. Grosfeld and Hare (1991), Jackson (1991) or Portes (1991), now point to the importance of restitution, whereas previously no one recognised 'how dangerous restitution would be as an obstacle' (Portes, 1991, p.4) for privatisation.

In the face of such an obstacle, some of the economies have not yet tackled it,[7] others have increased its priority[8] and others have postponed privatisation.[9] The scope of restitution has also varied,[10] as has the amount involved and the method.[11] Most economies have favoured compensation over the return of property, and vouchers or points rather than cash payments, and all have excluded foreigners who have not returned.

Small privatisation
Small privatisation refers to the sale of existing small and medium-sized state-owned enterprises to new owners. This form of privatisation includes enterprises employing up to 150, and it usually refers to the privatisation of consumer and producer services and less to industry and manufacturing.

Small and medium-sized units in the economies under consideration are in a special position in two important aspects. The 40-year-old 'bias to bigness' (Bicanic, 1989), 'empire building' (Nove, 1983) or 'bureaucratic rent collection' (Winiecki, 1989) among the policy-makers in these economies has led to an anomaly in the size distribution of firms. The distribution shows a significant under-representation of small and medium-sized units, which has been referred to as the 'black hole' (Vahcic, 1989), and an over-representation of large units.[12] Furthermore, in these economies both consumer and producer services, which tend to operate in small units, are under-represented (see Bicanic and Skreb, 1991a).

Thus, if small privatisation can increase efficiency and act as an engine, it can contribute significantly to the elimination of numerous possible bottlenecks. In spite of this, all these economies have not given 'bottom–up' (or 'spontaneous') and 'ground–up' privatisation adequate attention. Ground–up privatisation, i.e. the founding of new private firms, is outside the scope of this paper (and here policies have largely been passive and concerned with eliminating barriers to entry, because with stabilisation policies in place and inflationary pressures it is difficult to give other incentives). Bottom–up privatisation, i.e. where privatisation initiatives come not from government but from the employees or other buyers (domestic or foreign), is only organized (managed) by the state. In spite of measures to stimulate it – in some of the economies funds were set up[13] while some have let it be run on a regional basis[14], all have allowed more than one path for small privatisation[15] – there has been no extensive small privatisation.[16] Perhaps even more importantly, small privatisation is not a self-regulating process.

Policy options of large privatisation

History offers no experience of the kind of privatisation facing the previously Soviet-type economies. In peacetime till now no economy has attempted a transition from a centralised command economy with dominant state ownership to a decentralised market economy with mixed ownership. The experiences of privatising public companies in developed Western economies occurred in a quite different economic environment. In most of these cases the number of publicly owned firms was relatively small, they often were not dominant in their markets, private ownership was clearly dominant in the economy as a whole and all the institutions of factor and commodity markets already existed. For the countries under consideration here, the opposite is true: the economies are not developed, the state sector is dominant (if not the only one), the firms have monopoly powers and there are no capital markets, while prices are heavily distorted.

Perhaps this is why so many distinguished economists have taken up the challenge of offering prescriptions and blueprints for privatisation and why many of them were not area specialists.[17] This also, probably, explains why so much of the literature is speculative and normative, offering scenarios and prescriptions, and why in a quickly developing field of study some of the most valuable contributions have not been made in the more usual academic manner through journals and books.

After two years it is possible to distinguish some common features regarding privatisation in these economies. The issues discussed in relation to privatisation, both in the economics profession and among politicians, centred on the following inter-related features of the process: (i) its speed, (ii) revenue raising, (iii) its extent, (iv) equity, (v) preparation, and (vi) the role of foreigners.

Concerning the speed of privatisation, the discussion has centred on whether to privatise quickly (shock therapy) or slowly (by targeting and gradually). Arguments have been put forth for both, and both policies have been chosen and implemented. It is the common experience of all the countries concerned, with the exception of Hungary and to a certain extent Yugoslavia, that they opted for policies of rapid privatisation. However, in all cases the laws enacted favoured less haste than the policies envisaged and the actual implementation was even slower. The process of privatis-ation required continuous revitalisation. Numerous such plans were passed up until the autumn of 1991. The slow-down affected even the economies which had chosen a gradual approach.[18]

Advocates of rapid privatisation argue that the purpose of the transition is to create efficient market-oriented firms and that this is impossible without private property. They seem to argue that transition is an 'instant package' in which lagging behind in one goal brings the others into question, especially the two other 'grand' goals of markets and democracy. Privatisation is also claimed to contribute significantly to another 'grand' goal in that it makes the decomposition of Soviet-type economies irreversible, which gives the process important political dimensions. Rapid privatisation prevents a dual system from emerging with producers simultan-eously dependent on two types of microeconomic relations, the first based on markets and profits and the second on commands and tutelage. Furthermore, rapid privatisation is supposed to reduce uncertainty and adjustment fatigue, as well as avoid the political paralysis of gradualism, while enabling very scarce resources to be allocated to other goals.

The arguments for gradualism point to the need to minimize overall (through time) transition costs and the requirement that the transition should achieve other goals apart from merely changing property rights. Indeed, gradualists point out that the overriding goals of efficient production and market exchange can be achieved by alternative policies and that private ownership does not in itself 'deliver' any of the expectations placed upon it. They also argue that privatisation in itself is a poor policy instrument and is inferior to other policies in most aspects bar efficiency goals. Gradualism argues in favour of a controlled and policy-oriented privatisation, which is frequently reduced to case-by-case privatisation. Proponents of gradualism also point to the negative side-effects of rapid privatisation (inequity, undervaluation of resources, policy errors due to speed, etc.).

Since rapid privatisation dismisses most of its negative side-effects as being of secondary importance in comparison with the positive effects of speed, most of the remaining aspects concerning privatisation are discussed by the advocates of gradualism.

If privatisation is to earn a revenue, which is always the case when foreign capital is involved, then gradualism is necessary; indeed, privatisation can be reduced to the case-by-case approach.[19] If it is to succeed in earning a revenue, privatisation must address at least three extremely complex issues: (1) valuation of the capital stock, (2) finding potential buyers and (3) determining the beneficiaries in the sale. Valuation problems of the existing capital stock seem insoluble[20] in an environment of administered prices, non-existent capital markets, uncertainty about future tax and monetary policies, and inadequate knowledge-intensive producer services.[21] Finding buyers is no easier. The domestic market does not have the capital (and those that do raise equity issues) while foreign capital expects many 'sweeteners' and is in a dominating bargaining position. Furthermore, when revenue is an important goal, the governments are under continuous populist pressure not to allow a give-away sale of the national wealth. The beneficiary of these sales is the state administration, whether directly through budgets or indirectly through funds managing the resources under the close tutelage of government.[22] It is difficult to imagine a successful privatisation of loss-making enterprises. The question of preparing enterprises for privatisation has been addressed through 'commercialisation' (making firms profit oriented), 'demonopolisation' (breaking up national monopolies), 'decomposition' (breaking up enterprises into potentially profit-making entities and loss-making ones) 'corporatisation' (establishment of tangible property rights) and 'liquidation' (allowing the capital stock to be used in new firms[23]). Most of these economies have attempted demonopolisation and decomposition[24] at the national level, but the question of local monopolies has not yet been addressed.

The extent of privatisation has been a sadly neglected topic. Public discussions seem to indicate here more than elsewhere, the influence of the 'pendulum effect' where policies swing from one extreme (complete state ownership) to the other (no public ownership). Not only are the possible positive effects of mixed ownership of producers within a sector disregarded (see Chapter 4 of this volume, for example), but the supply of services and utilities is being replaced by their private provision which erodes the welfare level. This privatisation is probably strongly influenced by budget deficits, stabilisation policies and falling real wages and production.

Equity issues related to privatisation are important not only because of the political appeal of populist policies but also because of inherited egalitarianism and the deteriorating economy. An important issue addressed in all these economies has been how to distribute the deserts of privatisation fairly, how to prevent the emergence of large economic inequalities, and how to protect the national wealth. The first is based on the notion that all members of society contributed to the existing capital stock and national wealth and should therefore enjoy the consequences of its privatisation. The idea is expressed in the notion of 'people's capitalism' or 'popular capitalism' and reflected in give-away schemes (like voucher schemes and workers' shares) or reserving shares for small shareholders or workers. Some form of this has been advocated in each of these economies.[25] The fear of large inequalities emerging during the transition is real and fosters populist egalitarianism. There are many reasons for this and the more outstanding ones are: inherited low inequality levels; the fear that only racketeers and 'old regime' beneficiaries have the capital to buy newly privatised firms;[26] the further stimulus privatisation can give to 'savage capitalism'; and the fear of the social costs of the transition and the inequalities inherent in markets.

The role foreign capital can play in privatisation is closely related to the valuation and equity questions. With domestic sources of capital very limited (as well as being frequently of dubious origin), great expectations in all these economies are placed on foreign capital. At the same time, there is a fear of selling off the national wealth and some need for protection. This has lead to a double-handed policy in these economies. Thus there have been major policy changes removing limitations on foreign capital involved in ground–up privatisation,[27] while at the same time many bureaucratic limitations and regulations remain when foreign capital is involved in privatisation from above.[28] These restrictions are an expression of the fear that an economy starved of domestic capital can offer foreigners undervalued capital stock on more favourable terms than that offered to domestic capital.

The expectations from privatisation

The expectations from privatisation by the politicians (and many economists) as well as by the population of these economies have been very big. Indeed, many treated it as one of the three equal components of the 'magic wand of transition' (the other two being markets and democracy). This was especially true during the early days of 'heady optimism' when it was expected the transition would be easy, relatively costless and with low barriers. That is why privatisation was one of the first issues addressed by all the newly elected governments once they came to power.

It was expected that privatisation would be one of the main instruments for irreversibly decomposing 'socialist production relations', or more precisely the centralised command economy and its tutelage system. Private property, independent profit-maximising firms and competitive markets would, it was claimed, thought and believed, be sufficient to irreversibly dismantle rigid bureaucratic centralised planning and decision-taking. The two were thought to be incompatible, hence rapid privatisation had to be high on the agenda.

A further important role of privatisation was to be its contribution to depoliticising society in general and the economy in particular. The all-embracing power of 'the party' and, especially, its interference in the economy by determining personnel and investment policy and reducing all issues to political considerations, were thought to be incompatible with a mixed economy with dominant private ownership, where there is a clear division between economics and politics. Politics is dominated by democratic rules and economies by competitive profit-seeking entrepreneurs.

Lastly it was expected and hoped that privatisation would in its own right provide a much-needed engine for growth. Property restructuring would free the entrepreneurial animal instincts, enabling industrial restructuring.

Privatisation was thus seen to be as important as and inseparable from political democracy and market exchange. This was especially true during the early days of transition. The expectational burden of privatisation is very heavy and it shares something with another component of the 'magic wand'. Like market exchange, private property is seen in an idealised form. The vision that policy-makers and many economists in these countries have regarding the efficiency of production under private ownership, the success with which shareholders can control and influence managers of corporations, and the absence of political considerations in economic decision-making is closer to textbook paradigms than to real-world economics. This kind of idealisation led to the burden being heavy.

Privatisation has not fulfilled its expectations. This is not just because it was impossible to satisfy such expectations or because of the short period in which it has been taking place, but also because it has not become a self-regulating process in any of the economies. Indeed, the opposite is true. The privatisation process has had to be continuously recharged and has been much slower than envisaged. This is one of the important reasons why the transitional period, and with it the interregnum, has been extended.

The role of the state in a prolonged 'interregnum' period[29]

In all these economies, numerous pressures (economic as well as social and political) have appeared which lead to the deceleration of the speed of transition. It has been shown how these are reflected in privatisation that is not yet a self-governing process but is continually slowing down and requires new policy drives. The fear of large social costs during the transition, adjustment fatigue, inherited risk-averse behaviour and a new political landscape favouring populism also favour deceleration. The behaviour of managers and workers further adds to this. But perhaps most importantly a reassesment of the magnitude and complexity of the transition as well as its barriers and constraints, both of which were underestimated, provides the main pressure which will lead to a prolonged interregnum.

Such an extended transition from one growth path to another will not only give the state additional tasks to the important ones it already has, but may also provide some important policy opportunities. Such a prominent role for the state may seem a paradox given the long-term policy objectives of deregulating a command economy and building a market one instead.

During the transition from a state-owned to a mixed ownership economy the state has many important tasks which are not path dependent (see also Chapter 2). These are primarily related to building the underpinnings required by a market economy. For their orderly and efficient functioning, markets require underpinnings that are still non-existent in these economies. Not only are there no laws, but there are no market institutions, regulating bodies or accumulated experiences.[30] This is especially true for factor markets (e.g. for capital markets there are no bourses, financial banking or regulatory agencies) but is true for all markets (there are no anti-monopoly laws or legal experience nor is bankruptcy regulated satisfactorily). The time available has prompted some economists to propose a simple translation and application of EC laws in these areas. The role of the state concerning 'market failure' issues is also path independent. Whereas developed mixed economies have a long history, both practical and theoretical, of solving market failure problems, this experience is lacking in the economies under consideration. Since indivisibilities and public goods and services are included under market failures it is clear how important these questions are. Housing has already been mentioned as an important source of inequality, while the difficulties concerning public goods and services will be discussed later. Another path-independent role of the state is connected to devising a framework for macreconomic policies (stabilisation policies especially), because until now economic policy was based on quite different principles.

The very nature of a prolonged interregnum adds, however, new path-dependent tasks for the state. Two seem especially important. The first is the role the state has as a consequence of gradual privatisation and the second is a result of the gradual introduction of markets.

As has been said, gradual privatisation assumes the sale of profitable state enterprises to voluntary buyers. Making existing state enterprises profitable operations through their 'commercialisation', 'demonopolisation', worker shedding, decomposition, etc. and introducing efficient monitoring and control of managers are all decisions which involve the state as a prominent participant. Gradual case-by-case privatisation involves, furthermore, the state in its supervision and the issuing of permits. The experience of most of these economies shows that the role of the state is increasing, as the state is not only managing privatisation[31] but is reasserting its position in the economy,[32] managing the reorganisation[33] and commercialisation[34] of enterprises and permitting very low levels of decentralisation.[35]

The gradual development of markets that is inherent in a prolonged interregnum requires the state to exercise significant regulation[36] before the markets become a self-regulating process.

On the other hand, an extended interregnum provides the state with new policy opportunities. A proactive industrial policy for restructuring, a regional policy decreasing the impact of regional asymmetries during transition and a welfare policy minimising social costs seem most probable. While the last two will not be discussed here, the first will be briefly.

The 40 years of postwar development policies have left all these economies with major structural deformities which are well known. Thus all these economies share an over-representation of heavy industry and large enterprises and an under-representation of services, agriculture and energy. The capital stock has been run down and is largely technologically out of date, energy intensive and environmentally dangerous, while human capital is lacking as well. Management is risk averse and together with labour shows a very low rate of innovation. The organisation of production has been neglected, leading to high X-inefficiency and low productivity.

Such circumstances and a prolonged interregnum do provide a challenge for designing an active industrial policy. Gradual privatisation can use the extensive state sector for other goals, for it must be remembered that privatisation as a policy is a poor instrument. For policy goals other than efficiency gains, it is inferior to other policies (see Yarrow, 1986, p.363). Hence a well-designed gradual privatisation policy could go a long way towards sectoral restructuring by selecting propulsive sectors and firms. Defining the as yet undefined behavioural rules of managers in state-owned firms and the relationship between state firms and the state could also be done with economic policy in mind. Existing labour relations and work discipline could also make the task of manpower and retraining easier.

However, for a successful industrial policy opportunities are not enough. Success depends on implementation and credibility as well as on the choice of correct policies. There are three main reasons why the state's success is doubtful. The first concerns 'state failure', the second the lack of human capital, and the third is a credibility gap. To this one must add political considerations. While the lack of human capital and political considerations have been dealt with, the other two require comment. State failure has largely been analysed in relation to development policy,[37] and from a long list the most important in the present context are allocational errors (due to ignorance, lobbying, sectarian and regional interests or 'elitism'), bureaucratic rigidity and slowness (in a fast-changing world), imperfect information and limited capacity for its use, and the state blocking initiatives and entrepreneurship. The credibility gap comes from the undoubtedly unsatisfactory past experience of central planning, development policies and state overhang.

Notes

1   In Yugoslavia, as a consequence of applying the self-management paradigm, the capital stock was owned by 'society' and hence there was 'social ownership'. In this paper, unless otherwise stated, for simplicity's sake, when referring to state ownership of the capital stock, in the case of Yugoslavia this will mean social ownership.

2   Referred to also as reprivatisation or denationalisation.

3   Even though the term was coined in the CSFR for describing any privatisation for cash to a single owner, it is now used in reference to all these economies to describe any privatisation of small or medium-sized enterprises.

4   Even this is more complicated that it seems. Unclear present land ownership (especially of plant sites) has been one of the main causes for the failure of small privatisation and even its temporary suspension in Hungary, (see Jackson, 1991, p.44).

5   Romania has renamed and protected them (see Topor, 1991), Bulgaria has increased the role of machine-tractor stations (see Nikolaev, 1991) and in the CSFR their land has been excluded from privatisation (see Martin, 1991).

6   In Bulgaria a 30 ha maximum (20 ha in the most fertile regions) has been imposed (see Nikolaev, 1991); in the CSFR up to 150 ha can be reclaimed but only 36% of land is included in privatisation and restitution (see Martin, 1991): Romania permits a maximum reclamation of 10 ha and imposed a 10-year re-sale ban (see Topor, 1991); in Yugoslavia the federal land maximum has been abolished and various republics have introduced different limitations. Croatia and Slovenia have abolished the maximum, while Vojvodina has increased it from 10 to 30 ha (see Bicanic and Skreb, 1991b).

7   None of the republics which constituted Yugoslavia (see Bicanic, and Skreb, 1991b) or Romania (see Topor, 1991).

8   Fearing long disputes it has been speeded up in the CSFR (see Wellisz, 1991) and in Poland the new government installed in early 1991 has given it higher priority (see Fallenbuchl, 1991).

9   In Bulgaria, discussion over it has prevented the privatisation law from being passed (see Nikolaev, 1991), while in Hungary the application of the privatisation law was held up until it was passed (see Okolicsanyi, 1991).

10   In the CSFR, restitution applies only to small business (see Grosfeld and Hare, 1991), while in Hungary large enterprises, church and the largest agricultural co-operatives have been excluded (see Wellisz, 1991).

11   Hungary has opted for compensation through vouchers. Their value is regressively related to the value of the asset, a maximum voucher value has been determined, and, although the vouchers cannot be redeemed for cash, they can be used in property auctions envisaged in the future (see Wellisz, 1991). Poland has chosen to give each asset points, which later determine the share in a special fund (see Wellisz, 1991). The CSFR has chosen to compensate previous owners in cash (see Wellisz, 1991). Bulgaria has decided to compensate both by returning assets comparable to the previously nationalised assets and through cash payments (see *Report on Eastern Europe* RFE/RL, No. 17/II).

12   And, in economies with extensive private agriculture (e.g. Poland and Yugoslavia), an over-representation of small (subsistence) peasant plots, making the distribution of productive units 'double humped'.

13   In Poland, see Jackson (1991), in Yugoslavia, see Bicanic and Skreb (1991b) and in the CSFR, see Obrman (1991).

14   The CSFR, Hungary, and to a limited extent Poland.

15   Choosing from among many options (auctions, liquidation, leasing, worker buy-outs, direct sale, direct privatisation or self-privatisation), Poland has chosen worker buy-outs, leasing, liquidations and direct sales, the CSFR auctions and direct sales, Hungary self-privatisation and direct sales, while Yugoslav federal law has permitted partial worker buy-outs and direct privatisation.

16   In the CSFR, out of 70,000 small enterprises offered in auctions only 3,000 were privatised (see Jackson, 1991). In Poland, only 28% of state-owned stores and 243 medium-sized industrial enterprises have been privatised (see Jackson, 1991). In Hungary, a self-privatisation drive has not affected more than 350 enterprises (see *Report on Eastern europe*, RFE/RL, No 27/II.

17   The American economist Jeffrey Sachs, probably the most influential economist among politicians and a consultant to the Yugoslav, Slovenian, Polish and Soviet governments, is a specialist on Latin America and debt.

18   Hungary is the example of gradual privatisation while all other economies have opted for rapid privatisation. In the latter, the slowing down of privatisation has required frequent government privatisation drives, campaigns and plans. In Poland, the Act on Privatisation was passed in July 1990 and the first minister in charge of privatisation, Jacek Kuzcinsky, following a pilot privatisation project in September 1990 (in which the seven planned privatisations of the most profitable enterprises were reduced to five; see Fallenbuch, 1991), announced a privatisation plan in December 1990 (with targets of privatising 50% of the economy in three years and approximating the ownership structure of developed economies in five; see Jackson, 1991). The new government and new minister, Janusz Lewandowski, announced a new plan in March 1991 (retaining global targets and aiming to privatise 400 enterprises in the third quarter of 1991 and 300 in the fourth; see Bielinski, 1991), and a privatisation drive in June 1991 (planning to privatise 25% of the GDP and 12% of employment in six months; see Wellisz, 1991). In Hungary, the government plan was announced in the summer of 1990 (aiming to privatise 50–60% of state assets; see Grosfeld and Hare, 1991). In September 1990 the State Property Agency announced the First Privatisation Programme (privatisation of 20 companies with good potential; see Grosfeld and Hare, 1991), and a second programme for 1991 (predicting the privatisation in 1991 of 400 enterprises involving 20% of state assets; see Jackson, 1991). But by July 1991 there were no fixed plans (see BBC Monitoring, EE. No. 1123/B). In spite of a commitment to rapid privatisation in the CSFR and the legal structure being in place by mid-1991, by the autumn of 1991 there was only a June 1991 plan (earmarking 50 enterprises for sale to foreigners (see *Report on Eastern Europe*, RFE/RL, No. 33/II)). The other countries are committed to rapid privatisation but the legal framework is still being discussed. The exception is Croatia, which has passed the laws but the war prevented any further development (see Bicanic and Skreb, 1991b).

19   Hungary is the only one of these economies that has explicitly stated revenue as a major goal of its privatisation (see Grosfeld and Hare, 1991) and largely reduced its large privatisation to a case-by-case approach. Poland, the other country fairly far along the privatisation road, has also recently started favouring a case-by-case approach (see Jackson, 1991).

20   Because of the insoluble difficulties involved, valuation problems have provided an important incentive for give-away schemes which by-pass them (see Portes, 1991).

21   In all these economies, foreign banks, accountancy firms and consultants play a prominent role.

22   Frequently some quasi-government agency or fund.

23   This method especially gained popularity in Poland (see Bielinski, 1991) and Yugoslavia (see Bicanic and Skreb, 1991b). Both economies inherited workers' councils and forms of self-management, with the consequent pressure for worker buy-outs and employee ownership. Liquidation was a means of addressing these pressures.

24   For Poland and Hungary (in sugar refining) see Jackson (1991), for Bulgaria (where 100 enterprises were broken into 800 smaller business and it seems the most extensive programme was set up under the Council for Demonopolisation) see Engelbrekt (1991).

25   Poland has opted for vouchers (up to 30% of the value of assets) and reserving some shares for small stockholders (see Fallenbuchl, 1991). In the CSFR the initial heavy reliance on vouchers was reduced in the laws that were actually passed (see Obrman, 1991). The federal plan in Yugoslavia introduced a complicated system of non-transferable internal (worker) shares which was muted in Croatia and Slovenia, (see Bicanic and Skreb, 1991b), while Romania has started discussing privatisation which includes a widespread voucher system (see Topor, 1991). Only Hungary has refused any form of a give-away scheme (see Grosfeld and Hare, 1991).

26   The negative experience of 'nomenklatura privatisation' (Levitas and Strzalkowski, 1990) acted as a pointer. It was possible from 1988 in Poland, Hungary and Bulgaria, and involved asset-stripping, large quasi-rents and insider knowledge creating a small rich stratum whose wealth was based on shady deals. The Romanian government has come under attack for favouring 'old regime' applicants (see *Report on Eastern Europe*, RFE/RL, No. 16/II).

27   All these economies have attempted to attract foreign capital in similar ways: profit repatriation has been liberalised, permitting the export of profits in a foreign currency; ownership restrictions have been lifted or reduced, allowing the possibility of complete foreign ownership of new firms and majority ownership in existing ones; bureaucratic red tape has been reduced by raising the value ceilings requiring permits and by simplifying procedures; etc. (see Grosfeld and Hare, 1991, and Jackson, 1991).

28   In Poland, foreigners need approval if they buy more than 10% of shares (see Fallenbuchl, 1991), in the CSFR they were excluded from the 1991 privatisation auctions (see Obrman, 1991), while in Romania the proposal excludes them for five years (see *Report on Eastern Europe*, RFE/RL, No. 26/11). In Hungary, the case-by-case approach imposes similar constraints.

29 This section is based on Bicanic and Skreb (forthcoming).

30 For example, the lack of legislative experience has led to inefficiencies (see Jackson, 1991) and frequently legal regulation 'has been slow and uncertain, with legal provision often correcting and changing processes that were already under way' (Grosfeld and Hare, 1991, p. 138).

31 In all the economies, ministries (in Poland the Ministry for Privatisation and in the CSFR the Ministry of National Property Administration and its Privatisation) or government agencies (in Hungary the State Privatisation Agency, in Croatia the Republic Restructuring Agency) manage privatisation by proposing rules, drawing up plans, earmarking enterprises for privatisation, negotiating with foreign partners and issuing the necessary permits.

32 In Hungary, the state reasserted state property, placing any reorganisation under most government control (see Grosfeld and Hare, 1991), in the CSFR there was a renationalisation as the workers' councils were dissolved (see Grosfeld and Hare, 1991), in Croatia the state took direct ownership over many enterprises (see Bicanic and Skreb, 1991b).

33 Demonopolisation especially in Poland (see Jackson, 1991) and Bulgaria (see Engelbrekt, 1991).

34 Which is happening in all these economies as the government appoints managers and takes direct responsibility for the operation of many enterprises.

35 Neither Poland nor Hungary has regionalised privatisation in spite of bottlenecks and accumulation of power in the centre (see Grosfeld and Hare, 1991), Croatia has also kept decision-making power in the centre (see Bicanic and Skreb, 1991b), while in the CSFR the nature of the economy is more conducive to regional decentralisation, which has not yet taken place (see Obrman, 1991).

36 Portes (1991) points to the need to control the conduct of managers, provide transparency, determine efficiency tests and enable equal operating conditions.

37 See World Bank (1983), Stern (1989) or Krueger (1990)

References

Bicanic, Ivo (1989), 'Systemic aspects of the social crises in Yugoslavia', in Stanislaw Gomulka *et al.* (eds), *Economic Reforms in the Socialist World*, London: Macmillan.

Bicanic, Ivo and Skreb, Marko (1991a), 'The service sector in the East European economies: what role can it play in future growth', *Communist Economies and Economic Transformation*, III (3), 221–34.

Bicanic, Ivo and Skreb, Marko (1991b), 'The private sector in the Yugoslav economy', mimeo, paper written for the World Bank project on System-Related Issues in Measuring Economic Performance, *Module* 6: Measurement of the private sector's contribution.

Bicanic, Ivo and Skreb, Marko (forthcoming), 'A paradox of the transition to a market economy: how will the role of the state change?' in Franco Targetti (ed.), *Privatisation in the Transition to Post-Socialist Development*, Aldershot: Dartmouth.

Bielinski, Jarzy (1991), '*Commercialisation of Polish enterprises*', mimeo, paper presented at the central European university seminar on privatisation, Prague, July.

Brus, Vladzimierz (1986), 'Postwar reconstruction and socio-economic transformation', in Kaser, Michael and Radice E. A. (eds) (1986), *The Economic History of Eastern Europe 1919–1975*, Vol. II, Oxford: Clarendon Press.

Engelbrekt, Kjell (1991), 'Bulgaria: economic reform: results and prospects', *Report on Eastern Europe*, Vol. II, No. 34, 1–8.

Fallenbuchl, Zbigniew (1991), 'Poland: the new government and privatisation'. *Report on Eastern Europe*, Vol. II, No. 12, 11–16.

Grosfeld, Irena and Hare, Paul (1991), 'Privatisation in Hungary, Poland and Czechoslovakia', *European Economy*, Special Edition, No. 2, 129–56.

Jackson, Marvin (1991), 'The progress of privatisation', *Report on Eastern Europe*, Vol. II, No. 29, 10–14.

Krueger, A. O. (1990), 'Government failures in development', *Journal of Economic Perspectives*, IV (3), 9–24.

Levitas, Anthony and Strzalkowski, Piotr (1990), 'What does 'uwlaszczenie nomenklatury' ('Propertisation' of the nomkenklatura) really mean?' *Communist Economies*, II (3) 413–16.

Martin, Peter (1991), 'Czechoslovakia: new law on land privatisation passed', *Report on Eastern Europe*, Vol. II, No. 29, 10–14.

Nikolaev, Rada (1991), 'Bulgaria: The new law on farmland', *Report on Eastern Europe*, Vol. II, No. 19, 1–5.

Nove, Alec (1983), *The Economics of Feasible Socialism*, London: Allen & Unwin.

Obrman, Jan (1991). Czechoslovakia: two landmark bills on privatisation approved', *Report on Eastern Europe*. Vol. II, No. 11, 12–16.

Okolicsanyi, Karoly (1991), 'Hungary: the compensation law: attempting to correct past mistakes', *Report on Eastern Europe*, Vol. II, No. 19, 7–11.

Portes, Richard (1991), 'Introduction', *European Economy*, Special Edition, No. 2, 1–16.

Stern, Nick (1989), 'The economics of development', *Economic Journal*, XCIX, 597–685.

Szelenyi, Ivan (1983), *Urban Inequalities under State Socialism*, Oxford: Oxford University Press.

Topor, Gabriel (1991) 'Rumania: the post communist land law', *Report on Eastern Europe*, Vol. II, No. 35, 36–40.

Vahcic, Ales (1989), 'Prestrukturiranje jugoslavenske privrede pomocu poduzetnistva', *Nase teme*, XXXIII, 2906–15.

Wellisz, Christopher (1991), 'Poland: the perils of restitution', *Report on Eastern Europe*, Vol. II, No. 33, 1–5.

Winiecki, Jan (1989), 'Large industrial enterprises in Soviet-type economies: the ruling stratum's main rent-seeking area', *Communist Economies*, I (4), 363–85.

World Bank, (1983), *World Development Report 1983*, New York: Oxford University Press.

World Bank (1991), *The Transformation of Economies in Central and Eastern Europe: Issues, Progress and Prospects*, Socialist Economics Unit, Washington DC, April.

Yarrow, George (1986), Privatisation in theory and practice', *Economic Policy*, II, April, 323–79.

The transition process in Eastern Europe

Some lessons from Germany

Economic reforms in Eastern Europe – induced by the process of democratisation – aim at closing the gap in living standards compared with Western European countries and at catching up in productivity. There are two main lines of political action. First, the rules of a new economic constitution have to be established. Economic reforms are directed towards adapting the constitution of a market economy: private property with productive resources; liberalisation of markets; rules of competition policy; reform of the public sector, i.e. tax reform to finance public expenditure and redistribution policy; a social security system; last, but not least, reform of the monetary sector and the banking system. Second, policy is pursuing a strategy of integration: opening up the markets to Western products and knowledge and at the same time striving for access to the Western European markets, especially the EC.

Although the reform concepts applied differ greatly by country, these guidelines form the bases of development policy in all of Central and Eastern Europe. There is reason to suppose that such a strategy might be successful: historical examples like the 'Wirtschaftswunder' of West Germany after World War II suggest that the joint effects of economic reforms and integration have been important determinants of economic development.

This paper is part of a research project which intends to compare the Central and Eastern European countries' approaches of a more or less gradual transition with a development strategy from scratch – German reunification. The project being in its initial phase, no results can be presented. Rather, different concepts of transition are analysed with respect to the underlying theories. In addition, it is asked what lessons can be drawn from the German experience for socialist economies in transition in Central and Eastern Europe.

Theoretical concepts of transition

What does theory tell us about transition? The most striking fact is that nobody had foreseen the problem. It is true that the poor performance of socialist economies has been a subject of economic analysis. Technological backwardness and chronic shortages have been traced back to systemic defects. Nuti (1988), for example, underlines the inability of a socialist system to cope with complex problems – i.e. to co-ordinate the divergent objectives of society – and its lack of adjustability and innovative capacity. However, theoretical and empirical research since the von Wiese/Lange debate on planning has been preoccupied with the issue of efficiency. As is well known, the source of this debate was the question whether or not a socialist, centrally planned economy can be efficient. Of course, if the proper information requirements are fulfilled and the economy is under the control of the planning authority, a socialist economy can be organised according to neoclassical efficiency criteria. Neoclassical theory, therefore, has always been fascinating for Marxist economists. The controversy on efficiency provided the theoretical background for research in comparative systems. The message of the research programme was that, under realistic conditions, systemic defects could be resolved by convergence.

Hence, much research on transformation was directed towards the partial implantation of systemic elements. For example:

- The question was discussed of creating incentives for economic efficiency by decentralising the decision process within a system of central planning; relatively early on this induced a new economic policy in the GDR (economic leverage) and similar reform policies in Czechoslovakia and the Soviet Union.
- On similar terms, but with more far-reaching consequences, the programme of a 'third way' (Ota Sik, 1979) for a socialist market economy was a result of the convergence debate.
- This debate on convergence was further stimulated by the insight that private property was evidently not an essential part of an efficient market economy. In the West, institutionalism created the notion of 'managerial capitalism' (Robbin Marris,

1964), which relied on the division of private property rights and the power of decision-taking in the capitalist corporation (joint stock corporation). The work of John Galbraith, with his notion of the 'industry structure', underlined this view. Along this line of reasoning, a capitalist manager was not very different from a socialist functionary.

This tradition of research in comparative systems with a stance on convergence has evidently had much influence on current explanations of the transition process in Eastern Europe. In particular, it has been postulated that a socialist system can be transformed gradually, i.e. by pursuing a step-by-step approach to a market economy (see also the previous chapter). Moreover, it has been assumed that this process of transformation can be designed and controlled by policy in an optimal way (the welfare theory approach of rational economic policy). There are several reasons for questioning this theoretical approach. Experiences in Eastern European economies, in particular Poland and the Soviet Union, show that gradual reforms have made economic performance worse for a very long period. Furthermore, the focus on efficiency may be justified in an environment where there are stable institutions. In a world of change, however, society lacks a framework for defining and evaluating marginal steps.

A different approach is needed, therefore, to explain the process of change. In particular, the fundamental issues of uncertainty and information requirements in society have to be recognised. Consequently, an appropriate theoretical concept of transition has above all to take into account the fact that transition is an open process. Moreover, the concept of gradual transition neglects the fact that reform steps are not interchangeable but rather have to be seen as set in an hierarchical order. Certain fundamental requirements have to be fulfilled in advance if a market economy is to evolve.

Against this background, the following propositions are made. First, a socialist planning system and a capitalist market economy are mutually exclusive, with the consequence that a gradual transformation avoiding the social cost of structural change is not feasible. Second, after the socialist system has broken down, the task of transition is to establish a market economy from scratch – the outcome of which is uncertain. Hence, the crucial question of sequencing is to define the elementary conditions of economic development and to open up options for future change.

There are two lines of theoretical support for the proposition of mutual exclusiveness which provide the basis of transition requirements.

The first line refers to the Austrian tradition of economic theory. The methodological individualism of the Austrian tradition stresses uncertainty and the fact that the use of information within society is restricted. In particular, Hayek's (1948) judgement that only markets provide the necessary information 'of time and place' for innovative activity delivers a theoretical explanation for the lack of innovative capacity of socialist economies. According to the Austrian tradition, 'the lack of knowledge' needed to pursue a rational economic policy is 'constitutional' (Witt, 1991). Hence, the market's capacity of adjustment cannot be replaced by state intervention (Hayek describes the market as a method of discovery).

On the other hand, the methodological individualism of the Austrian tradition constitutes a theory of economic evolution. In a constellation of uncertainty it is the Schumpeterian entrepreneur, undertaking innovative enterprise, who gives momentum to evolution. However, the 'constitutional lack of knowledge' means that the results of evolution cannot be determined in advance. This theoretical position provides for a different background for the explanation of transitional change. It is in line with a liberal position upheld by Ralf Dahrendorf in his recent book *Reflections on the Revolution in Europe*, which states that the process of transition is basically an open process the results of which cannot be foretold. At the same time, the possibility of error has to be taken into account. The most important, therefore, is 'to keep our matters open for change' (Dahrendorf, 1990).

The second line of argument concerns the monetary conditions of transition. Only recently did monetary theory clarify the conditions of mutual exclusiveness of a socialist planning system and the market economy. The theory of convergence, and the proposition of a 'third way' in particular, could not tackle the problem of efficient capital allocation. In a socialist market economy there was no market for capital, as investment funds were subject to government distribution. By contrast, managerial capitalism provides leeway for the control of managers by shareholders and the banking system, thus guaranteeing efficiency conditions in that respect. Incidentally, proposals for transition stressing the issue of shares and the establishment of capital markets underline the importance of an efficient control of capital allocation (Newbury 1990: Sinn, 1990).

On the other hand, monetary theory clarified the decisive difference between a shortage economy and a money economy, which typically is in excess of goods supplied. In a capitalist economy, scarcity is manipulated by the monetary system. Money, if it is to fulfil its functions, has to be a scarce factor. Hence, monetary theory explains not only the inflationary bias of socialist economies (pump-priming by the state) but also their systemic allocative inefficiency and lack of innovative strength. Take the role of liquidity. The functioning of the market system rests on the confidence that an enterprise which is liquid is able to react to unforeseen events by a market transaction. If, on the other hand, a manager cannot trust in the purchasing power of his liquid assets – the case of a shortage economy – a market transaction will be a high-risk option. Consequently, firms will amass stocks as surrogates for liquid balances – this is the role of secret stocks (Lohmann, 1985) – and, on the other hand, will reduce their need for market transactions by vertical integration: each and every nail is produced in-house. This was – apart from the ideology of people's ownership – the main systemic reason for the vertical integration of industry in the former GDR (so-called 'Kombinate'): the number of small and medium-sized enterprises in the GDR was reduced from about 10,000 in 1971 to fewer than 1,000 by 1987.

The result is a backwardness in productivity which has two different aspects:

(1) a lack of specialisation (which uses comparative advantage of the division of labour); the dominance of bilateral relations in the former Comecon has been the outstanding indicator of a lack of money scarcity;
(2) the allocative condition of development – diversity in the economic structure – is missing; hence, by lacking scarce money, socialist economies suffer from a systemic backlog in their innovative potential.

Consequences
If we accept this approach in explaining the nature of the transition process, three propositions follow:

(1) According to the Austrian tradition, development is essentially an open, competitive process. This should be understood as a long-run proposition. There is much short-termism in the notion of sequencing. David Newbery was one of the first to analyse the sequencing problem (1990). He recently expressed the key concerns of the transition process as:

- macroeconomic stability;
- retained options for future change, specifically to increase the competitive performance of the economy;
- maintenance of government support for continued reform with a long-term view of decentralisation.

This clearly indicates that strengthening the competitive forces is a long-term issue. Above all it implies trade liberalisation, i.e. tackling the inefficiencies resulting from national monopolies by opening up markets to international competition, that is, economic integration. It is exactly what we hear from Eastern Europe. Rita Klimova (Karls University, Prague), ambassador of the CSFR to the USA, recently made a remarkable speech at a Stanford symposium in Berlin. She specified three major problems:

(i) the breakdown of the former markets in Eastern Europe (USSR, GDR);
(ii) the CSFR government wants not aid or debt relief, or preferential treatment in the first place, but open access to markets;
(iii) whether or nor a parliamentary system can cope with unemployment (macro-stability).

She recognised that market integration provides for the competitive forces which are an essential precondition for sustained economic development.

Karel Dyba, the Czech minister of economics, argues in the same direction. His proposed programme of economic reforms (see Charap and Dyba, 1991) has as its main issues: (i) price liberalisation (started early in 1991), (ii) opening the economy, (iii) devaluation of the crown to retain convertibility and accompany liberalisation of markets (also early 1991).

These statements have in common that the long-term issues have to be tackled first.

(2) Development by innovation requires a strong monetary system and, in particular, assigns a dominant role to the banks in allocating financial resources. Here Austrian theory (Schumpeter's development theory – 1911) and monetary theory (Keynesian-monetary, by the way) coincide. A monetary reform, therefore, establishing a two-tier banking system, is of utmost importance:

(a) An independent central bank has to provide for a stable currency which is accepted as a medium of deferred payment, i.e. lenders must be prepared to give up liquidity. In particular, the central bank must not be committed to financing the public deficit.

(b) A credit market has to be set up, where private banks intermediate between lenders and borrowers. The banks play a crucial role in development in providing for an efficient allocation of funds for investment purposes (Morishima and Catephores, 1988).

(3) As far as economic evolution is concerned, two aspects of technological innovation should be taken into account (Allen, 1988):

(i) The momentum of evolution is enhanced by diversity. Innovation is to a large extent a re-combination of best-practice techniques. A diversified industrial structure thus provides favourable conditions for the innovative process.

(ii) Social learning, i.e. adjustment to new knowledge, plays a central role in an evolutionary, open society. This implies that an innovative process, to be set in motion, requires leeway for making 'errors'. Here, we see a peculiar role for the Schumpeterian entrepreneur. Even if the innovations which are introduced by entrepreneurs fail on average, the process of selection by the market may induce evolution. However, evolution is not a mere process of Darwinist selection. On the contrary, in the social field, learning is above all a matter of imitation.

A main issue of an industrial strategy would therefore be, to provide favourable conditions for social learning and imitation.

Development strategy: some lessons from Eastern Germany

If we stress market integration, monetary reform and social learning as the decisive elements of transition, what lessons can be learnt from the German experience? In a sense, there are two historical examples: first, the transition from a fascist war economy, which had many features of a planned or regulated economy, to the market economy of the postwar period; and, secondly, the German reunification after 1989.

The process of German reunification is particularly interesting because of its rapid implementation. It is true that in Eastern and Central Europe countries are in no position to proceed along these lines. The example illustrates, however, what consequences and requirements a rapid transition will have.

The peculiar circumstances of German reunification were the following:

The process started with an integrated labour market. When the wall was opened on 9 November 1989, it meant that the West German labour markets were opened up to East Germans. Large income differentials and a high demand for qualified labour in Western Germany induced emigration from East to West. This constellation was highly unstable and pressurised the government to speed up the restructuring of the GDR economic system.

As a main response to those tensions, a monetary reform exchanging the former currency by the DM took place in mid-1990. Hence, even before German unity (3 October 1990) a monetary union was established supplying a hard and convertible currency.

Thereby the signals were set for a fundamental structural change. The federal government provided for massive income transfers to build up a social security system in East Germany and – after much political pressure had been applied – the East German states were fully integrated into the system of tax revenue redistribution ('Finanzuasgleich') by February 1991. At the same time, considerable administrative support was provided to establish an administration at state and local levels. The government privatisation agency, the Treuhand, was taken over by West German staff. This indicates that a rapid process of social learning was initiated both in public administration and in the enterprise sector.

The German Monetary Union (GMU)

The main transition problems of a monetary union were (1) how to convert money assets and liabilities (the stock problem), (2) how to restore the competitiveness of the GDR economy (the flow problem). First, as to the conversion of money assets, the money stocks accumulated in the past represented an obstacle to further development in that there were no real capital values of equivalent size (money overhang). However, it was clear that within a GMU the money overhang would no longer be a GDR problem but would be transformed into a common German problem.

There are two (conflicting) aspects of this problem. On the one hand, conversion of Mark to D-Mark at a favourable rate could create an inflationary potential. An additional money supply in excess of an amount determined by the increase of productive capacity would have violated the Bundesbank's quality-of-money rule. The expansion of the money supply due to GMU was estimated to amount to 120 billion DM (10% of M3), approximately the additional potential output (Deutsche Bundesbank, 1990). In fact the money supply increased at a higher rate (14%). None the less, inflation was still moderate in the autumn (annual rate: 3%), partly owing to the fact that supply in tradable goods markets is presumably rather elastic. Hence, part of the additional demand was matched by an import increase that helped to reduce Germany's huge current account imbalances. In some narrow markets, for example the market for second-hand cars, prices increased sharply, however.

On the other hand, the conversion rate for money assets determined the extent of the capital transfer flowing from West Germany to East Germany. This transfer has usually been regarded with respect to its distributional consequences but it has a developmental role as well. Money assets were in the hands of private households and small-scale enterprises. A favourable conversion rate for money assets would indeed have provided for equity finance to small business, thus stimulating economic growth. As for private households, incentives to save (a right to buy their dwellings or shares of 'people's ownership' in the productive sector) could have produced similar effects.

The government introduced neither such incentives nor a scheme of freezing private households' savings, tolerating a temporary boom in private consumption. The conversion rates for money assets were differentiated according to social criteria only. Up to a limited amount per person, a 1:1 rate was applied; above that amount the rate was 2:1 (Table 15.1).

Table 15.1 *Consolidated balance sheet of the GDR banking system as of 31 May 1990*

Assets	Marks billion	DM billion	Liabilities	Marks billion	DM billion
1. Credits to domestic debtors	397.4	180.7	1. Deposits by domestic non-banks	249.9	156.6
of which:			of which:		
State	60.6	12.3	State	10.8	5.4
of which:			Firms	57.0	27.8
Credits from revaluation of external liabilities	31.2	—	Private citizens of which:	182.1	123.4
			Demand and savings		
Firms	231.7	115.8	deposits of residents	165.6	115.2
Residential construction	102.6	51.3	Life insurance	14.2	7.1
Private citizens	2.5	1.3			
2. External claims	45.0	36.3	2. External liabilities	152.5	55.6
(a) COMECON countries	17.4	8.7	(a) COMECON countries	1.1	0.6
(b) Western industrialised and less developed countries	27.6	27.6	(b) Western industrialised and less developed countries	55.0	55.0
			(c) Provisions for specific exchange rates	96.4	—
3. Other assets	4.2	2.6	3. Notes and coins in circulation (excluding cash holdings of banks)	13.6	6.8
			4. Accumulated surplus/ reserve fund/liability cover	23.4	23.4
			5. Other liabilities	7.2	3.6
Total	446.6	219.6	Total	446.6	246.0
Balancing item	—	26.4			
Total	446.6	246.0	Total	446.6	246.0

Source: Deutsche Bundesbank (1990); English version in Siebert (1990).

Whereas the conversion of money assets actually increased the real wealth of private households and small-scale enterprises, the West German government did not intend a net capital transfer of equivalent size to the East German economy. Rather, the Deutsche Bundesbank proposed (and the governments, by the State Treaty, approved) that liabilities should be converted at the same rate (2:1) that was in general applied to money assets. Hence, a compensatory item amounting to not more than 26.4 billion DM was necessary to balance assets and liabilities after the conversion act (Table 15.1). However, by limiting the banking sector's claims against government – and, accordingly, limiting the interest burden on the federal budget – the credit banks were left with overvalued assets. In particular, the Deutsche Kreditbank (DKB), a credit bank founded as a daughter of the former GDR Staatsbank, inherited dubious credits to industry and the housing sector which amounted to 330 billion Mark (before conversion). It should have been clear that the DKB, which was obliged to undertake profit-oriented banking activities, could not reach a sustainable position under these conditions.

The basic shortcoming in the Bundesbank's proposal was to calculate the conversion of money stocks by simply adapting the socialist accounting system without questioning the rationale of evaluation. In the socialist planning system, firms' debt burden had no economic meaning as investment risks were non-existent. The underlying reason for the firms' debts was taxation: firms were not allowed to accumulate profits and the 'value added' accrued to the government. In exchange for the fiscal drag, the government granted loans, thereby controlling the overall and allocation of investment activities.

A market economy, by contrast, requires equity finance in order to provide for a firm's ability to bear investment risks. Hence, by simply transforming the past pattern of liabilities at a 2:1 rate into hard currency the government ended up with a systemic over-indebtedness of firms. It has been argued that a 'general' debt release would not be in order, since it would induce misallocation. It runs the other way round: the government imposed a general tax on firms to finance the burden of a generous conversion of money assets. This major transition problem has only recently been recognised. The Treuhandanstalt, the state's trustee agency responsible for privatisation, will take on these liabilities. Hence, firms will be able to start new activities without the burden of past debts reflecting the peculiar financial relationships of the socialist system.

Wage policy
As regards the flow problem, the main determinant of the East German economy's competitiveness – after monetary union – was wage policy.

Initially, on the basis of (dubious) productivity calculations, an evaluation of income flows at a rate of 1:1 seemed to leave industry with a competitive cost level. However, markets for Eastern tradable products broke down completely as East Germans showed frantic demand for Western products; Eastern Europe was no longer willing to pay in hard currency for East German goods. Moreover, in expectation of the monetary union, substantial wage increases had been negotiated in several industries. That pushed up the overall wage level in East Germany by an estimated 20% in 1990. As the wage rise was based on short-term contracts, further substantial increases had to be expected.

In early 1991, a new wage settlement negotiated by IG Metall, followed by ÖTV and other trade unions and their employers' associations, clarified the situation. Essentially, long-term contracts were agreed upon, fixing wages per hour to the West German level, starting with an initial 60% ratio followed by annual increases up to 100% until 1994. These contracts provide reasonable perspectives for both sides. From the employee's standpoint a catching-up process of income is guaranteed. Furthermore, real income differentials are smaller owing to subsidies on non-tradables in East Germany, especially housing. On the other hand, employers can count on substantial wage differentials for at least the next three years. In particular, fringe benefits and a shortening of the working week have been excluded from the contracts. Hence, total labour costs per hour will still be 20% points below West German costs by 1994.

These wage settlements have been questioned on the neoclassical assumption that lower wages would have avoided the sharp rise in unemployment which is actually under way. In particular, this argument was raised in a study undertaken by Akerlof *et al.* (1991) and was underlined by a recent OECD (1991) study on Germany.

The Akerlof study argues on the basis of some 400 inquiries in East Germany. It therefore suggests that wage increases are counterproductive as they cannot prevent migration. On the contrary, that migration is driven by unemployment, not by wage differentials and would be reinforced by such a wage policy. The question is to what extent this argument holds. The wage settlements led to a price–cost squeeze on the basis of the old productivity standards. By stressing the price–cost squeeze it is assumed that products produced by the old techniques will find a market. That may apply as long as the choice of production technique does not influence product quality (the neoclassical case of factor substitution). That is not typical for industrial markets, however. In these markets, monopolistic competition, product differentation and high quality standards prevail. The decisive argument here seems to be that customers paying in hard currency will demand high-quality standards.

In any case, the problem of macroeconomic stability, i.e. stabilising employment, is a serious issue in the transition process. In particular, the question has been raised whether unemployment will hold back the process of democratisation (Klimova).

The Akerlof study recommends a scheme of wage subsidisation. There are two arguments against financing unemployment on the job. First, from the employers' point of view, low wages diminish the pressure for productivity increases and delay the catching-up with Western productivity standards. To avoid this kind of adverse incentive the Akerlof study recommends a scheme of decreasing subsidisation. However, if the objective is to keep firms sustainable, the subsidy should be bound not to wage levels but to investment. Second, there are other adverse incentives in such a scheme even for the subsidised workers. The recent government policy of subsidising unemployment on the job by paying wage differentials (of up to 100% in the case of short-term labour) is evidence of that. Many firms complained that workers had no incentive to accept retraining or re-education programmes because participation in such a programme would reduce their income.

The government stopped the programme of financing unemployment on the job in mid-1991. As a main provision against rising unemployment, it is planned to separate labour contracts from the employment relation. Firms are allowed to lay off workers and end contracts if that is what is required for restructuring. On the other hand, contracts are offered by specific associations to the laid-off workers, providing them with remuneration and employment in communal programmes. These associations are temporary and should stimulate retraining of the labour force.

Privatisation
The privatisation programme, which was simply to sell firms by a government trust agency (Treuhandanstalt), did not work properly until recently, for the following reasons:

(1) The agency has been inclined to sell businesses in their present form rather than decomposing them.

(2) The agency requires that purchasers should be existing enterprises. No use is being made of the capital market in the form of offering shares to the public. Only recently has the agency responded to the mounting pressure for management buy-outs. However, there is no adequate provision of capital or risk-bearing support for the buyer in this case.

(3) Employment guarantees were required in some regions to protect the employment structure.

(4) Unsettled property claims hindered the privatisation process.

(5) Administrative shortcomings – a centralised decision-taking process within the Treuhand and corruption – delayed and misdirected the privatisation process. Generally, there has been no public control of the procedure as there would have been with auctioning.

(6) In some major cases the Treuhand delayed privatisation and damaged the sustainability of the firm by demanding high prices for fiscal reasons.

(7) Medium-sized firms have hidden their economic potential to avoid a take-over and to improve their chances for management buy-outs. In such cases, the bureaucratic Treuhand approach decelerates restructuring instead of promoting it.

To summarise, the Treuhand was created as a state agency to manage 'people's ownership' under the Modrow government. But now, with privatisation as the new objective, it has to act like a market agent. Apart from administrative deficiencies, however, its policy is restricted by its other objectives:

- monitoring economic structure, following the structural policy aims and objectives of regional employment;
- applying fiscal constraints on behalf of the federal government, which may hinder the adoption of a developmental role.

Furthermore, the Treuhand takes on all managerial and entrepreneurial functions before privatisation is conducted – a task it can barely fulfil as a bureaucracy.

References

Akerlof, G.A. *et al.* (1991), 'East Germany in from the cold: the economic aftermath of currency union', Paper presented at the Conference of the Brookings Panel of Economic Activity, Washington DC.

Allen, P. M. (1988) 'Evolution, innovation and economics', in G. Dosi *et al.* (eds), *Technical Change and Economic Theory*, London and New York: Pinter Publishers.

Charap, J. and Dyba, (199), 'Transition to a market economy: the case of Czechoslovakia' *European Economic Review*, 35.

Dahrendorf, D. (1990), *Reflections on the Revolution in Europe*, New York: Times Books.

Deutsche Bundesbank (1990), 'Die Währungsunion mit der Deutschen Demokratischen Republik', *Monatsberichte*, 42 (7) July.

Hayek, F. A. (1948), *Individualism and Economic Order*, Chicago: University of Chicago Press.

Lohmann, K. E. (1985), 'Ökonomische Anreize im Staatssozialismus [Economic incentives in state socialism]', Dissertation, Berlin.

Marris, R. (1964), *The Economic Theory of Managerial Capitalism*; Reprinted with a foreword by J. K. Galbraith, New York: Basic Books, 1968.

Morishima, M. and Catephores, G. (1988), 'Anti-Say's Law versus Say's Law: a change in paradigm', in H. Hanusch (ed.), *Evolutionary Economics. Applications of Schumpeter's Ideas*, New York: Cambridge University Press.

Newbery, D. M. (1990), 'Reform in Hungary: sequencing and privatisation', mimeo.

Nuti, D. M. (1988) 'Perestroika', *Economic Policy*, 7.

OECD (1991), *OECD Economic Surveys: Germany 1990/91*, Paris.

Schumpeter, J. (1911) *Theorie der wirtschaftlichen Entwicklung*, Berlin (5th edn 1952).

Siebert, H. (1990), The economic integration of Germany – an update' *Kiel Discussion Papers*, 160a, September.

Sik, O. (1979), *Humane Wirtschaftsdemokratie*, Hamburg; For a Humane Economic Democracy, New York: Praeger Special Studies, 1985.

Sinn, H.-W. (1990), Macroeconomic aspects of German unification', *Münchner Wirtschaftswissenschaftliche Beiträge*, Discussion Papers, November.

Witt, U. (1991) 'Überlegungen zum gegenwärtigen Stand der evolutorischen Ökonomik [Reflections on the present state of evolutionary economics]', Paper presented at the meeting of the Evangelische Akademie Tutzing, 'Evolutorische Ökonomik – Normen – Institutionen – Neuerungen', 4–6 March.

Index